BRIAN LENIHAN

BRIAN LENIHAN

IN CALM AND CRISIS

MERRION
PRESS

First published in 2014 by Merrion Press
an imprint of Irish Academic Press
8 Chapel Lane
Sallins
Co. Kildare
Ireland

British Library Cataloguing in Publication Data
An entry can be found on request

978-1-908928-97-9 (cloth)
978-1-908928-98-6 (PDF)
978-1-908928-99-3 (EPUB)
978-1-908928-32-0 (MOBI)

Library of Congress Cataloging in Publication Data
An entry can be found on request

Printed by ScandBook AB, Sweden.

CONTENTS

Acknowledgments

In the first instance, we want to thank the authors of each of the individual essays for taking the time out of their busy schedules to contribute to this project, for doing so on time and with such care.

We also wish to gratefully acknowledge the wisdom and friendship of Seamus Browne, whose advice is reflected in many facets of this book.

We would like to express our gratitude to Jonathan Williams for his faith in this project and to Conor Graham, Lisa Hyde and all at Irish Academic Press, whose professionalism and attention to detail has made the final publication such a fine production.

We are grateful to many who assisted us in sourcing the photographs included in this book and for permission to reprint them. David Conachy, the Photographic Editor of the *Sunday Independent*, was extremely generous in that regard. We also wish to thank Stephen Rae, Editor in Chief at Independent News and Media and Michael Hinch, Editorial Imaging Manager at Independent Newspapers Ireland. We are also grateful to Damien Eagers; Peter Cavanagh (irishphoto.com); Eamonn Farrell (RollingNews.ie); Susan Kennedy (Lensmen/Irish Photo Archive) and Irene Stevenson (Irish Times Library) for their permission to use photographs in this book.

Loughlin Deegan, Joe Lennon and Richard Aldous undertook the time-consuming task of reading much of the final manuscript. They were meticulous in so doing and made many useful suggestions for improvement. We want to thank our publicist, Peter O'Connell, for helping to market this book.

All royalties from this book are being donated to the Irish Cancer Society. We want to express our appreciation to Kathleen O'Meara and Orla Sheils at the Irish Cancer Society for their help in this regard.

Others who offered valuable assistance in one form or another include Mary Bailey, Olivia Buckley, Noel Dempsey, Eoin Dorgan, Vincent O'Doherty, Eoghan Ó Neachtain, Eoin O'Shea, John Pollock and Patricia Ryan.

We would each like to thank our families and friends for their support and patience while we committed time to this project.

Working on this book was never a chore, but, of course, at times it was a poignant task. We hope it does some service to the recognition of the legacy of Brian's too short life.

Brian Murphy
Mary O'Rourke
Noel Whelan
September 2014

LIST OF PLATES

1. Handing in his father's nomination papers for the 1989 General Election. (pic: Independent News and Media)

2. Canvassing in Ballyfermot during the 1996 Dublin West by-election (pic: Jack McManus, *Irish Times*)

3. At Dublin West by-election count 3 April 1996 with (seated) Sean Sherwin, National Organiser Fianna Fáil, and (standing l/r) Noel Dempsey TD, Director of Elections; Mary O' Rourke TD, Deputy Leader of Fianna Fáil; Marty Whelan, Fianna Fáil Press Office and Joan Keating, Fianna Fáil HQ (pic: RollingNews.ie)

4. Launching a report, as Minister for Children, at Government Buildings, November 2006 (pic: Tom Burke, Independent News and Media)

5. Receiving the seal of office as Minister for Justice from President McAleese with Taoiseach Bertie Ahern, 14 June 2007 (pic: Albert Gonzalez, RollingNews.ie)

6. Congratulating new Garda recruits, as Minister for Justice, at Templemore College July 2007 (pic: Eamonn Farrell, RollingNews.ie)

7. With Mary O'Rourke TD and Conor Lenihan TD at Fianna Fáil Parliamentary Party conference, Druid Glen, September 2007 (pic: Independent News and Media)

8. Shopper watches as the Minister for Finance delivers his first Budget 14 October 2008 (pic: Martin Nolan, Independent News and Media)

9. With Taoiseach Brian Cowen at Annual Fianna Fáil Wolfe Tone commemoration, Bodenstown, 18 October 2009 (pic: Donal Doherty, Lensmen/Irish Photo Archive)

10. Visiting the Mountainview Resource Centre, Blanchardstown, in his own constituency of Dublin West (pic: Frank McGrath, Independent News and Media).

11. Minister for Finance Brian Lenihan arriving at the Treasury Building, July 2009 (pic: Cyril Byrne, *Irish Times*)

12. Giving a briefing on the legislation to establish NAMA, November 2009 (pic: Brenda Fitzsimons, *Irish Times*)

13. At a media briefing with Eamon Ryan, Minister for Communications, Energy and Natural Resources, Government Buildings February 2010 (pic: Sasko Lazarov, RollingNews.ie)

14. Speaking at the Annual Michael Collins commemoration, Béal na Bláth, Co. Cork, August 2010 (pic: Eamonn Farrell, RollingNews.ie)

15. Making a point to Christine Lagarde, the French Finance Minister, EU Finance Ministers meeting, Brussels, January 2011 (pic: © Peter Cavanagh,www.irishphoto.com)

16. Waiting for the General Election result in Dublin West with supporters, including Mel Kelleher, Mary D'Arcy, and Margaret Kenny, Coolmine Leisure Centre, 26 February 2011 (pic: Damien Eagers, Damien Eagers Photography)

BIOGRAPHICAL NOTES
ON CONTRIBUTORS

Professor Alan Ahearne is Head of Economics at NUI Galway. He is an adviser to the IMF and a member of the Commission of the Central Bank of Ireland. He served as a special adviser at the Department of Finance from March 2009 to March 2011. He previously worked as a Senior Economist at the Federal Reserve Board in Washington, DC.

Jim Flaherty was a Canadian Member of Parliament from 2006 until his death in April 2014. He was a member of the Ontario Legislative Assembly from 1995 to 2005. He had served as the Canadian Federal Minister for Finance; Deputy Premier of Ontario; Minister of Finance of Ontario; Attorney-General of Ontario with responsibility for Native Affairs and Minister of Labour of Ontario.

Paul Gallagher is a Senior Counsel. He is a Bencher of the King's Inns and was formerly Vice Chairman of the Irish Bar Council. He was Attorney General of Ireland from 2007 to 2011. Paul is an Adjunct Professor of Law at University College Dublin, a Fellow of the International Academy of Trial Lawyers and a Fellow of the International Society of Barristers.

Cathy Herbert worked with Brian Lenihan as his special adviser from January 2006 to March 2011.

Professor Patrick Honohan has been Governor of the Central Bank of Ireland since September 2009. He came to this position from Trinity College Dublin where he was an Economics Professor. He spent twelve years on the staff of the World Bank. In the 1980s, he was Economic Adviser to Taoiseach Garret FitzGerald, and later spent several years at the ESRI.

Christine Lagarde is the Managing Director of the International Monetary Fund, taking up this position in 2011. She previously served in a number of ministerial positions in France. She joined the French Government in June 2005 as Minister for Foreign Trade. After a brief period as Minister for Agriculture and Fisheries, in June 2007 she became the first woman to hold the post of Finance and Economy Minister of a G-7 country.

Mary McAleese was President of Ireland from 1997 to 2011. She is a former Pro-Vice Chancellor of Queen's University Belfast and she was Reid Professor of Criminal Law, Criminology and Penology at Trinity College Dublin from 1975 to 1987.

Ray Mac Sharry is a retired public representative. He was a member of Dáil Éireann from 1969 to 1988 and a member of the European Parliament from 1984 to 1987. He has served as European Commissioner for Agriculture and Rural Development; Minister for Finance and Public Services; Tánaiste; Minister for Finance; Minister for Agriculture and Minister of State at the Department of Finance and Public Service.

Dr Martin Mansergh was Minister of State at the Department of Finance with special responsibility for the OPW from 2008 to 2011. He was a Fianna Fáil TD for Tipperary South from 2007 to 2011 and Senator from 2002 to 2007. He was a member of the Oireachtas Joint Committee on Finance and the Public Service, latterly vice-chairman, until 2008. As a special adviser to the Taoiseach, he was member of the Tax Strategy Group 1997 to 2002. He is the author of *The Legacy of History for Making Peace in Ireland*.

Rory Montgomery is Second Secretary General, Department of the Taoiseach, having previously been the Irish Permanent Representative to the EU and Ambassador to France. He is writing in a purely personal capacity as a long-standing friend of Brian Lenihan.

John Mullen is from Tinahely, County Wicklow, and served as Deputy National Organiser of Fianna Fáil until 2004.

Dr Brian Murphy is a former speech writer to two Taoisigh. He recently completed a PhD in the School of History and Archives, University College Dublin.

Dr Harman Murtagh is a native of Athlone and a former senior lecturer at Athlone Institute of Technology, where he is currently a visiting fellow.

Marie Louise O'Donnell was educated at Nottingham University, NUI Maynooth, and UCD. She lectured in the School of Communications at DCU. She trained in radio with the BBC and presented programmes for Radio 4 for several years. She has lectured in Ireland, Europe and the USA. She presents a weekly colour piece on *The Today with Sean O'Rourke Show*. Marie Louise is a published writer. In 2011, she was appointed to Seanad Éireann by Taoiseach Enda Kenny.

Feargal O'Rourke is Head of Tax Services in PwC Ireland and has been a partner in the firm since 1996. He was a member of the Government's Commission on Taxation (2008–9). He is a frequent commentator in the media on tax policy matters.

Mary O'Rourke is a best-selling author. She was a member of Dáil Éireann from 1982 to 2002 and 2007 to 2011. She was Leader of Seanad Éireann from 2002 to 2007. She has served as Minister for Public Enterprise; Minister for Health; Minister for Education; Minister of State at the Department of Enterprise and Employment and Minister of State at the Department of Industry and Commerce. She is a former Deputy Leader of Fianna Fáil.

Eamon Ryan is the leader of the Green Party. He was a member of Dáil Éireann from 2002 to 2011. He served as Minister for Communications, Energy and Natural Resources from 2007 to 2011.

John Trethowan is a career banker with 42 years of experience. He is a past President of the Institute of Banking in Ireland, and is currently head of the Credit Review Office which allows SMEs to appeal declined lending decisions up to €3 billion. John is also an experienced company director, and is currently chairman of the board of two large business organisations in Northern Ireland.

Jillian Van Turnhout is an Independent Senator nominated by Taoiseach Enda Kenny. She knew the late Brian Lenihan through her work as Chief Executive of the Children's Rights Alliance from 2005 to 2011.

Noel Whelan is a barrister, *Irish Times* columnist and author of a number of books on politics and elections.

INTRODUCTION

NOEL WHELAN

FEW PERIODS IN IRISH history are likely to be as extensively excavated by future historians as that from 2008 to 2011.The financial and banking collapse, the acute economic and social crisis and the potentially seismic political shifts that Ireland experienced in those four years have already attracted volumes of analysis. Much of that analysis is framed in the context of political charge and counter-charge and almost all of it is shaped by intense and justified public anger.

It is unavoidable that this book, focusing as it does on the life and work of one of the central, if not the central, political figures of those years, will feed into the early drafts of the history of this turbulent period. While that is inevitable, that is not the purpose of this book.

This collection of essays gathers the observations of some of those most proximate to Brian Lenihan during these crucial years. It will be obvious to the reader that all of the contributors had strong affection for Brian and many of them are, therefore, defensive of his memory. Some, however, are simultaneously (or alternatively) defensive of their own actions. In some places, the contributors are critical of what Brian and his government colleagues did or, at least, are critical of how it was done. As well as covering their dealings with Brian Lenihan, some of the contributors have given their broader recollections and reflections on key events, some of them for the first time. Each contribution is shaped by the angle from which each writer viewed events at the time and by adjustments in their perspective, which may have occurred since. Like everyone writing about this period, they have, even after this short interval, the benefit of hindsight.

Those looking for a definitive account of Brian Lenihan's life or detached judgement of his actions have come to the wrong place. In each of the following essays, the authors themselves set out their own particular connection to Brian Lenihan. It is for readers, each of whom will also come with their own pre-determined view of the man and the period, to decide the extent to which the contributors can be objective or the extent to which they may be over-compensating for being perceived as coming with inevitable bias.

While Brian Lenihan's tenure as Minister for Finance will fascinate readers most, this book ranges over his entire political career and, indeed, covers non-political aspects of his life and his personal formation. The choice of contributors was not strategic or deliberate. In most cases, they were obvious. A number of people were asked to write up to five thousand words about the Brian Lenihan they knew and their workings or contact with him. There were some who declined, honestly acknowledging that, although they liked and respected him, they felt they knew him insufficiently to justify writing in this volume.

Through a combination of design and happenstance, the final line-up of contributors collectively gives a comprehensive if inevitably benign picture of Brian Lenihan's political life and impact.

Harman Murtagh chronicles how Brian was shaped and initially schooled in Athlone, Mary McAleese and Rory Montgomery, as teacher and fellow student respectively, give some insight into how Brian's years in Trinity College shaped him for later challenges, in which each of them had ringside seats. Mary O'Rourke, his aunt and later a fellow parliamentarian, was similarly positioned to give insights on his youth and later career. Feargal O'Rourke, Brian's cousin and himself a leading expert on taxation issues, gives both a personal reflection and professional assessment of Brian.

Cathy Herbert was Lenihan's closest political adviser in all his ministries, and along with Alan Ahearne, was part of his core team within the Department of Finance. Martin Mansergh was his junior minister in that department, while Eamon Ryan and Paul Gallagher engaged and befriended him from different perches around the cabinet table. Ray Mac Sharry had been minister for finance during a previous economic crisis and Brian valued his advice. Patrick Honohan was appointed by Brian as Governor of the Central Bank and he worked closely with him in that role. John Trethowan was asked by Brian to establish the Credit Review Office. Christine Lagarde, the then French finance minister, was a close colleague in the decision-making councils of the European Union, while the late Canadian finance minister, Jim Flaherty, bonded with him at gatherings of the OECD.

Brian Murphy and John Mullen offer insights into two significant by-elections in Brian Lenihan's life and his undoubted talents for electioneering.

The various contributions draw a series of pictures of Brian in different times and places: a bright and curious young student sharing coffee in the Trinity Commons; a strong college debater, who later became a strong parliamentary performer; an ambitious young politician; a hardworking and innovative Minister for Children and then Minister for Justice and then an initially rattled, but ultimately fearless Minister for Finance.

For my own part, I didn't actually get to know Brian Lenihan until about a year after he entered Dáil Éireann. It was at a point when I was easing out of politics and he was easing out of the Law Library. Our paths had never really crossed in Leinster House or the Four Courts, but, from a distance, he seemed a jovial, able, bright barrister turned politician. My first ever extended conversation with him happened by chance when he offered me a lift back to Dublin from a by-election campaign in Cork in October 1998. Over the two-and-a-half hour journey, we covered a range of political topics, including the merits of various government and opposition politicians and long-term political trends in Ireland, England and the United States. We then covered a range of historical topics. All of this was interspersed with commentary from Brian on the social and political geography of various towns we were passing through or by-passing en route.

Having worked in politics since college, I had met many senior politicians and, indeed, had become cynical about most of them. It was clear, however, that Brian Lenihan was unique. The man's intellectual capacity was extraordinary and impossible to understate. The depth and breadth of his reading was phenomenal. He also had an impressive capacity to assess political nuances and shifts. One only had to engage with him for a short period to see that he also had a passionate commitment to politics and a yearning to apply his undoubted intellectual talents and political skills to improving the country.

I lived in Carpenterstown at this time and Brian developed an occasional habit of calling at the end of the day to reflect on the current political events, which often led to long, late night discussions.

In conversation, Brian could sometimes seem distracted, but only because his mind was like a computer with too many windows open simultaneously, such was his urgency in conversation and appetite for discourse. When talking to him, you might get a sense from his facial expression that he was no longer interested or engaged only to realise from some later reference that he had been following every detail.

A few years later, my wife moved to work in Belfast and the house in Carpenterstown became no more than a dormitory for me midweek. When Lenihan would telephone to say that he was dropping over, I would offer to shop or dial something to eat. He always declined and would again decline any offer of food on arrival. However, he would then proceed to spend much of his time in the house walking in and out to the kitchen scouring the fridge or presses for nibbles. During one such sequence of talking perambulation, I heard a shriek from the kitchen – he had stuck his hand into the under-used bread bin and found only green mouldy bread!

At this early stage in his political career, Brian was excited, active, engaged but impatient. Brian clearly, and in my view correctly, felt Bertie Ahern was thwarting his political advancement. Most politicians and commentators recognised Brian as cabinet material from the outset, but Ahern delayed appointing him even to junior ministerial office. Chairing the Oireachtas Committee on the Constitution certainly interested him and played to his strengths as a lawyer and consensus builder, particularly when the committee was tasked with dealing with the abortion issue, but he was impatient to have the direct impact on policy, which being a minister would bring.

He was also, at times, overwhelmed by the response he attracted from the Fianna Fáil grassroots or members of the public. Although a mere backbencher, he was often mobbed by well-wishers at Ard Fheiseanna or other events. He himself wondered whether this was merely a residue of the affection in which his late father had been held. The rest of us could see that it flowed from his own regular competent media performances and because he himself was seen as a rising star in the party, and even then as a future party leader.

Like all politicians, of course, he enjoyed this attention, but he was also nervous around it. He was a surprisingly shy man. This – and his occasional demeanour of intellectual distraction – sometimes gave rise to lazy suggestions that he was somehow remote or detached. This was simply nonsense. Brian had a passionate interest in people, their views, their concerns and their opinions. Above all, he had genuine empathy and never in a contrived sense that some politicians mastered.

When finally appointed a Minster of State with responsibility for Children in 2002, Brian quickly got stuck into a range of issues about which he was passionate, the details of which have been well chronicled by Jillian van Turnhout in her essay in this book. He continued as Minister for Children in 2005 when the portfolio was upgraded to a cross-departmental role enabling him, although not a member of the Cabinet, to attend cabinet meetings.

The day that Brian Lenihan was appointed Minister for Justice was, perhaps, the happiest of his political life. He thrived in the role; he loved the department, its officials, and working with the Garda Síochána. As well as implementing a programme of law reform, he viewed as an important part of his brief the need to make the right appointments at senior and middle-management level in the department, in the prison services, in the Garda Síochána and to the judiciary. He gave careful consideration to each recommendation made to him.

His time in Justice was too short to have an enduring impact and he would have loved to stay there. He resented, in part, being yanked out of his comfort zone to Finance. He once recounted how, in the days before he became Taoiseach, Brian Cowen summoned him to his office then in the Department of Finance: 'What's this I hear about you wanting to stay in Justice? I want my best minister next door,' Cowen said. The two Brians then had an intense conversation about some of the challenges he was likely to face in Finance, where fiscal contraction was inevitable. It seems that neither appreciated then the scale of the banking problems with which they would also have to deal. Lenihan actually took a private moment, as he walked back to his own office on St. Stephen's Green, to reflect on the magnitude of the task he had just agreed to take on. The task demanded all of his extraordinary intellectual, political and communications skills, day and night, for the remainder of his too short life.

Caught up in pre-Christmas travel and other arrangements in December 2009, I missed a hint from Cathy Herbert on Christmas Eve that I should give Brian a call. On the afternoon of St. Stephen's Day, TV3 began to run promos flagging a significant news bulletin and I started getting phone calls from Dublin saying there was growing speculation that it related to Lenihan.

Appreciating that something significant was happening, I rang him to let him know what the talk was. He answered the phone, no doubt fielding a series of calls, jokingly saying: 'The Minister for Finance is enjoying Christmas at home with his family and will be making no comment.' His upbeat demeanour, however, quickly fell away. It was clear that he was distressed at the situation in which he had been put, deprived of the space and time to enjoy a family Christmas and to tell those closest to him the details of a diagnosis he, himself, had only had days to absorb. It was just devastating news and devastating to watch it play out within hours on national television.

Many of us close to him had a sense that dealing with the illness was easier for him because he stayed working, but who can judge what really operates in the mind of a person living under the shadow of a fatal cancer. Brian had interrogated the best doctors in the field on the nature and inevitable consequences of the diagnosis. He had accepted that outcome intellectually. Emotionally, of course, at least for another year or so, he could not resist holding on to some hope.

Several of those who worked closely with him confirmed then – and go out of their way in their contributions to this book to confirm again – that he suffered no diminution in his intellectual capacity as a minister during his remaining two years in office. I concur with that assessment, but it is also clear that the diagnosis, while it did not impact on his capacity, certainly impacted on his frame of mind.

There is no doubt that he did adjust to a longer view. As the extent of the economic crisis became clear, Brian recognised before most people how traumatic the economic and social consequences would be. He also recognised the political consequences for Fianna Fáil. He knew too that his reputation would be damaged by the inevitable outcomes. His focus, however, was on the national challenge. 'Dublin West doesn't matter now,' he used to say, 'Fianna Fáil doesn't matter now either. It's only what works for the country that matters now.' It was not just a mantra. He meant it and he meant it even more after his diagnosis. It was reflected, for example, in his determination to get Budget 2011 and the associated Finance Act passed before the looming general election date.

The narrowing of his mind-set also had an impact on his political ambition. He had, for a time, flirted with the idea of challenging Brian Cowen to become Taoiseach. Indeed, around the autumn of 2010, he more than flirted with it and deliberated aloud on the mechanism of how this might be achieved with many – in fact, too many – in the parliamentary party and elsewhere. Lenihan accepted, indeed, at times, touted the analysis of the growing number of Cowen critics in the party that failings in political leadership and disastrous communication were contributing to the national sense of crisis. Lenihan felt a less partisan, more coherent, more media-friendly and more popular leader would not only be in Fianna Fáil's interest, but also in the national interest, at least until the next election.

When encouraged to act on this analysis, Lenihan vacillated. Among his stock answers to those who suggested he should lead a push was that the Minister for Finance challenging the Taoiseach, at such a time of economic uncertainty, would precipitate a constitutional crisis. He was also uncertain he would succeed in toppling Cowen and then it was simply too late. A factor which may have impacted on his prospects of success in a leadership challenge, but also on his attitude to initiating such a challenge, was that he could only ever be a stop-gap leader. Lenihan also had a loyalty to Cowen, who had promoted him and who, whatever his failings in Finance and as Taoiseach, had supported the tough decisions necessary to address the crisis.

Brian was giddy, almost childlike, about the invitation to speak at the Michael Collins commemoration at Béal naBláth. The Cork South West Fine Gael TD, Jim O'Keeffe, had sought to clear the way by enquiring in advance whether Brian would accept such an invitation if it was issued. He accepted instantly. O'Keeffe swore him to secrecy for a few weeks, but Brian could not resist sharing the historic news. That sunny day in August 2010, at the site of Collins's assassination, was the highpoint of Brian Lenihan's political career and of his public standing. Brian had worked carefully on his speech, but the fact that he was giving the oration was actually the most significant statement. For a long time after he spoke, people came up to him in small groups to shake his hand, have their photograph taken with him and to wish him well. He was almost the last to leave – fired up, visibly tired, but clearly touched.

The last paragraphs of the Béal na Bláth speech sat uncomfortably with the rest of the text because they dealt with very contemporary banking issues. They were inserted late in the day at a time when Lenihan felt he needed to publicly address the worsening picture of the banking debt, which had emerged over that summer. Brian always felt that it was inevitable Ireland would need to turn to the IMF-ECB-EU Troika for some level of support. He hoped it would be a less intrusive form of support and that it would wait until the spring of 2011. Events overtook him. Ireland was backed into a corner by the ECB in particular and, with money fleeing the country, he was bounced into a bailout.

The events surrounding the announcement and negotiation of the bailout are recounted by some of the participants in later essays in this book. The shambolic way in which the entry into negotiations with the Troika was communicated to the Irish people is something for which Lenihan himself must carry some of the responsibility. He contended afterwards that he had warned other ministers to be careful in their utterances during those crucial days, but failing to keep all ministers fully informed, ideally by means of a special cabinet meeting over that crucial weekend or on that Monday after stories about an Irish bailout began circulating in the international press was wrong, and not only in hindsight.

As the economists Donal Donovan and Antoin Murphy acknowledge in their 2013 book, *The Fall of the Celtic Tiger*, the motives for delaying the public announcement of a bailout were benign. Lenihan was hoping to obtain some alternative support mechanism short of a formal bailout or hoped, at least, that delaying a formal letter of application would strengthen the Government's hand in the subsequent negotiations. The manner in which it was mishandled did much to compound the impact on an already traumatised Irish public.

The bizarre series of event, which subsequently gave rise to the collapse of Brian Cowen's government, are also recounted in this book. Lenihan was bemused and, at times, angry about the turn of some of these events. He had known, once Ireland had entered the bailout programme, that the Government could not last long, as its popular mandate had dissipated. His primary focus during this time was to get as much of the budgetary process as possible completed before the election was called. In doing so, he bequeathed a great gift to the new government and made a significant contribution to Ireland's ultimate emergence from the bailout in a relatively short period.

Brian Lenihan's decision to contest the leadership of Fianna Fáil after Brian Cowen's resignation was curious. He talked, it seems, to none of those to whom he usually turned for advice that crucial afternoon, but, it seems, after holding back from challenging, he now felt obliged to contest the vacancy. It was a pointless exercise always doomed to failure. Micheál Martin, who had resigned a week earlier when his challenge to Cowen's leadership had failed, was set to be the beneficiary, such as it was, of the Fianna Fáil leader's resignation. Lenihan had been damaged by association with the bailout and by suggestions that he had conspired against the Taoiseach.

When I did get hold of him early that evening, he was dealing with departmental matters, but he realised that he needed a base from which to do some leadership campaigning. I invited him out to our house, in Ranelagh, where he spent three hours simultaneously negotiating a new timescale for the Finance Bill with the Greens and ringing Fianna Fáil TDs seeking their support for his leadership candidacy. In most cases, he was calling his party colleagues several hours after Micheál Martin or the other leadership contenders. Feeling a need for momentum in his already stalled and doomed leadership bid, he decided to call a press conference for the following morning. I worked up some words for that press event – the only lines I had ever written for him in fourteen years – and Cathy Herbert reworked them with us over email. In framing those few short pages, it was apparent to all three of us that Brian, damaged by the bailout and limited by his diagnosis, had little to offer Fianna Fáil TDs and Senators as leader, except to front a containment mission in the forthcoming election.

The following Wednesday Micheál Martin won, as predicted, and he did so decisively. There was further humiliation for Lenihan in the fact that a cohort of Brian Cowen loyalists threw their support behind Eamon Ó Cuiv in the leadership vote (not at Brian Cowen's instigation, it should be said) and Lenihan was nudged into third place.

Brian Lenihan decided to stay and fight the 2011 election, although he knew Fianna Fáil would be out of power and he himself would struggle to be re-elected. He was privately critical of other senior Fianna Fáil figures, who he felt had walked off the pitch in the final stages of the match. He enjoyed that one last campaign and had a sense of reconnecting with his voters in what he used to call 'the barony of Castleknock,' but he was philosophical throughout, as Marie Louise O'Donnell captures in her essay in this volume. Brian was touched by the fact that the voters re-elected him and took it as a mark of the regard in which he was held locally. He knew also that there was an element of sympathy in that support: the voters of Dublin West had decided to shield him from one final blow.

For the short few months in opposition after the 2011 election, Brian was sanguine. He enjoyed the additional time at home greatly. He continued to visit Leinster House regularly and jokingly reminded colleagues and opponents that he had not yet gone away.

In late April 2011, we had our last chat in person over a quiet cup of tea in the Westbury Hotel. His form was very good, his mind was sharp, but his physical presentation was weak. Among the things we discussed that afternoon was his need to get down on paper his own account of some of the events of the previous years. We talked, in code, about how he should do so while the events were fresh in his mind, but, of course, we both knew it was for the purpose of the historic record before time ran out on him.

He was content that he had already given his take on the background to the Bank Guarantee at the meeting of the Joint Oireachtas Committee on Finance and the Public Service on 26 February 2009. He had also dealt extensively with the economic and international dimensions of more recent events in an off-the-record interview with Dan O'Brien, for BBC Radio Four, some weeks previously. He had cleared a short extract of that interview for broadcast in a documentary O'Brien made on the bailout and he was shortly to receive a transcript of the entire interview to decide what to do with the rest of it. He had a sense, however, that he still needed to give his perspective on the political dimensions to many of the key events. We agreed that, when the Whit break in the court calendar came in early June, he would come and sit before a tape recorder in my offices near the Law Library and I would prompt his recollections on his time as minister and get it typed up for him. It was not to be; fate had a different momentum.

As we said our goodbyes outside the hotel, he to head to Leinster

House and me to the courts, I took a last minute notion to walk with him over to Kildare Street. I was concerned, I suppose, in part, that he might not be physically up to getting there safely, but concerned, in reality, I think now that I might not see him again. As we strolled the few blocks, I noticed that people stopped as he passed – in their eyes I saw recognition, then affection and then concern.

After that I didn't ring him, but waited for him to ring me for fear I might be intruding. We spoke a couple of times on the phone. They were short conversations, in which he struggled to be animated and, in which, I dared not ask him whether he was at home or in the Mater because to hear he was at home would probably have been more upsetting. The last such call faded out on some talk of a Fianna Fáil front bench reshuffle.

1 THE DOCTOR ON DUTY

ALAN AHEARNE

BY THE TIME BRIAN LENIHAN arrived at the Department of Finance in May 2008, the Irish banking system was doomed. Over the previous five years, the domestic Irish banks had ballooned their loan books to a staggering €400 billion from €150 billion in 2003. Most of this new credit was extended to the property sector, including a nine-fold increase in lending for speculative development and a doubling in mortgage lending. Lenihan remarked that unlike other capital cities around Europe, there were no foreign buyers of property in Dublin during the boom years – a tell-tale sign that real estate was overvalued.

The banks funded this lethal expansion in credit by borrowing on international money markets. They attracted corporate deposits from all over the world and sold large amounts of bonds and commercial paper. They pumped this money into the Irish economy, thereby fuelling a surge in consumer and government spending. Ireland's banking bosses gambled everything on the expectation of a soft landing in the property sector and continued benign conditions in international funding markets. Few people shouted stop. The domestic property crash and international financial crisis revealed in the starkest terms the recklessness of the banks' business models and the failures of those tasked with regulating the banking system.

Now the chickens were coming home to roost. Ireland's banks were about to hit the wall. Lenihan would spend nearly the next three years performing radical surgery on the Irish banking system. The international experience with systemic banking crises provided some guidance, but the complexity of the emergency facing Lenihan was unparalleled. Ireland's banks were unusually large, with loans standing at more than twice the country's total annual income. They had grown exceptionally dependent on international funding markets, just as the global financial system plunged into the most severe crisis since the Great Depression. An additional dimension to Ireland's crisis was the country's membership of a poorly constructed – and at times dysfunctional – currency union. The external environment and the rules of the game were constantly changing. Decisive, courageous and difficult decisions would be required to stave off disaster.

THE BANK GUARANTEE

I first met Brian Lenihan at his office in the Department of Finance in August 2008. Property values were already falling, the construction sector had come to a 'shuddering halt,' and the banks were struggling to fund themselves on money markets. During a wide-ranging discussion, I found Lenihan remarkably frank. It was clear to me that he was working on a plan. Among other things, we discussed the pros and cons of using money from the National Pensions Reserve Fund to strengthen the banks' balance sheets. We agreed it was crucial that Lenihan had an accurate picture of the financial condition of the banks. We spent some time discussing the prospects for Anglo Irish Bank and Irish Nationwide Building Society – the two financial institutions most exposed to the crumbling property sector.

We met again in Galway some weeks later, on 15 September. I had been invited, along with economist Philip Lane from Trinity, to speak at the Fianna Fáil Parliamentary Party meeting about the Irish economy. That same day, the US investment bank Lehman Brothers filed for bankruptcy, sending violent shockwaves through the global financial system. On the fringes of the meeting, Lenihan and I chatted again about the state of the banks. Lenihan mused whether it would be possible 'to knock over two dominoes without knocking the other four.' I assumed at the time that he was contemplating the closure of Anglo and INBS, but was concerned about the knock-on effects on the other banks of such a move. He was exploring a wide range of alternatives, which I later learned was his *modus operandi* in making decisions. (He himself would have described it as his method of operating, as he disliked the unnecessary use of Latin in popular speech.)

Two weeks later, with the banking system on the brink of running out of cash, the Government introduced a blanket guarantee of the debts of the six main domestically owned financial institutions. The guarantee was identical to a successful scheme introduced in Sweden in the early 1990s. The emergency measure was aimed squarely at helping the banks to retain and attract new funding. In signing the guarantee order, Lenihan said: 'The guarantee has as its central objective the removal of any uncertainty on the part of counter parties and customers and gives absolute comfort to depositors and investors that they have the full protection of the State.'

European finance ministers on 7 October announced a coordinated response to the financial crisis, though undoubtedly a clear message had been sent out from Brussels and Frankfurt to European capitals weeks earlier that there was to be no repeat of the Lehman's debacle in Europe.

Although in the public mind the guarantee is most closely associated with the two Brians, it is often forgotten that the scheme was overwhelmingly supported by the Oireachtas. The introduction of the guarantee was also widely welcomed in the media. Criticisms of the move at the time were few and far between.

Judged against its immediate objective of keeping enough cash in the banks to forestall a widespread closure of the financial system, the guarantee worked a treat. With repayment of debt guaranteed by the (then) AAA-rated Irish State, the banks were able to raise €40 billion in new funding within six weeks. Lenihan described the bank rescue scheme as 'the cheapest bailout in the world so far,' a phrase that later was thrown back in his face many times as the cost to the State of shoring up the banks mounted.

Lenihan did not believe that rescuing the banks would involve no outlays. He speculated some time later that the resolution of Anglo and INBS would cost the State about €5 billion, but that the State would, in time, profit by a similar amount from its investments in the other banks. He realised that the State would incur substantial up-front costs as a result of the intervention to save the banks, but he expected that most of this outlay would eventually be recouped.

Many others shared this assessment. The Financial Regulator, Patrick Neary, in late 2008 described the banks as well capitalised, though he acknowledged that the banks might need more capital if the economy deteriorated further. Outside commentators were also relatively sanguine about the prospects for the banks. Not long before the introduction of the guarantee, the ratings agency Fitch affirmed Anglo's long-term rating at A+ and maintained its outlook on that bank as stable. Later, in an article in *The Irish Times* in November 2008, ten academics specialising in finance and banking recommended that the State inject €10 billion of capital into the banks to repair them. They predicted a 'good prospective return' for the State on this investment.

All of these projections proved optimistic. To be fair, the ultimate cost of a banking crisis is impossible to determine early on. In the end, the State would inject €64 billion into the banks, much of which will probably not be recouped.

The higher-than-expected cost of saving the banks in part reflected the greater-than-expected severity of the recession. In Budget 2009, which was announced two weeks after the introduction of the bank guarantee, the Department of Finance projected a small decline of 1 per cent in economic activity (measured by GNP) for 2009, followed by a rebound to positive growth of 2.5 per cent in 2010 and 3.5 per cent in 2011. The Department anticipated that the unemployment rate would peak at 7.3 per cent in 2009.

Other economic forecasters were also pencilling in a relatively soft landing for the economy. In the ESRI's Quarterly Economic Commentary (QEC) for autumn 2008, released just before Budget

2009, the QEC team forecast a modest contraction of less than 1 per cent in GNP in 2009 and a small increase in consumer spending. The Central Bank of Ireland and the IMF published similar projections.

In the event, GNP plummeted more than 9 per cent in 2009 and consumer spending slumped more than 5 per cent. By the end of 2013, the depth and length of the economic downturn was such that both these measures of economic activity were still far below their peak levels in 2008. Unemployment soared to roughly twice the rate that economists had forecast.

If the economy had performed as anticipated in late 2008, banks' losses would have been contained. But the exorbitant cost of shoring up the banks was also due to another factor. Reckless lending practices by the banks during the bubble years meant that the underlying quality of the banks' loan books was much worse than could be gleaned by reading the banks' financial statements. The detailed loan-by-loan due diligence examinations of the banks' loans carried out in late 2009 and 2010 as part of the NAMA valuation process revealed a disturbing picture of poor loan documentation, of loans not properly legally secured and of marked deficiencies in the banks' measurement and management of risk. The banks' books were laden with landmines hidden beneath the financial accounts.

The blanket bank guarantee covered some €440 billion of banks' debt. Deposits and bonds that were scheduled to be repaid by the banks over the next two years were covered. If the banks were not in a financial position to meet these obligations, then the State promised to make good on the repayments. The scheme categorically ruled out imposing losses on senior bank bondholders – also known as burden sharing with or bailing in bondholders – for a period of two years. Contrary to claims from some quarters, the blanket scheme was not extended beyond September 2010. Two other bank guarantee schemes were still in operation at that time and were extended well beyond 2010, but neither covered bank bonds issued before 2010. The two-year duration of the scheme meant that there would be no opportunity to bail in bondholders until October 2010. By that time, however, most of the bonds had reached their maturity dates and had been repaid in full.

Some people have argued that a narrower guarantee scheme which excluded existing senior bonds would have allowed burden sharing and reduced the cost to the State of rescuing the banks. At an abstract level, this might be true. In practice, however, this argument ignores the European Central Bank's entrenched position regarding burden sharing with senior bank creditors. The ECB vehemently opposed bailing in bondholders. The ECB's stance on this issue would later frustrate Lenihan's plans to impose losses on senior bonds after the blanket scheme expired. Although promises to burn the bondholders featured in the general election campaign in 2011, to date no losses have been imposed on senior bonds of any bank in the euro area. At this remove, it is clear that the State would have had to make good on senior bank bonds, even if they had been excluded from the blanket guarantee.

More generally, there are mixed views among observers today as to whether the blanket guarantee was a mistake. A well-researched book by Donal Donovan and Antoin Murphy concludes that the guarantee was the least-worst option and that critics have failed to supply evidence that other solutions would have worked. The former President of the European Central Bank, Jean Claude Trichet, recently described the decision by the Government as 'justifiable given the situation it found itself.' In contrast, European Commissioner for Economic and Monetary Affairs Olli Rehn recently said: 'In retrospect I think it is quite easy to spot some mistakes like the blanket guarantee for banks.' Rehn's comment is puzzling since the European Commission approved the guarantee scheme for state-aid purposes. To conform to EU state-aid rules, government intervention in the banking system 'has to be necessary, appropriate and proportionate.' How can a policy that is deemed to be necessary, appropriate and proportionate be a mistake? Moreover, the Commission later sided with the ECB against Lenihan and the IMF staff in protecting senior bank bondholders. It is not clear how these apparent contradictions can be explained.

One cannot help feel that for many people it is convenient to blame the country's entire economic woes on the blanket guarantee. Many people are uncomfortable discussing what they said and did –

and in some cases what they did not say and did not do – during the years of the bubble. If the public can be convinced that our problems began on the night of the guarantee, then nearly everyone is off the hook. The simplistic narrative that the bank guarantee cost the State €64 billion and that we ended up in an EU/IMF bailout programme because of the guarantee is too often used to distort the truth.

BATTLE TO RESTORE MARKET CONFIDENCE

The introduction of the guarantee bought time for the banking system, but by early 2009 the banks' funding position was becoming strained again. For sure, the banks were supported by the State, but investors were becoming concerned about the sustainability of the State's finances. During the first quarter of 2009, the economy lost nearly 8,000 full-time jobs per week. The bulk of these jobs were in construction and other property-related sectors. Economic activity plunged, led by a collapse in new homebuilding, and the public finances deteriorated at an alarming pace. The economy was falling off a cliff. Ireland's costs of borrowing on international markets rose steeply.

The deepening recession affected investor confidence in the banks. In turn, the weakening banking system further depressed the economy and damaged the public finances. The toxic inter-relationship between the State and the banking sector was threatening to bring both of them down. It would be another four years until European leaders would agree to begin to build a banking union in Europe to break the link between sovereigns and banks. In the future, we may see a common backstop for banks in the European Union. But during Lenihan's tenure at Finance, each member state was responsible for stabilising its own banking system.

Lenihan believed that the battle to restore market confidence and stabilise the financial system had to be fought on three fronts. First, the public finances had to be put on a sustainable footing. The transient taxes of the boom had evaporated, revealing a huge structural gap between government spending and revenues. To that end, Lenihan 'executed' (as he put it himself) €21 billion of budgetary adjustments, pushing the enormous boulder of fiscal correction more than two-thirds the way up that particular mountain.

Second, the country had to regain international competitiveness to improve its potential for growth. As Lenihan put it: 'Unless we regain our competitive edge, we will be unable to return to the tried and tested strategy of export-led growth that ushered in the boom in the early 1990s. We must be able to compete and win again in the international marketplace.' To measure competitiveness, Lenihan put a great deal of stock in Ireland's unit labour costs. He studied these data regularly and was encouraged by the marked drop in costs in Ireland relative to our main trading partners during 2009 and 2010.

Despite the tight constraints imposed by the need to reduce the fiscal deficit, Lenihan's Budgets contained initiatives to boost the competitiveness of various sectors of the Irish economy, including tourism, agriculture and agri-food, forestry and bio-energy, construction and the retail trade. He also enhanced the incentives for R&D and intellectual property to help the country to attract new business and new jobs.

Lenihan was an optimist. He was convinced that the Irish people could work their way through the crisis. Lenihan could see light at the end of the tunnel when many others could see nothing but unrelenting economic gloom. He often reminded those around him how important it was to give people hope of a better economic future, lest they give up the fight to restore order to the public finances. Some of his more positive public comments about the future reflected this view.

NAMA

The third set of actions to repair the banking system involved recapitalising, shrinking and restructuring the banks. Lenihan wanted to ensure that the banks had enough capital to enable them to make loans to support the real economy. Lenihan also recognised that because of their large and risky loan books, the banks would constantly struggle to attract badly needed funding and capital. He also knew that a return to sustainable economic growth in the medium term would require a functioning banking system. In response, Lenihan set up the National Asset Management Agency

(NAMA) to help to deleverage and de-risk the banks.

The establishment of NAMA was strongly supported internationally by those with experience in resolving banking crises. When the plan for NAMA was outlined to visiting officials from the IMF in April 2009, they responded by saying: 'If you hadn't suggested NAMA to us, we would have suggested it to you.' International support was hardly surprising, as a 'bad bank' was a standard tool to assist in the resolution of troubled banks.

The domestic reaction to the announcement of NAMA was more sceptical, however. Ireland had never experienced a systemic banking crisis, and few people here were familiar with the resolution toolkit employed by policymakers in such circumstances. Lenihan welcomed and encouraged constructive debate about NAMA, but despaired at the opportunism and cheap point-scoring that sometimes poisoned the political and wider debate. He remarked on how casual and ill-informed some of the media commentary was about banking issues. Lenihan had hoped to achieve political consensus around NAMA in order to improve international confidence, but to no avail. Nonetheless he was buoyed by the public support given to NAMA by people such as Alan Dukes, Garret FitzGerald and Ray Mac Sharry. Lenihan more than once called for a united national effort to confront the difficulties the country faced.

The charge that NAMA was a bailout for developers and bankers was politically potent. At this remove, the charge seems absurd. Nowadays, critics accuse NAMA of being overzealous in dealing with debtors and it would be difficult to find a banker or bank shareholder who would claim to have been enriched by NAMA. But critics made a populist appeal by misrepresenting NAMA as a novel construct established by a crooked government to protect narrow sectional interests. The debate intensified in the weeks and days before the internal Green Party vote on the policy on 14 September 2009. Opponents reckoned that if the Greens voted against NAMA, the coalition government would collapse. They made a big effort to affect the vote, but were unsuccessful.

Others had different reasons to oppose the setting up of NAMA. Lenihan was annoyed when he learned that some people at AIB were covertly briefing the media against NAMA. The NAMA process would force the banks to face up to the reality of their property losses; some at AIB would doubtlessly have preferred if the unpalatable truth about the state of that bank's loan book had remained concealed. Lenihan was also exercised by an article critical of NAMA by financier Dermot Desmond published by *The Irish Times* on 16 September 2009, the same day the Dáil commenced second-stage debate on the NAMA bill. During that debate, Lenihan provided estimates of how much NAMA would pay for the loans. It was not clear how useful these high-level estimates would be, since under EU law the actual purchase price would be determined by detailed loan-by-loan valuations. But the Opposition had demanded estimates, and in any event Lenihan believed it was wrong to ask the Oireachtas to vote on a bill without some indication of the potential up-front cost involved.

Lenihan believed that effective rebuttal of critics' arguments was the key to winning the debate over NAMA. Time has proved Lenihan right and the critics wrong. No serious commentator today could claim that investor confidence in our banks has not benefitted from the transfer of loans to NAMA. One shudders to think how the banks would have managed their development property loans had they remained on their books, given how slowly they have tackled mortgage arrears. The Spanish government three years later established a bad bank identical to NAMA to aid recovery from that county's property crash, and Slovenia took NAMA as a model in late 2013. In both cases, the bad banks were set up with little or no controversy.

REFORMING BANKING REGULATION

The banks needed to be restructured, and so too did the system of banking regulation which had failed the country. Lenihan had no time for light-touch regulation of banks. He restructured the Central Bank and gave it new powers. He made an inspired choice in appointing Patrick Honohan as governor and brought in Matthew Elderfield from Bermuda as financial regulator to help restore much-needed credibility to the Central Bank. Honohan would later be central to securing a deal to restructure the IBRC promissory note. Lenihan also set up the Credit Review Office under John Trethowan to encourage more lending to the essential SME sector.

Lenihan was always eager to examine alternative policies and approaches. I recall a long conversation over the phone one weekend about a proposal by Citi Chief Economist Willem Buiter for a so-called 'good bank/bad bank.' Lenihan was open-minded about whether that model could be applied to Anglo. He eventually decided in autumn 2010 to wind down Anglo.

As the year 2009 drew toward a close, the cost of borrowing for the State declined and banks' deposits stabilised. The global headwinds that were contributing to the recession began to abate, as world leaders delivered coordinated fiscal stimulus to the major economies. Ireland's GNP bottomed out in the final quarter of 2009 and rose moderately in 2010. I recall Lenihan saying: 'You know, I think this country has a future after all.' But Lenihan knew that the improvements in sentiment were fragile. More gains in competitiveness were needed, the budget deficit was still large, and the economy was susceptible to international developments.

Moreover, bank losses were mounting, as the true extent of the reckless lending during the bubble was revealed. Lenihan wanted to spread the cost of the property crash over as long a period of time as possible. He recapitalised Anglo with a promissory note, not with cash borrowed on international markets. If he had injected cash, there would have been no scope at a later stage to renegotiate that arrangement.

He saw as a priority the need to reinforce international market confidence in the banking system, not least because the banks faced a funding cliff at the end of September 2010 when the blanket guarantee was due to expire. He introduced a scheme that guaranteed newly-issued (but not existing) bank debt for up to five years to help the banks to reduce this funding cliff as market sentiment gradually improved. Banks successfully issued new debt in the spring of 2010 and bank deposits began to rise again. In fact, during the first four months of 2010, funding to Irish banks rose around €500 million per week on average, compared with average weekly drops of €3,000 million during the first half of 2009.

EU/IMF BAILOUT

But events were conspiring against him. The scale of banks' property-related losses continued to rise and rumours circulated in the markets that summer that the bailout of AIB could cost as much as Anglo. In a statement to the Dáil at the end of September 2010, Lenihan announced revised estimates of the cost of repairing the banking system. He wanted to provide reassurance to investors about the capacity of the Irish State to manage these costs. He began working on the four-year National Recovery Plan, which would later become the blueprint for the EU/IMF programme. He announced the first instalment of that plan would be a budgetary adjustment of €6 billion for 2011.

Abroad, fiscal stimulus was prematurely withdrawn from the world's largest economies and analysts began to mark down their forecasts for global economic growth, including growth in Ireland. With slower growth forecast for the coming years, the task of closing the budget deficit began to look even more daunting. The euro area sovereign debt crisis exploded, with Greece entering a (failed) bailout programme in May, amid growing market anxiety about the prospects for peripheral euro-area economies. The country's cost of borrowing rose to unsustainable levels, forcing the Government to withdraw from funding markets in September and rely on previously accumulated cash balances. The banks were unable to issue new bonds to address the funding cliff and relied instead on fresh borrowings from the ECB and the Central Bank of Ireland.

Angela Merkel and Nicolas Sarkozy's disastrously timed agreement at Deauville in October (which they later tore up) to force a country that applied for a bailout programme to default on its sovereign debt was the straw that broke the camel's back. Investors were now very concerned that the Irish State and its banks would default on their debts.

On the plane to Washington D.C. that month for the annual IMF/

World Bank meetings, Lenihan and I discussed at length the pros and cons of exiting the euro area. He was always willing to investigate alternative strategies. Lenihan concluded that an exit would be disastrous for the people of Ireland. He recognised that the European Central Bank was providing invaluable support to the Irish banking system, but he wanted the ECB to do more. He pointed out that if Ireland were a state in the United States, the Federal Reserve would be offering unconditional support. He admired the Fed as a genuine lender of last resort.

Instead, the ECB was pressurising Ireland to reduce the amount of emergency loans that the Eurosystem had extended to Irish banks. In frustration, Lenihan sometimes referred to the ECB as 'that bank in Frankfurt.' He became aware that senior people at the ECB were briefing market investors that the bank was considering the withdrawal of financial support to parts of the Irish banking system. Investors were alarmed. By now, funding in debt markets for the Irish banks had dried up and they were haemorrhaging deposits.

As the financial pressure on Ireland intensified, the Government hoped that the ECB would step up its purchases of Irish bonds under the Securities Markets Programme. These hopes were dashed. One-and-a-half years later, with Italy and Spain under severe financial pressure, the ECB, under new boss Mario Draghi, belatedly introduced a potentially limitless bond-buying programme. In response, market confidence in Italy and Spain improved dramatically.

In early November, Lenihan came up with a plan which he hoped would keep Ireland out of a formal EU/IMF programme. He pointed out that, unlike Greece months earlier, the Irish State was not about to run out of cash. In fact, Ireland was fully funded until the middle of 2011. Lenihan wanted the European Commission to endorse the National Recovery Plan and the ECB to provide unequivocal liquidity support to the Irish banks. He believed that such European support would boost investor confidence in Ireland and quell the financial panic. In return, he would agree to increased surveillance by the European authorities – including quarterly surveillance if necessary – and that Ireland would enter a formal bailout programme in 2012 if things hadn't turned around by then. He intended to discuss the plan with the French Finance Minister, Christine Lagarde, and the German Finance Minister, Wolfgang Schäuble.

But towards the end of the second week of November, a long-distance phone call from Olli Rehn, who had visited Dublin a few days earlier, confirmed that Lenihan's bespoke plan for Ireland was not going to work. Under pressure from the ECB, the Government shortly afterwards applied for a financial assistance programme from the EU/IMF. In the negotiations, Lenihan, supported by the IMF staff, wanted to reduce the cost to the State of recapitalising the banks by imposing losses on the banks' senior bonds. But the ECB would not countenance such a move. In fact, there was considerable opposition to bailing in bondholders in finance ministries across Europe and in the G7 group of countries. In the end, the Troika ruled out imposing losses on senior bank bonds. When the issue of burden sharing came up during the general election campaign in early 2011, Lenihan remarked that the new government would probably have more success pursuing other approaches at European level to reduce the cost to the State of rescuing the banks.

Europe's evolving response to the euro crisis was at times chaotic. Lenihan described a meeting of euro area finance ministers around that time in which the Finnish ministry wanted Ireland to offer the state-owned ESB as collateral for loans from the European rescue funds.

The measures for ending the banking crisis contained in the EU/IMF programme built upon Lenihan's efforts. As he put it himself, the programme meant 'more capital and more NAMA.' Lenihan had long wanted more support from Europe to repair the banks. 'A small sovereign like Ireland faced with an outsized problem that we have in our banking sector, cannot on its own address all those problems,' he said. By the time he left office in March 2011, the institutional arrangements in Europe to address banking crises were still not fully in place. Things are still evolving in that regard. As the head of the European Stability Mechanism (Europe's bailout fund), Klaus Regling, said in early 2014,the European-level responses to the crisis have evolved over time and that options that were not available to Ireland, Portugal or Greece have become available now, while new options may become available in the future.

CONCLUSION

Ireland's property bubble was one of the largest on record internationally. For nearly three years as finance minister, Lenihan lived with the consequences of the bursting of that bubble. The international experience provides plenty of examples of banking crises less severe and less complicated than Ireland's where bank depositors lost their life savings and businesses their working capital. Ireland did not suffer that fate.

Lenihan was the doctor on duty when the critically injured banks arrived at the A&E department. In working out the consequences of the property bubble, extraordinary measures were needed to meet extraordinary challenges. For sure, the Irish banks have not yet been restored to full health. History, however, will surely show that Brian Lenihan's incredible hard work and courage during the most acute phase of the crisis put the banking system and the Irish economy on the road to recovery.

2 A MAN OF CHARACTER

JIM FLAHERTY

IN 1985, CANADIAN PRIME Minister Brian Mulroney and American President Ronald Reagan met in Quebec City for a bilateral summit. Because of their shared Irish heritage, the meeting was dubbed 'the Shamrock Summit' – an amusing title which reflected the good-natured relationship between Prime Minister Mulroney and President Reagan. Since Canada's Confederation in 1867, Irish heritage has played a critical role in our history and our relationships. When I became Canada's Finance Minister, I wanted to continue the tradition of strong Irish-Canadian relations. Upon meeting my Irish counterpart, the late Brian Lenihan, I could tell that we would share a good working relationship. What neither of us knew at the time was that we were about to embark on one of the most challenging periods of our lives: the global economic crisis. Although Brian did not survive to see his good work come to fruition, I can honestly say that his steadfast leadership and commitment to fiscal responsibility helped Ireland to stave off the worst effects of the recession. His commitment to his country and his resolute leadership stand as important reminders for future generations of the Irish people – at home and abroad – of what it means to be a good public servant.

I became the Minister of Finance for Canada on 6 February 2006. We were elected as a minority government. This meant that we always had two strategies: a short-term one should our government be defeated in the House of Commons and a longer-term strategy focusing on long-term economic growth, jobs, and prosperity. This government was re-elected in October 2008, but again as a minority government.

I mention all of this because Brian Lenihan became Minister for Finance in Ireland in May 2008. Ireland forms part of the constituency led by Canada at the IMF and World Bank, along with the English-speaking countries of the Caribbean. Brian became Minister at a time when the credit crisis was well underway having first surfaced in the sub-prime mortgage market in the USA in August 2007. The developed economies, including Ireland and Canada, were also entering the crisis in the real economy, now referred to as the Great Recession. So, I had to deal with a minority government at home and a deteriorating economy at home and abroad. Brian was confronted by an Irish economy which experienced one of the worst recessions among developed countries, with growing unemployment and government deficits.

In the autumn of 2008, banks were failing in the USA, UK, and some regional German banks. On 30 September 2008, the Government of Ireland extended a bank guarantee designed to cover all deposits, covered bonds, senior debt, and dated subordinate debt. This initiative sent shockwaves outside of Ireland. Then, in December 2008, the Irish Government announced a capital injection of US $7.6 billion into the country's three main banks.

I discussed the bank situation and, of course, the housing bubble with Brian at the fall IMF/World Bank meetings in Washington in 2008 and at subsequent meetings. There was serious concern at the IMF that it was essential for Ireland to enter into a financial aid agreement with the IMF. Ireland resisted, knowing full well that many of the European governments that had accepted IMF 'packages' had been defeated in their next elections.

At one point, the IMF asked me to intervene as the leader of the Canadian constituency at the IMF to demand that Ireland raise its corporate tax rate as a condition of receiving IMF aid. Brian dismissed this suggestion. I did not press the point given not only that the lower corporate tax rate was a proven economic advantage for Ireland, but also the unemployment rate and public debt in Ireland were both rising dramatically. It was not the time to discourage investment in Ireland.

The Finance Minister took further steps, including the introduction of the National Asset Management Agency, which would buy roughly €81 billion worth of property development and commercial assets from participating banks at a significant discount, and stricter regulatory requirements.

We had many discussions about the IMF financial aid proposal. I learned about his family's history in polictics, met his brother, and enjoyed his company. I knew of his illness, although Brian never mentioned it to me or made a word of complaint. We lamented from time to time that we had both been Minister of Justice (Ireland for Brian, Ontario for me) and barristers. I believe that we shared the feeling that our work in the justice systems had perhaps been more satisfying than dealing with banks, developers, audit agencies, and the rest.

On a later golf round in Ireland, after Brian's death, with a few of my Canadian friends, the caddy commented on the diminished value of a property which he had visited in Dublin. He was not a young man. One of my golf partners (a Canadian Member of Parliament), who likes to create mischief, asked him what caused the housing price collapse. He replied that 'it was the fucking politicians and the banks – and the lawyers too!' I thought this covered my career (and a good part of Brian's) comprehensively. It was a few holes later when another of my golf partners shared with the caddy that I was a lawyer, a politician, and Canada's Minister of Finance. The caddy recovered quickly with 'well, we could use you here now that Brian Lenihan is gone.'

Back to the IMF and Ireland. Not only were there continuing discussions of Ireland 'taking a package,' but also there was a voting quota question. Ireland, Luxembourg, Canada, and others accepted reductions in our voting shares. Each country, not each constituency, vote independently on voting quota issues. Brian felt that the larger European countries had not wanted to give up more quota than they did to emerging economies and therefore, in effect, capped the smaller European economies. He always fought to defend Irish interests.

At the end of many discussions, the Government of Ireland chose to accept the IMF package of financial aid. I had encouraged Brian frequently to do so, but, as an elected person, I knew also that the consequences at the polls would be dire. But these are the tests of character in political life, are they not? If it is only about getting re-elected regardless of the public good, one will not run short of willing politicians. Brian Lenihan had character. He took the essential steps for his country's economic recovery. He has been proven right.

When Brian called to inform me that the Government of Ireland had taken the decision to accept the IMF financial aid package, I congratulated him on his courage and foresight. He sounded relieved and even a bit cheerful. I said that he seemed to be in good humour despite it all. He said: 'Ah, Jim, we weren't rich all that long!'

Brian, of course, was re-elected despite the government's defeat – a testament to his enduring commitment to public service. He was a fine man and an excellent Finance Minister. Moreover, I can honestly say that his leadership is greatly missed internationally.

3 IN MEMORY OF BRIAN LENIHAN: A PERSONAL REFLECTION

PAUL GALLAGHER

AFTER THE CONCLUSION OF our last Cabinet Meeting on 8 March 2011, it was Brian Lenihan's turn to speak and say his goodbyes. He began with a short recitation of Milton, effortless and poignant. He finished exuding his usual confidence and positivity. He was the only Fianna Fáil TD from a Dublin constituency to retain his seat. He was still working hard. There were difficult outstanding banking issues to be dealt with. Brian had his papers with him and he had earlier been discussing an issue that needed to be resolved prior to the change of government. He was still energised and quietly defiant. Though he knew death was approaching, it was difficult for the rest of us to believe this to be the case. He spoke and acted as if, like his colleagues, he were merely moving on to the next chapter of his life.

This reflection is offered as a personal insight derived from my very significant contact with Brian in the last few years of his life. The focus is on Brian and the context in which he discharged his public duties.

Brian was a remarkable man. His courage and determination were evident in the manner in which he met, without complaint, the great trials and obstacles he faced in the last few years of his life. Brian's life changed utterly in the summer of 2008. From then, until his death three years later, his life was dominated by political and personal challenges. He has left a great legacy of courage and

determination and provided an example of what the human spirit can achieve no matter how constrained by circumstances.

It will take much calmer reflection at a national level to recognise the true enormity of the challenges, arising from the financial and economic crisis, faced by Brian Lenihan and his Government colleagues between June 2008 to March 2011. The challenges were unrelenting in their ferocity, their scale, their complexity and their novelty. There was little guidance to those who had the unenviable task of dealing with the challenges and of making urgent and critical decisions on matters of great complexity and consequence. There was no consensus amongst experts here or abroad as to how those challenges should be met. There were so many uncertainties and so many unknown and uncontrollable factors rendering any decision difficult and risk prone. The one certainty was that avoiding decisions was not an option.

In this personal reflection, I do not attempt to portray in detail the atmosphere and environment of the time or the context in which Brian had to operate. It is important, however, to understand that context in a general way in order to understand Brian and his achievements. It must also be recognised that throughout his period of office, as is well known, Brian received great support from his colleagues in government and, in particular, from the Taoiseach. The Minister for Finance is a member of government and the major decisions that he takes are approved by government. Brian also received great support from the Secretary-Generals in the Department of Finance and from so many other civil servants and advisers. In reflecting on Brian's achievements, it is very important that the role of others should not be overlooked.[1]

Brian was a brilliant young barrister, but it was clear that politics was the great love of his life. He could have enjoyed great and enduring success at the Bar. He had, in fact, become a Senior Counsel in 1997 but ultimately the call of public service drowned out any thought of personal gain. Brian's reward for this selfless public service came when he was appointed Minister for Justice on 14 June 2007.

Brian was a dynamic and very hard-working Minister for Justice. He was full of new ideas and had very definite views on what he needed to do as Minister. I was always impressed by his deep understanding of his responsibilities and, in particular, his great respect for the law and the Constitution. He also had a deep understanding of politics and of the political system. This was of immense help to him in proposing and securing the passage of legislation. He had an intense interest in the legislative agenda and committed himself to some critical legislative projects (which his short time in the portfolio prevented him from bringing to a conclusion), including Civil Partnership and Immigration,[2] the latter being designed to implement very significant reforms in immigration law and procedures. He had an excellent understanding not only of the legal problems which his legislation sought to address, but also of the technicalities of the legislation and of the practicalities in terms of what could be achieved. Above all, Brian had great integrity and a deep belief in the Rule of Law.

In 2008, during the Slovenian Presidency of the European Union, I accompanied Brian on a trip to Ljubljana for a Council of Ministers' meeting in the area of Justice and Home Affairs. At the meeting, he was fully in command of his brief and was clearly highly respected by his European colleagues. My abiding memory of the trip, however, related not to the official business, but to Brian's deep interest in a little known Irish saint, St. Coloman of Stockerau, who as an Irish pilgrim travelling to the Holy Land was tortured and hanged near Vienna on suspicion of being a spy. St. Coloman had travelled through Slovenia on his journey to the Holy Land. Brian, being deeply interested in history and all things Irish, was interested in learning more about St. Coloman's connection with Slovenia, despite the fact that, at best, St. Coloman was one of history's footnotes. I was struck by Brian's effortless knowledge of this little known saint and his quite extraordinary hunger for more knowledge about him. This, of course, was very characteristic of Brian. There was no subject, however, arcane or esoteric, in which he was not interested and very few matters about which he did not display a very impressive

knowledge, not only of the general subject matter, but of the detail. This ability to store and assimilate information was to stand him in good stead in the forthcoming challenges of which he was then blissfully unaware.

Brian had great enthusiasm for all aspects of his Justice brief and displayed the surefootedness and insight of a longstanding and very experienced minister. A life in politics had prepared him well. These were qualities that were very apparent to his colleagues. Taoiseach Brian Cowen made an inspired decision in choosing Brian as his Minister for Finance in May 2008. It was in this latter office that Brian will be long remembered. Much has been said about Brian in that role. Much has been made of Brian's ministerial inexperience, his lack of any qualifications in finance or economics and of the fact that he had little time to prepare for the financial maelstrom, which hit the financial systems of Europe and the United States in late summer 2008.

Those comments are usually stated by way of an implied criticism, but, in my view, they miss the point. It is true that Brian had been a Minister for less than a year when he was appointed Minister for Finance, but few elected representatives ever had such a profound and instinctive knowledge of the operations of government and of parliamentary democracy. Brian had been acquiring political knowledge all his life, having grown up in a deeply political environment. It is also true that Brian had no formal qualifications in finance or economics, but very few Ministers of Finance in Ireland or, indeed, elsewhere have had such qualifications. He had other qualities which were of equal if not greater importance. He had the ability to rapidly absorb complex information and to apply it to the practical reality confronting him. He also had the confidence and judgment to make decisions. He knew when to listen and when to act. He canvassed many opinions from many different people. These served not to impede his decision-making process, but contributed to it. He readily segregated good and bad advice and was not afraid to reject advice from any quarter if, after consideration, he did not agree with it. He was open to ideas and to suggestions, but never feared having to make a decision and to take responsibility for it.

From time to time, I have heard commentators suggest that Brian may not have had an understanding of technical details. I do not agree. There were, undoubtedly, many things he had to learn. He, undoubtedly, made mistakes. He did, however, possess the capacity to master technical information and issues confidently and quickly and, when he needed to make important decisions, he ensured that he had a thorough understanding of the technical complexities.

In order to understand the context and, more particularly, what Brian and the Government faced in September 2008, it is necessary to describe briefly some of the international events which brought much of the western world's financial system to the brink of destruction. It must be remembered that Ireland initially faced this crisis entirely on its own and without the financial or economic resources enjoyed by the large states and without the monetary tools necessary for this purpose. Ireland was a member of the Economic and Monetary Union, (EMU), but it retained sovereignty and responsibility in respect of its own financial system. Under the then European Treaties,[3] the European Central Bank (the ECB) was responsible for monetary policy, but it not only had no responsibility for intervening to prevent the collapse of a Euro member's financial system, but was expressly prohibited by law from doing so.[4] In fact, as Governor Mario Draghi was later to demonstrate, the ECB could have done much more than it did in those early critical months. Jacques Delors, one of the Euro's chief architects, in a speech in Brussels on 28 March 2012, criticised the ECB's approach at that time. When Governor Draghi took over the ECB he reversed the interest rates increases in November/December 2011 and expanded the pre-existing longer term refinancing operations (LTRO), which permitted banks to borrow large amounts of money from the ECB for terms as long as three years and demonstrated that much could be done by the ECB within its legal constraints.

Many would say that the financial crisis, which led to what is now known as the 'Great Recession,' began in 2007 in the US with the collapse of the sub-prime mortgage market.[5] The problems in financial markets gathered pace in 2008. In March 2008, the US Federal Reserve, supported by the Treasury, contributed almost

3 In Memory of Brian Lenihan: A Personal Refection

$30 billion to facilitate the takeover of Bear Stearns by JP Morgan. International financial markets were getting very uneasy. However, there was still great optimism with regard to the future and little sense of the impending calamity. Governor Jean-Claude Trichet, in June 2008, at a ceremony in Frankfurt's Opera House to celebrate the tenth anniversary of the ECB, hailed the Euro as a 'remarkable success' and stated that he had no wish to name and shame those who predicted it would fail.[6] However, unlike other Central Banks, such as the US Federal Reserve Bank and the Bank of England, the ECB could not act to regulate liquidity and interest rates in capital markets by making large-scale purchase of government bonds. Under the then interpretation of its mandate and powers, it in effect was an interested but powerless bystander. As mentioned above, the ECB's legal mandate to address the dramatic events of September 2008, which triggered, certainly in this country, a financial and economic crisis of unprecedented proportions, was limited. The ECB did, of course, have power to cut interest rates, but it refused to do so until October 2008. The 4 per cent overnight rate that prevailed in August 2007 did not fall to 3.25 per cent until November 2008 and did not get as low as 2 per cent until January 2009. By contrast, the Federal Reserve was virtually 0 per cent by December 2008. This situation undoubtedly made it more difficult, particularly for a small country like Ireland, to address the problems created by the financial crisis.

On 16 September 2008, the US Federal Reserve had to extend a loan of $85 billion to AIG, the American insurance giant to save it from collapse. Morgan Stanley was also in trouble. It borrowed heavily from the Primary Dealer Credit Facility set up by the Federal Reserve's Board of Governors to lend money to securities firms by broadening the range of eligible collateral. Morgan Stanley and Goldman Sachs applied to the Federal Reserve to become banks in order to obtain the protection which was available to banks. Merrill Lynch was about to collapse and was sold to Bank of America in order to save it. Washington Mutual, the nation's largest savings and loan association and the sixth largest bank of any kind, failed on 25 September 2008. All this followed the collapse of Lehman Brothers on 15 September 2008.

Around the same time in Germany, Hypo Real Estate Bank had to be supported with a €35 billion credit arranged by the German Finance Ministry because of a liquidity run. The proposed deal fell apart on 6 October 2008 and the Bundesbank had to arrange a new line of credit, this time for €50 billion and subsequently the bank was nationalised in 2009.

Following the collapse of Washington Mutual in the United States, there was a silent run on Wachovia, the US's fourth largest bank (it was twice the size of Washington Mutual). The market value of Wachovia's ten-year bonds dropped from 73 cents in the Dollar to 29 cents. In effect, the bonds of America's fourth largest bank were then junk bonds. Wells Fargo stepped in on 3 October 2008 under government pressure to save Wachovia and, on the same day, the US Congress passed a modified version of the Troubled Assets Relief Programme ('TARP').[7]

On 25 September 2008, rumours circulated that Fortis, a gigantic banking insurance investment conglomerate, based in the Benelux countries, was in difficulty. The Belgian, Luxembourg and Netherlands Governments offered support to Fortis. They announced that the banking division would be nationalised, with the three countries investing a total of €11.2 billion in return for about two-thirds ownership. A few days later, Dexia, a substantial Belgian bank with worldwide operations, came under severe pressure and sought State Aid. It received a capital injection and State guarantee of its liabilities and subsequently had to be nationalised in October 2011.

On 29 September, the US House of Representatives rejected the TARP. After its rejection, the US Stock Market fell almost 9 per cent the next day, destroying about $1.25 trillion of wealth – representing twice the monies for which TARP had provided.

On 11 October 2008, an emergency meeting of the Euro Group launched a comprehensive plan in an attempt to save their banking systems. The plan consisted of thirteen points and provided for the ECB to intervene in the financial turmoil to boost liquidity. Eurozone governments undertook to underwrite bank debt until the end of the following year and committed to preventing the collapse of 'systemically relevant institutions through appropriate means, including recapitalisation.'

The Euro Group had been encouraged to adopt this rescue plan by the British Prime Minister, Gordon Brown, who emphasised that government guarantees for inter-bank lending were 'absolutely critical' to freeing up the banking paralysis. The French Government announced that it would legislate on similar guarantees, while Chancellor Merkel and her government prepared draft emergency plans which were reported to factor in up to €300 billion for underwriting German bank debts issuance.

The UK Government the previous week announced a three part £550 billion programme, which involved the injection of £50 billion into bank capital reserves, £250 billion to guarantee loans between banks and involved lending another £250 billion directly to commercial banks.

On 23 November 2008, the US Treasury, the Federal Reserve Bank and the Federal Deposit Insurance Corporation (FDIC) issued a joint press release bailing out CitiGroup, the giant conglomerate which was the nation's largest bank at the time, and they agreed to guarantee a designated pool of US$306 billion in assets.

The great Central Banks of the world, the most experienced of politicians and finance ministers and the most celebrated economists struggled to cope with and control 'the Great Recession.' There were no tried and tested solutions to the problem. The ECB had no answer and its powers were limited. The scale of what was emerging, the enormous uncertainty created by the events which were occurring, the difficulty in predicting what would happen and the inability to control exogenous factors and, in particular, developments in other states and international market forces, posed an enormous and unprecedented threat to Ireland's financial and economic survival.

It is easy at this remove to lose sight of Ireland's isolation and its complete inability to control international events and, in particular, events on the financial markets having the most profound consequences for Ireland and its financial system. This lack of control coupled with the inherent difficulty in devising workable solutions made the problems faced all the more intractable and daunting.

Added to these problems were the difficulties in predicting financial markets and their ongoing impact on the economy.

The instantaneous assessments and reactions of international markets, the suddenness of financial economic developments and the frequent imminence of potentially catastrophic consequences required decisiveness and a clear vision and, above all, the courage and ability to make decisions and, when the occasion demanded, to make them quickly. Brian had these qualities in abundance and when making decisions he had the ability to consider varied and multifaceted problems and to assimilate great volumes of information. The scale of what faced him and what needed to be done would have overwhelmed most people, but not Brian. He was never daunted by the circumstances in which the decisions had to be made, by the necessity to make immediate decisions, by the impossibility of being certain as to the effect or outcome of the decisions or by the requirement to make decisions when there were so many matters relevant to that decision over which he had no control. I found it remarkable that during this period he never once sought to avoid issues or problems. In fact, the contrary was the case. He was always looking ahead to identify the problems that were likely to develop and he would consider how they might be addressed if they did develop. This ability to think ahead and to anticipate problems was of immense importance because it provided an additional opportunity for consideration of issues and problems which ultimately had to be confronted. Most people would have wished existing problems away and would not have had the time or the energy or the willpower to begin thinking about problems that had not yet emerged. Brian was very different from most people.

Added to these external pressures on Ireland was the domestic collapse, the scale of which was enormous. Real GDP fell by 3 per cent in 2008, 7 per cent in 2009 and unemployment rose to almost 14 per cent by the end of 2010. These domestic developments and the rapidity with which they occurred, greatly exacerbated the problems for the domestic banks. They also created great difficulties in developing a budgetary strategy that could cope with, on the one hand, the huge collapse in public finances and, on the other, the continuing demands on those public finances – not least because of the large increase in unemployment. This and the financial support for the banks led to a huge increase in Ireland's budget deficit. Ireland moved from a surplus of 0.1 per cent GDP in 2007 to deficits of 7.3 per cent and 14 per cent of GDP in 2008 and 2009 and plunged to a 31.2 per cent deficit in 2010.[8] The resulting budgetary challenges were immense, both at the level of principle and at a political level. At the level of principle, a means had to be found to bring public finances under control. At a political level, great care had to be taken to ensure that not only would the necessary measures be approved by the Oireachtas, but that the cuts would not lead to social disruption and a breakdown of societal cohesion. Brian understood what needed to be done and never flinched from these challenges. Again his understanding of what was politically possible and what would be accepted by the people was of vital importance. Brian was very conscious of the effect of cutbacks on those who needed State support and it required great determination and focus to take the necessary steps to address the budgetary problems. I remember Brian speaking to me about this with great sadness and compassion on a number of occasions.

By the middle of 2009, it was clear that the Irish banks had a large number of problem loans which were not being addressed and, unless some solution was found, it was feared that this would result in 'zombie' banks, which would be unable to engage in the lending which a real economy required. In a situation where the value of troubled assets was continuing to decline, some action was required to address the problem. There was no tried and tested formula anywhere for solving the problem and the financial and legal issues that needed to be addressed as part of any solution were of immense complexity. There was also the political reality that any attempt to remove bad loans from the banks would be seen and represented as helping the banks and, worse still, helping the developers whose loans were now so severely impaired.

The proposal for the National Asset Management Agency Bill was published for the purpose of public consultation at the end of July 2009. The proposal was quite unique. It contained the detailed provisions of the Bill which were to be subject to further change and refinement following public consultation and further internal review. The proposal described in detail how NAMA was to operate and how it would affect the participating banks and their debtors. Between the publication of the proposal and the eventual passage of the Act on 22 November 2009, Brian participated in the very animated and, at times, bitter public debate on the proposal and provided careful explanation of what the NAMA Act would involve and how it would affect the banks and others. The change in public attitude to the proposed NAMA Act, which ultimately facilitated its passage through the Oireachtas in November 2009, was in large part due to his indefatigable defence of the proposal and his willingness to engage in public on the detail of the proposals and on the concerns raised about them. His mastery of the detail of the complex legislation and his deep understanding of the rationale for the legislation and its necessity, in terms of dealing with the problems created by the volume and extent of impaired bank loans, enabled him to respond to the trenchant criticisms of the proposal and to convert many who were sceptical about it. When Brian spoke, people listened and trusted him. Brian was convinced, as was clear from his public statements, of the necessity of this Bill in order to deal with the problems of the financial system, but it took great courage to be so publicly associated with a proposal that initially looked as if it would certainly be defeated. It also took great courage to champion a proposal that involved such an enormous commitment by the State and the success or otherwise of which would only be determined many years in the future.

NAMA was, of course, only one of the many challenges Brian faced in 2009. In legislative terms, Brian also introduced legislation to provide for a substantial reduction in the remuneration of public servants. This meant that all persons employed or holding office in public service bodies, which embraced in effect the wider public service and, therefore, a very significant part of the electorate, were to be subjected for the first time to reduction[9] in remuneration from 3 per cent to 10 per cent, depending on their salary. Ensuring the passage of such a measure through the Houses of the Oireachtas was a major achievement. In 2009, Brian was also responsible for the introduction and passage of a number of other very important legislative measures affecting financial matters, including the Finance Act, the Financial Services (Deposit Guarantee Scheme) Act, and the Financial Emergency Measures in the Public Interest Act, (No. 2) Act, 2009.

Brian's work rate in 2009 was astonishing. He was indefatigable and continued to engage fully in all aspects of political life. He was always optimistic that the measures taken would improve Ireland's financial situation. Nothing could have prepared him, or the rest of us, for the tragic news that Brian was to receive a few days before Christmas 2009 and nothing could have prepared him for what was to be the greatest challenge of his life. Brian had no inkling in December 2009 that he had any serious illness. The diagnosis of his illness came as a complete shock. Brian's reaction to his illness was as awesome as it was inspiring. I remember talking to Brian about his diagnosis shortly after it was made. He was his usual courteous self and appreciative of the inquiry and concern. He was able to talk about his illness and what it meant in a detached but very focused and realistic way. He made no complaint about his diagnosis. Above all, there was no element of self-pity.

The diagnosis was very serious and the prognosis for recovery was very poor, as he well knew. His decision to continue in office and to carry out his public duties was a reflection of his sense of public duty and of his great personal courage. He spoke of his decision as if it were the only obvious decision to make and certainly expected no thanks or commendation for it. It was, in fact, a momentous and courageous decision. He could so easily have given up the struggle against the unremitting tide of financial and economic problems battering the State and nobody would have blamed him for doing so. To gain any appreciation of the courage involved in the decision, one has to understand the scale of the challenges he continued to face and the enormity of the burden, which he continued to carry and that he knew was unlikely to diminish.

Throughout 2010 I would have seen Brian at cabinet and would have met him or spoken to him every few days. His performance levels were remarkable. He had no difficulty meeting the tremendously tight timelines in which decisions had to be made and issues confronted and had no difficulty in confronting the issues. He did not waste time lamenting his condition nor did he seek sympathy. I remember mentally remarking on many occasions that, if I did not know he was ill, I would not have even suspected it. He behaved precisely as he did before and even when he appeared at cabinet after treatment he conducted his usual workload. I did not notice any diminution in his capacity or determination. His only apparent concession to his illness was to bring a couch into his office to enable him to take a rest during the course of the day, when he needed to do so, and to develop a passion for green tea, but apart from these nods to his illness and a reduction in the large number of public and political commitments which he undertook, he continued to perform at a level which made it very difficult to believe that there was anything really wrong with him. Every now and again there would, however, be some little reminder of what he was confronting. I remember one day sympathising with him over some problem he had to deal with. He looked at me, smiled and shrugged and said that every day you are alive is a great day. I will never forget the remark. It was, as usual, made without self-pity or sorrow. It was a remark as simple as it was inspiring.

Many remember the dispiriting days of November 2010, but few remember the important external events which transformed the cautious optimism of early 2010 into the deep pessimism of November. As Donovan and Murphy point out,[10] in a narrow and financial sense 2010 began relatively well for Ireland. Although the economy was still in deep recession, the NTMA continued to borrow at rates which, although slightly higher than normal, were well within an acceptable range. In the spring of 2010, it became clear that Greece was in real trouble and it applied, in April 2010, for a bailout. The emergency support for Greece did not calm the markets. In May 2010, shortly after the launch of the Greek Programme, EU member states decided on the creation of a €750 billion support fund for states cut off from market funding.[11]

As the true scale of the Greek problem became apparent and as it emerged that Greece had entered the EMU on the basis of fraudulent government statistics and had continued to report false numbers, the markets reacted angrily and Irish Government bond yields rose steadily from May 2010. In August 2010, Standard & Poors issued a very unfavourable rating assessment of Ireland. Market sentiment was worsened by the Deauville Declaration which followed a bilateral summit between Chancellor Merkel and President Sarkozy. The Declaration issued on 18 October 2010 suggesting that lenders in the sovereign debt market might face losses in future bailouts, had the effect of causing immense increases in Irish bond yields. These external developments created enormous problems for Ireland. In addition, the ECB was greatly concerned with its financial exposure to Ireland and the statement by ECB President Trichet in September 2010 expressed concern about the amount of Emergency Liquidity Assistance (ELA) outstanding to Anglo Irish Bank.

The Cabinet decided on Sunday 21 November 2010 to apply for financial assistance from the EU. Brian had to fly out to Brussels that Sunday morning to finalise the agreement and the bailout terms. He rang me from Baldonnell airport. Weather conditions were appalling. He had been up late the night before and had attended the Cabinet meeting at which the decision to apply for a bailout was made. As always, he was very focused. He was aware of the immensity of what he was doing and its consequences for Ireland. He gave no consideration to himself or what it might mean for him. His only concern was to achieve the best possible outcome for his country. Again, there was no sense of self-pity or regret that he had to discharge this unenviable task. It was an extremely poignant and historical moment. He was doing something which no other Finance Minister ever had to do. He knew too that he would forever be associated with this event and that all of his decisions since becoming Minister for Finance would be closely questioned and evaluated. He realised this evaluation would be conducted, in many cases, by those who were only too willing to criticise with the benefit of hindsight and with the luxury of never having had to make such difficult decisions and, particularly, decisions in such extraordinary and unforgiving circumstances. He also knew, only too well, that the bailout would have huge political consequences for him and his party. Again, however, there was no trace of self-pity or despondency and, above all, no regret that he had continued to fight the battle after the diagnosis of his illness.

Following the bailout, there was still much for Brian and the Government to do. A budget had to be introduced based on the economic programme prepared by the Government prior to the bailout and which was, in substance, adopted by the Troika, as the basis for the financial conditionality reflected in the Memorandum of Understanding to which Ireland was obliged to subscribe in order to obtain the benefit of the bailout. This budget inevitably carried very serious political consequences, as he and the Government acknowledged publicly at the time.

In December, Brian also introduced the Credit Institutions Stabilisation Bill, an extremely important and complex piece of legislation designed to provide a resolution framework for failing banks, while avoiding the ever-present risk of triggering a bond default consequent on such resolution, which would have had disastrous consequences for the banks and the economy generally. This was in large part unchartered territory. Brian steered this Bill through the Dáil and Seanad under an immensely tight time schedule. Its passage was essential to facilitate urgent State investment in the banks, including a vitally important investment in Allied Irish Banks the following day, and its passage was a condition of Troika support. The legislation was extremely controversial, but it provided a resolution framework for dealing with the troubled banks and for reducing the entitlements of subordinate bondholders.

The events of November and December 2010 would have overwhelmed even the strongest of people. It had been a truly momentous year for Brian, who must have encountered the full range of human emotions and, in addition, great stress and personal anxiety. It was a year which would have been mentally and physically exhausting for the toughest and fittest person. One can only wonder how any person could have survived all of this while undergoing treatment for his illness and yet perform so remarkably. Late on the evening of 23 December 2010, when most had given up any thought of any work until after Christmas, Brian contacted me and asked that we go for a drink to discuss important work that needed to be completed over the remaining life of the Government. By this stage, it was clear that the Government had only a very limited lifespan, as the Green Party had indicated its desire to leave Government after the budgetary measures had been passed. We went over to a nearby hotel together. Brian explained in detail and with clarity what he wished to achieve.

Brian's only focus was on the country's interest. He displayed no consideration for his personal convenience or comfort. Completing his public duty was his only objective. The meeting was relaxed and convivial, but there was no mistaking his determination to achieve these objectives and his willingness to do whatever was required of him in order to achieve them. Shortly before we got up to go, Brian spoke to me in words which are indelibly etched in my memory and which were said without self-pity or fear. He said: 'You know I have only a very short time to live.' That was the first and only time he had ever said that. He had always conducted himself as if his own survival was never an issue. It was impossible to respond in any meaningful way. I do not know what defines heroism or what makes people heroic and we should be very slow to use such an exalted term but for me that was the closest encounter I ever had with heroism.

Given Brian's fondness for Milton, it is perhaps ironic that Milton's *Lycidas* best expresses the overwhelming sense of loss at the passing of one who did so much and promised even more:

> Bitter constraint and sad occasion dear
> Compels me to disturb your season due;
> For Lycidas is dead, dead ere his prime,
> Young Lycidas, and hath not left his peer,
> Who would not sing for Lycidas? he knew
> Himself to sing, and build the lofty rhyme.
> He must not float upon his wat'ry bier
> Unwept, and welter to the parching wind,
> Without the meed of some melodious tear.[12]

4 THE BATTLE TO RESTORE FISCAL STABILITY

CATHY HERBERT

AT A CONSTRUCTION INDUSTRY conference in Dublin Castle in June 2008, a month after his appointment as Minster for Finance, Brian Lenihan mused laconically, and not a little wistfully, that it had been his misfortune to have been appointed Minister for Finance just as the building boom was grinding to a 'shuddering halt'.

All hell broke loose. He was accused of throwing a wobbler, of wallowing in self-pity, of talking down the economy. For months, one national newspaper referred to him as the 'gaffe-prone' Minister for Finance.

At this remove, it seems extraordinary that such a blindingly obvious observation would cause such a furore. But it was the beginning of a pattern. Throughout his two years and nine months as Minister for Finance, Brian Lenihan coaxed a reluctant public and his fearful government colleagues to face the unpalatable truth about the extent of our economic crisis and to accept the need, however grudgingly, for the toughest budgets in our history.

Around the time he made his unguarded remark, he was finding out just how bad the figures were. He quickly realised the severe shortfall in tax revenue required an immediate response. On 13 June 2008, as news of the defeat of the Lisbon Treaty was filtering through from count centres around the country, he walked across to the Taoiseach's office to brief him about the need for emergency measures to address the rapidly deteriorating budgetary position. It was a dark day for both men. Back in his office, Lenihan's natural ebullience had given way to a deep gloom about the task that lay ahead. He was shaken by the gulf that lay between the triumphalism of the crowd that had drowned him out during a brief visit to the count centre in Dublin Castle and the harsh reality of the budgetary position outlined to him by his officials in the previous month. He despaired that he could ever bring a population that believed it could defy the expressed will of 500 million fellow EU citizens to accept the difficult decisions he knew he would have to make.

He did what he always did when he was worried: he telephoned a list of people – colleagues, close friends, acquaintances and people whom he barely knew but respected – and discussed the sorry position upside down and inside out until he could see a way through to the next step. This habitual, informal consultation process with a variety of touchstones was his coping mechanism throughout his torrid time in Finance.

On 8 July, he announced a series of measures to achieve immediate savings of €440 million. It was the first of six bouts of increasingly painful budgetary correction in his constant battle to stabilise the public finances. Two years and four months later, he lost that battle. But his dogged efforts made our bailout programme considerably less drastic than it might otherwise have been.

It became clear almost as soon as the July package was announced that it was inadequate. In September, it was decided to bring forward the budget by two months to October. That decision has since been blamed for the controversy that the budget provoked, swiftly leading to a number of high profile reversals. It certainly was an inelegant budget but it is doubtful that more time for greater deliberation would have made the kind of measures that needed to be taken any more palatable. Our position was pretty dire and our choices severely limited. We simply had to tax more and spend less: there was no painless way to do either, particularly after seven years of giveaway budgets.

As Lenihan was grappling with this budgetary dilemma, he was also dealing with the mounting liquidity crisis in our banks, which had intensified following the collapse of Lehman Brothers on 15 September. Two weeks later, the Government made the decisions to guarantee virtually all of our banks' liabilities.

Notwithstanding the enormous consequences of that decision for our economy and for the Irish people, it was the alarming growth of our budget deficit that was uppermost in the minds of most of us in the Department of Finance in those weeks leading up to Budget Day on 15 October. The extent of the solvency issues in the banks had yet to emerge and the ferocity and depth of the international financial crisis could not have been foreseen. By contrast, the threat posed to our financial stability by our ballooning deficit was real and pressing.

Lenihan had hoped that bringing forward the budget would demonstrate to the public the gravity of this threat. In that respect, at least, it certainly failed. Almost all of its elements were deemed unacceptable by those affected and the consensus was that the budget was unfair and picked on the most vulnerable. Few put their heads above the parapet in defence of a politically toxic but economically necessary set of measures. October 2008 was a lonely month in Merrion Street.

The decision to abolish the universal entitlement to medical cards for over seventies was derailed by protesting pensioners, the most effective political lobby group of this long and deep recession. The fact that the State pension was increased by €7 in that budget made no impact at the time and has long since faded from memory.

The truth is, in late 2008, the public and the political system had yet to grasp the full extent of our economic difficulties. To be fair, neither was the severity and depth of the recession fully appreciated internationally and forecasts everywhere turned out to be wide of the mark. The Department of Finance forecast of a mere 1 per cent contraction in GNP in 2009 was in line with the projections of the ESRI, the Central Bank and the IMF. There was an expectation that we would return to growth as early as 2010 and that unemployment would peak at just over 7 per cent.

Never having served in an economic ministry and having no background in economics or business, Lenihan had no special insight into the likely twists and turns of an international crisis. But he was obsessed with one thing: the need to bring public spending back to levels that reflected our available resources.

In the summer of 2008, he had watched from the sidelines as decisions on public service pay, the biggest element of public spending, were being taken in another arena across the courtyard from his office. Although officials from his Department took part in the talks, the Department of the Taoiseach was firmly in the driving seat. Privately, he was aghast that the rituals of social partnership were being played out, the actors apparently oblivious to the deteriorating economic backdrop. But a mere two months in his role as Minister for Finance, I suspect he was more reticent about his views around the cabinet table: social partnership was at the core of the political process and had become the preserve of the most powerful figures in the administration.

In the event, the talks broke down, earning the Taoiseach sharp criticism for his failure to do what every other Taoiseach had done since 1987: cut a deal with the unions. There was little acceptance either in the media or among the opposition that our circumstances had changed utterly. The talks reconvened in September and within days of the collapse of Lehman's, the Government conceded an award of 6 per cent over twenty-one months. I recall Lenihan asking two of his senior officials if we could afford the pay increase. If it was the price of industrial peace, he was told, it was worth it.

The exchequer returns at the end of 2008 showed a drop of more than €8 billion in tax receipts over the year. In January, the Government said immediate savings of €2 billion would have to be found. In early February, five months after it was granted, the pay increase was suspended and the Government introduced a public sector pension levy, which amounted to an average cut of 7.5 per cent in the pay of public servants without the agreement of the unions. A short time later, the social partners walked away from the process.

Lenihan had been in cabinet for just under a year when he was appointed Minister for Finance. I had worked with him since January 2006, just after the Office of the Minister for Children was set up and, as its political head, he began to attend Cabinet meetings. He was fascinated by the business of government and had an in-depth knowledge of how the system worked, much of which he learnt from his father, who had held seven different portfolios in his long political career. It was as if he had been training to be a minister all his life and when his time came, he was completely at ease in his role and supremely confident in his exercise of ministerial power. He loved Justice: as a well regarded lawyer, he was a natural fit and he knew many of the personnel, having served in that Department as a junior minister.

By contrast, the Department of Finance was more reserved and hierarchical. The offices with their doors closed; the echoes of footsteps on the marble floors: he used to say it reminded him of a monastery. Although he never said so, he must have found it daunting. Critics, and there were many, especially in the first year, pointed to his inexperience in cabinet and his lack of knowledge of financial matters: although some of the most experienced figures in finance and politics around the world lost their footing in this most intractable of crises. The criticism did not bother him much. He had a job to do and he set about his work in the Department with alacrity.

Finance was now centre stage having been sidelined during the boom. The Department was under the media spotlight as never before. Scarcely a day went by without some negative piece of commentary. It had come to the point where at least one official said he had stopped telling people where he worked. Merrion Street had been knocked off its stride by the speed and depth of the crisis.

Inevitably, a siege mentality took hold and there was defensiveness. But there was a healthy self-doubt and questioning at senior level that made it an interesting work environment. The idea of setting up an independent review of its performance over the previous decade came from the Department. The hubris for which Finance was known was gone and in its place was a refreshing honesty. I recall one senior official saying to Lenihan about some banking matter: 'Minister, we cannot advise you because we have never been in this position before.' In the white heat of the crisis, there was no time for 'Yes Minister' games.

Those officials, senior and junior, who worked closely with the Minister, strove incessantly to meet the unrelenting demands. Against a background of intense criticism in the media, a strong camaraderie developed and relationships strengthened. The younger group of senior officials in Finance and in the Department of the Taoiseach recognised the political imperative of communicating the seriousness of the crisis to the public and of providing a rationale for the actions that had to be taken. As never before, civil servants and political advisers worked together on communications strategies for the budgets.

Lenihan held most of his senior officials in high regard. A small number were slightly bemused by him: the messy state of his desk and the fact that he conducted his meetings mostly from his armchair – he only ever sat at his desk to take an important phone call. His notorious timekeeping was another source of annoyance.

They seemed surprised by his openness and informality. His often hilarious post-cabinet debriefs, were something of a novelty. His agile mind and his capacity to scrutinise issues through different lenses made him wonderful company, but sometimes difficult to manage, especially when officials were under time pressure to get decisions. A few never really adjusted to what they regarded as his unorthodox way of doing business.

He consulted widely outside of the department among economists and business people. From an early stage, he had regular meetings with, among others, Patrick Honohan, then in Trinity College and his colleague Philip Lane, Jim O'Leary, Colm McCarthy and Alan Ahearne, whom he later hired as an economic adviser. Some in the Department were uncomfortable about these meetings; one official remarked that the Minister was being too liberal with budgetary detail.

He went to the ESRI offices to exchange views and discuss policy options, apparently, the first Minister ever to have done so. That annoyed some in the Department, who read it as an indication of his distrust of their advice. In fact, Brian Lenihan was simply doing what he always did: taking soundings from a broad spectrum of opinion before coming to his own conclusions. He had a list of people he used to telephone most Sunday afternoons to discuss whatever was current or on his mind.

Among his confidantes was Ray Mac Sharry, the last Minister for Finance to have dealt with a major fiscal crisis. It was from one of his many conversations with Mac Sharry that the idea of a reprise of the Bord Snip exercise emerged. Apart from the obvious benefit of seeking out waste and inefficiency, Lenihan saw it as a powerful symbol. Bord Snip of the late eighties had gained an almost cultish status as a no-nonsense purge of a sclerotic system. Key to that reputation was the plain speaking economist Colm McCarthy, Bord Snip's public face. By asking McCarthy to do national service again, Lenihan hoped to leverage that reputation.

In effect, An Bord Snip Nua, as it quickly became known, was a souped-up, rolling estimates process under the baton of Colm McCarthy and his fellow Bord members. For officials in the Department of Finance, who did all of the leg work, it was an opportunity to resurrect all the cuts they had been proposing, however ineffectively, throughout the boom years. Lenihan was aware the subsequent report by the Bord would make politically unpalatable recommendations, which would never have a chance of being implemented. But he believed a forensic, independent, critical analysis of all public spending was needed to open up a debate and create a climate that would strengthen his hand in framing future budgets. He had also taken the precaution of committing to the publication of the Bord's report at the time of its establishment lest there be any danger of it not getting into the public domain.

There was little appetite in Government for An Bord Snip Nua, either at ministerial or senior official level and not everybody shared Lenihan's enthusiasm for the Colm McCarthy effect. But it resonated with the public mood and, and when its report was published in July 2009, it was a bestseller.

Lenihan had always been something of a fiscal conservative. As Minister for Justice, he resisted demands for a Court of Civil Appeal, at least in part because he believed the solution lay in making the existing structures more efficient, rather than creating an additional costly judicial layer. As Minister for Children, during discussions about the proposed amendment to the constitution on children's rights, he firmly ruled out the idea of independent legal representation, or Guardians ad Litem, for children in legal disputes. It was, he said, a lawyer-fattening exercise. (Both these ships have since sailed). So, when he arrived in the Department of Finance, he already had a developed sense of fiscal discipline and an unerring nose for a vested interest.

A number of themes ran through his budgets. One was the need to serve the common good. In December 2010, he told the Dáil: 'The job of the Government on behalf of the State is to ensure that the common good is served: that requires saying "No" at least as often as saying "Yes."' Those in power, he believed, had a duty to interrogate all demands to ensure they did not damage the State's ability to provide for all citizens.

In one discussion on this subject, he instanced the Hepatitis C scandal of the mid-1990s. It was his view that Michael Noonan, then Minister for Health, had been treated badly by the political system, including by Fianna Fáil. While allowing that the controversy had been handled disastrously, he argued that all Noonan had been endeavouring to do was to protect the interests of the State, which was his duty. Lenihan's view was that no matter how deserving or worthy the cause, in a world of limited resources a government had to act proportionately in the best interests of all the citizens.

Another theme of his budgets was the principle that everybody should pay some direct tax. This went against the prevailing orthodoxy that low income earners should be kept out of the tax net. It was his firmly held belief that citizens only feel they have a stake in the State if they pay, according to their means, for the services it provides. In this context, he referred to the bin charges strike in his own constituency in the late 1990s. His analysis was that those engaged in the protracted protest at that time regarded the State as alien precisely because they had no sense of ownership.

He believed a broadly-based tax at a low rate should be applied to all income. He first introduced this concept in Budget 2009 when he brought in a levy on all income earners starting at 1 per cent up to €100,000 and at 2 per cent on income above that level. There was widespread criticism of the measure and the social partners lobbied successfully to have those earning less than €18,304 excluded. In Budget 2011, the Universal Social Charge which replaced the income and the health levy was applied to all gross income above €4,000. Despite all the opposition at the time, the charge continues to apply, although the threshold has been raised to €10,000.

At the other end of the spectrum, he was appalled when he was lobbied on behalf of one multinational to allow its PRSI bill to be written off against R&D tax credits. 'For God's sake, this is a social insurance tax. Do these people not see the need to pay any tax at all,' he reacted. He was genuinely shocked by a paper written by one of his senior officials, which documented the cumulative impact on the tax system of the reductions and reliefs that had been introduced over the previous decade. The erosion of the base and the imbalance in the sources of taxation had left the economy mercilessly exposed when the property bubble burst.

He occasionally expressed his frustration at the narrow focus of his job on cutting the deficit. It annoyed him that it fell to him to look after 'the financials' while others in government drew up a strategy for economic growth that he regarded as unconvincing. The 'Smart Economy,' the buzzword of the time – or 'An Eacnamiochta Glic,' as he liked to call it – cut little ice with him. He was deeply sceptical about the ability of the Science and Innovation strategy to deliver a return on the very considerable amount invested in it.

His own strategy for economic growth was to concentrate on our three biggest indigenous sectors: agriculture, retail and tourism, which, he believed, would be the engine for balanced economic growth across the country. He did what he could, with the limited resources available, to support them through government initiatives and the taxation system. That is why he reversed the VAT increase introduced in his first budget: he had been dubious about the measure at the time and soon afterwards admitted it was a mistake. In Budget 2010, he ran the gauntlet of the anti-alcohol lobby when he reduced excise duties on drink in order to stem the flow of cross-border shopping, primarily driven by the availability of cheaper alcohol in Northern Ireland.

As Minister for Finance, he never got a lucky break. The ever-deteriorating state of the banks continually undermined his consistent efforts to deal with the growing imbalance in the public finances. But he did have one piece of good fortune: he had no direct responsibility for the management of the economy in the previous ten years. He used to joke that Bertie had, after all, done him a big favour by keeping him out of the cabinet for so long. And the idea that he had been excluded by Bertie Ahern appeared to have seeped into the national political consciousness. The public seemed, by and large, not only to have absolved him of any blame for the collapse, but also to have placed considerable trust in him.

He, in turn, understood that to gain acceptance of the very unpalatable steps that had to be taken, the public had to be given a comprehensive explanation of our economic difficulties. A key aspect of his budget speeches was a forthright analysis of what had gone so badly wrong in the Irish economy. In his Supplementary Budget, in April 2009, he was going out on a limb within his own government when he offered this diagnosis: 'With the benefit of hindsight, it is clear that more should have been done to contain the housing market. We became too reliant on the construction sector for growth and tax receipts.' So, when, in February 2010, he commissioned Klaus Regling and Max Watson to do their *Report on the Sources of Ireland's Banking Crisis*, he was already well on his way towards the conclusions they were to reach three months later. Reacting to the publication of the report, he told RTÉ's *Morning Ireland* he was not surprised by its findings and that he had been living with the consequences of the mistakes made over the previous decade since his appointment as Minister for Finance.

Understandably, this led to some tensions between himself and the Taoiseach as well as some other government colleagues. Any critique of the causes of the collapse implied criticism of his predecessors. It was tough medicine for Brian Cowen, in particular and, to his credit, he never flinched from taking responsibility or from defending the difficult decisions taken by his Minister for Finance. Most members of the Government were in a politically impossible position because they were identified in the public mind with the decisions that caused the crash. In the end, and especially when it came to banking policy, it was mostly left to Lenihan, Eamon Ryan of the Green Party and a group of able and ambitious junior ministers and backbenchers to fight the government's corner. Not many queued up to sally forth for the government side on the increasingly hostile airwaves.

Notwithstanding these tensions, Lenihan and Cowen worked much more closely together throughout the crisis than is commonly understood. They respected each other and were both acutely conscious of their duty to work together in their respective positions in government, in the interests of economic recovery whatever the political cost to themselves. The stories of deep divisions between them circulating at the time were wide of the mark: part of the soap opera that surrounds leaders in times of crisis.

Certainly, there were clear political differences between them. For instance, Cowen was a strong believer in social partnership while Lenihan was not convinced the unions were prepared to play a part in solving the crisis.

Cowen had a strong attachment to the accretion of social policy that had been built up under the partnership process. At a Saturday morning meeting to discuss the Four Year Plan in late autumn 2010, he made known, in no uncertain terms, his deep unhappiness with the proposal to cut the minimum wage, which he described as a clear breach with traditional Fianna Fáil policy. Lenihan saw the level of the minimum wage as a barrier to employment, particularly in the hospitality and retail sectors, both of them on their knees at that time. It was not that Cowen was not seized of the need to respond to the economic crisis; he just seemed to jib at the idea that market forces or economic imperatives outside of our control should dictate the pace and the specifics of the required changes.

Notwithstanding these differences, there was no evidence of any personal rancour between the two men and they stood together on whatever decision was reached. Lenihan often remarked upon the support he got at Cabinet from the then Taoiseach and was very grateful for it. Both were political professionals to the end.

Lenihan's talent as a communicator was an enormous asset to the Government in dealing with the crisis. His ability to go into a studio in the most difficult circumstances and deliver a top class performance was exceptional. He set out the Government's strategy for dealing with the crisis with clarity and authority.

As the crisis went on, he formed the view that the Taoiseach and senior members of government should brief newspaper and broadcast editors on the Government's strategy. When he took it upon himself to do so, it became a source of contention with some in Government Buildings. In certain instances, they had a point: Lenihan was never good at circumspection and there were times when he should certainly not have returned journalists' telephone calls. But there is no talking to a politician with a headline in his sights.

He generally liked journalists and counted a number of senior members of the press among his friends. He would telephone them, on occasion to take issue with something they had written, but more often to exchange views. Sometimes, he was on a fishing exercise. He understood how the media worked and was acutely conscious of its influence even at times of enormous personal difficulty.

Within two days of his cancer diagnosis in December 2009, his thoughts had turned to a strategy for dealing with the inevitable media reaction. From the outset, he accepted the public's right to know, but he wanted to avoid intrusive regular updates. He prepared himself for those who would argue that he should resign and the accusation that he was hanging on to office. 'Don't worry,' he said, as I tiptoed around these delicate issues: 'I saw all this with my father. I know what to expect.'

We agreed that a frank interview with Sean O'Rourke on RTÉ's *News at One* in the first week of the New Year was the best way to put the matter into the public domain. Those plans were scuttled by TV3's decision to broadcast the details of his illness on St. Stephen's Day. He greeted this development with extraordinarily calm: by comparison with his precarious medical condition, TV3's editorial decisions must have seemed a trifling matter. With characteristic magnanimity, he quickly put the whole business to one side. It was left to the rest of us to bear a grudge on his behalf.

Budget 2010, delivered just a week before he became ill, had been well received as a tough, decisive budget that had grasped difficult issues, such as public service pay and reductions in social welfare, while also introducing much needed reform of public sector pensions. The deficit was reduced very slightly for the first time since the crisis began. His declaration at the end of his speech that we had 'turned the corner' was thrown in his face in many a subsequent debate. It did not bother him unduly. It was right at the time, he argued, in his indefatigable way. And it is true that the Greek crisis in the late spring of 2010 changed everything.

The seriousness of our economic position was, at this stage, by and large, well understood. The measures introduced were certainly very difficult and it is easy to forget the magnitude of the adjustment that had been visited on the country: between July 2008 and December 2009, savings and taxation measures amounting to €14.6 billion on a full year basis had been achieved. But amid all the bitterness and the anguish of the public discourse, there began to emerge that remarkable stoicism which characterised the response of the majority of Irish citizens to the crisis.

The perilous state of our banks remained a constant worry and absorbed an increasing amount of Lenihan's time. But, at least until the late spring of 2010, it looked as if the plan to bring stability to the public finances was finally working. Then the backwash of the constantly mutating international crisis, this time with Greece at its epicentre, rolled in on our shores. In May 2010, interest rates on Irish government debt jumped in response to the Greek crisis and from then on, it was all about the spreads on our bond yields which ebbed and flowed all summer. Following a downgrade by Standard and Poors in August our bond yields rose sharply and events began to take on a momentum of their own.

Returning to the Department after a summer holiday, the anxiety was palpable. 'I'm afraid that after all our efforts we are going to end up in the place we have been striving so hard to avoid,' an official confided. As the economic indicators rolled in, it became clear that the hope in the spring of a nascent recovery had melted away. Lenihan became worried about the politics of the crisis. He was deeply concerned that the Government had no mandate for the action that he feared would now need to be taken. Very early in September, he went to the Taoiseach to argue the case for calling an immediate general election, but Cowen was firmly of the view that it was the job of government to bring forward a budget and deal with the fallout.

For the next two months, Lenihan and senior officials engaged in almost constant discussions with the Commission and the ECB on our budgetary preparations. This oversight by Brussels was partly due to changes introduced earlier in the year increasing surveillance of individual member states' budgetary planning. But it was also a clear indication of the growing concern in Europe about our budgetary position and the state of our banks. Lenihan hoped that by embracing their involvement in our budgetary process we might avoid the need for a formal Programme. The Government's lack of a democratic mandate continued to worry him as he tried to make his way through uncharted waters.

He forged ahead with the decision to publish a four-year plan, which would set out in detail the measures to be taken to restore order to our public finances. He wanted a plan that could be read and understood by every citizen. He believed our own people, as much as the international markets and our masters in Europe, needed to be given certainty about the immediate future and confidence that we had a coherent strategy to get the country back on track. In effect, Lenihan's plan was to become the blueprint for our bailout programme. Adherence to it over the last four years has played no small part in the improvement of our economic outlook.

A small group was given responsibility for writing the plan and, in between his constant engagement with Europe and the ever-worsening position of our banks, he would meet with us to review progress. Meanwhile, events were gathering pace: as our borrowing costs continued to rise, we withdrew from the international markets; the adjustment required to return us to a deficit of 3 per cent of GDP by 2014 went from €7.5 billion to €15 billion; the cost of bank recapitalisation increased; the ECB became ever more uncomfortable about its level of exposure to Irish banks; and Angela Merkel and Sarkozy made unhelpful comments at Deauville. There was beginning to be an inexorability about where these events were leading us and a feeling that we were losing control.

In early November, Commissioner Olli Rehn paid a brief visit to Dublin during which he endorsed 'convincing measures' by the Government and the parliament to deal with the crisis. Within days, Commissioner Rehn, who had travelled from Dublin to the G7 meeting in Seoul, rang Lenihan to say a lot had changed since his visit to Dublin. The precarious position of our banks had been discussed by the finance ministers of the largest economies in the world and they were worried. There followed ten days of rumour, international manoeuvring and some heavy media manipulation. It was difficult not to conclude that we were being railroaded into a programme. On 18 November, three days before the Government announced its intention to request financial support from the EU and the IMF, the Governor of the Central Bank, Patrick Honohan, rang RTÉ's *Morning Ireland* from Frankfurt to tell the nation that arrangements were being made with external agencies for a Programme of Assistance for Ireland.

However irritated Brian Lenihan might have been by the Governor's interview at the time, he bore him no ill will. In a conversation soon afterwards, he said Patrick Honohan had his own dilemmas and he understood that he did what he felt he had to do.

The whole business was badly handled: more information should have been made available to the public at an earlier stage. But in the Government's defence, the circumstances could not have been more appalling. We were being swept in the direction of a bailout, even though we had access to funding; some EU member states were taking the opportunity to throw our corporation tax rate into the mix; and there was no agreement with the ECB about how our banking crisis should be addressed. The fact that media outlets were being briefed by sources in various European capitals made it particularly difficult to devise a communications strategy. The Government was in a very difficult position. But whatever about accusations of ineptitude, suggestions that it was playing for time to save its own political skin were unfair. Those at the most senior Government levels had no illusions about their political prospects: they already knew their goose was well and truly cooked.

Just over a week after the formal application for external assistance, Lenihan delivered his fourth and final budget speech. He presented the arguments in favour of the bailout he had fought so hard to avoid and he pointed out the Joint Programme was based on the four-year plan, which had been produced by his Department under his direction. He finished on his customary optimistic note: 'A Cheann Comhairle, there is every reason to be confident about the future of this economy and this country if we could only have confidence in ourselves.' As he frequently said: 'you have to give the public hope.'

He had a routine in the hour or so before delivering his budgets. Having run through his speech with a few key officials, he would then regale them with the reply he would deliver were he in opposition. He would deconstruct his own arguments with great rhetorical flourish and heap derision on the Government: his way of relaxing before the big occasion. For some reason, I missed the performance in December 2010, but an official who was present later described how, from his reclining chair, he delivered a highly entertaining but hard-hitting attack on himself and his Government. He must have wondered if he would ever get to deliver that budget reply for real.

This essay is an account of my observations of a man with whom I worked for five years and held in the highest respect and no little affection. It's not an exhaustive account of Brian Lenihan's budgetary policy; nor is it impartial. Others will, in time, provide a more objective perspective. But whatever critical analysis there will be of his legacy, partial as I am, I remain convinced that no other political figure could have done more to stabilise our public finances.

5 BRIAN LENIHAN AND THE NATION'S FINANCES

PATRICK HONOHAN

The three years of Brian Lenihan's tenure as Minister for Finance saw some of the most dramatic macroeconomic and financial developments in the history of the State. When appointed in May 2008 he seemed to have inherited robust public finances generated by a rapidly growing economy. But appearances had been deceptive. By the time he left office in March 2011 the landscape had changed utterly. Public debt was surging past 100 per cent of GDP, the unemployment rate had about tripled to almost 15 per cent and the banking system's solvency had collapsed.

As conditions rapidly deteriorated, it would no longer be enough to keep a steady hand on the tiller while deciding where the fruits of a growing economy should be distributed. Indeed, large parts of the economy of 2007 would prove to have been built on sand. The seemingly healthy public finances, with a low debt and deficit, had been achieved only thanks to unsustainable tax revenues coming from the property and construction bubble. Deflation of that bubble was by mid-2008 already well under way. It would bring down the banks with it, along with thousands of over-indebted borrowers.

Unwittingly, Brian Lenihan had been handed the unenviable task of limiting the fall-out of an economic implosion, which had already been primed, and which would soon be detonated by the global financial crash.

That detonation occurred at the height of the post-Lehman's crisis in the chaotic days of late September 2008. Faced with the imminent inability of the Irish banks to meet their payment obligations, as the foreign funders on whom they so heavily relied declined to rollover their maturing deposits, the Irish Government and its advisers saw no alternative to providing a blanket guarantee to the banks. Though they recognised some weaknesses in the Irish banks, none of the policymakers dreamt that the loan-losses latently embedded in the banks could be so great, and that the guarantee therefore entailed such large risks as subsequently materialised.

The primary responsibility for this miscalculation cannot be placed at Brian Lenihan's door. He was entitled to rely on the advice proffered without dissent by all of the official advisers and buttressed by costly consultancy reports from the pens of elite investment banks.

The alternative was not palatable either: the damaging effects of a default, whether of the banks in September 2008, or of the sovereign guarantee later, would have been felt not only in Ireland, but all over Europe and further afield. It is easy to exaggerate, as many have, the damage done to the Irish economy on the night of the guarantee. Still, by proceeding unilaterally and in such an expansive manner, the Irish Government weakened its legal and political ability to lever a greater degree of burden-sharing from bank creditors and from official European partners.

It was largely to Brian Lenihan that the task fell of seeking to restore equilibrium, first by moving quickly to start the process of cleaning up the banks' balance sheets; second, by planning and initiating the necessary fiscal adjustments; and third by being prepared to face up to the need for an international financial rescue package. It was characteristic of the man that, faced with a difficult challenge, he would act decisively, boldly, with an assured sense of confidence. The steps he was able to take in the two-and-a-half years that were left to him after the guarantee, helped the gradual process of rebuilding national and international confidence in the Irish economy.

In what follows, we look in turn at the three key elements of Brian

Lenihan's period in charge of the nation's finances. We begin with the banks, then move to budgetary adjustments before turning to the financial assistance programme with the EU and IMF.

THE BANKS

THE CONTEXT FOR THE GUARANTEE

Rightly or wrongly, the banking guarantee will always dominate discussion of Brian Lenihan's period as Minister for Finance. Although we do not have a full written contemporary record, the meetings and deliberations of the fateful night of the bank guarantee, on 29 and 30 September 2008, have been much recounted and raked-over. The broad elements are clear: the convergence of official and private views around the idea that a State guarantee was the only available policy action that would stem the outflow of funds from the Irish banks in the coming days and prevent their doors having to close; divergent views over whether Anglo Irish Bank should be immediately nationalised (rather than leaving it in private ownership); squabbles over how much the banks should have to pay for the guarantee and about what debts should be excluded; heavy reliance on the views of investment bank consultants, in contrast to insufficient communication with foreign official partners.

It is important to bear in mind the international context as it had developed in the dramatic days of late September 2008. For an economy and a banking system so strongly integrated into the global financial system, with more than half of the banks' funding coming from abroad, the seizing up and virtual collapse of international money markets amid an atmosphere of general financial panic that month both represented a contextual background and revealed the finances of the Irish banks to be a house of cards.

The financial crash of September 2008 had its epicentre in the United States. There, and in Britain, in Germany, in the Low Countries and elsewhere, policymakers scrambled to stem the panic, understand why traditional relationships were being interrupted and why the plumbing of international finance had stopped working. Nobody had definitive and immediate answers. The role of governments in backstopping the system and unblocking the flow of liquidity was acknowledged everywhere, even by the conservative administration of the United States, which was pressing an unwilling Congress for funding approval on an unprecedented scale.

In high policy circles in Europe, the view that national governments must not allow another significant bank closure had become general.[1] This view was communicated to Brian Lenihan. It implied that he should take effective action to prevent the disorderly failure of Anglo Irish Bank when it had become unable to meet its payment obligations.

Were it not for the fact that huge inevitable future losses were already embedded in the banks' balance sheets, such a blanket guarantee might have proved fiscally costless, as indeed the Government hoped. And the guarantee did avoid the large economic costs – at home and throughout the euro area – which would have accompanied the disruption of the payments system that would have resulted from a deposit freeze on one or more of the main Irish banks. But before long it became evident that the losses assumed by the Irish taxpayer were too high, ultimately surely exceeding what would have been suffered by Ireland had Anglo's operations been suspended there and then with a view to liquidation.

Within a few weeks, the immediate global liquidity crisis had passed; banks and their creditors had been saved by government action, and the collapse in international trade and finance was beginning to reverse. For the US and most European countries the damage was quite deep and protracted, and several countries had to adjust to the unsustainability of previous spending patterns. Still, the Government support provided to the US financial system was largely repaid within a few years and, while many other governments suffered permanent losses from propping up their banking systems in 2008, it was only in Iceland and Ireland that the scale of banking losses assumed by government had a really severe effect on the public finances and the economy as a whole.

WHAT ALTERNATIVES COULD HAVE BEEN TRIED?

Although tactically superior policy manoeuvres can by now be easily imagined, nothing that was available to Brian Lenihan on that night could have eliminated the largest part of the future economic damage packed into the several time-bombs which had been primed in the bank-driven property bubble, and which could now no longer be safely defused.

It was not as if no crisis management preparations had been made. Officials did react quickly to the alarming market suggestions in early September that the medium-sized lender Irish Nationwide Building Society (INBS) was in trouble, but failed at first to see that this was only the tip of the iceberg. Consultants from elite international investment banks were engaged to advise on options and to assess the condition, first of INBS and later Anglo. But the contingency planning was shallow and did not encompass a threat to the system as a whole.

Quick learner and acute intellectual that he was, Brian quickly understood all of the advice he was being given. It was the moment for action and Brian seized it. Unfortunately, the advice he was being given was based on the flawed premise that the banks had sufficient capital to absorb prospective losses and that the immediate problem was merely one of unjustified lack of market confidence. Instead, his advisers should have conveyed much greater uncertainty about the recoverable value of the banks' loan books. The risk that losses could be tens of billions higher than then envisaged, especially as property prices showed no sign of stopping their slide, should have been factored into a policy response that would have been more robust to such losses. Not enough thought had been given in advance to the question of allocating the burden of eventual losses between bank creditors and the taxpayer in the event that banks proved insolvent.

Bearing in mind that the guarantee was designed to stem an outflow of funds, there was no need to extend the guarantee to existing debt-holders who could not withdraw their funds until the debt matured. Sizable sums would not mature for years. If existing debt had been excluded from the guarantee, this would have left a materially larger cushion of creditors to absorb eventual losses, protecting the Irish taxpayer. This may be a moot point, given that the Troika subsequently (in 2010-11) blocked the idea of imposing losses on bank creditors; but by that stage, the negotiating position of Ireland had been weakened by the huge outflows of guaranteed money, as discussed below.

The banks[2] even argued that existing subordinated debt should be covered. This is hard to justify when the very purpose of subordinating debt is to rank it behind other creditors in the event of default. Subordinated debt had not been covered in the 2007 case of Northern Rock, often cited as a precedent used in Irish planning for the guarantee. Here Brian balked, and insisted on a modest carve-out, refusing to guarantee that portion of the subordinated capital instruments that had no maturity date (perpetual).

A further flaw, not often discussed, was the failure to word the guarantee in such a way as to prevent bondholders from being able to exploit any 'event of default' of a bank to force accelerated early payment of its debts not otherwise due for years. This flaw effectively froze any far-reaching resolution or restructuring of the banks for the following two years, as any such action would have been taken by foreign courts as an 'event of default' and would have triggered an immediate and impossibly large cash call on the Government under the terms of the guarantee as enacted.

Nationalising Anglo and somehow ring-fencing it from the rest of the system could have been a key element in such a policy response. This too had not been fully thought through, though. Nationalisation legislation was ready, but there was no worked-out view as to what would be done with the nationalised entity: Wind-down? Liquidation? Become the core of a new business bank? Would losses have been imposed on depositors and bondholders, or would nationalisation have been accompanied by an explicit or implicit guarantee anyway?[3] As he told me himself, Brian argued strongly for the immediate nationalisation of both Anglo and INBS – but officials cautioned that there would be operational risks in taking such action mid-week, and the idea certainly would not have appealed to all of his political colleagues; he was overruled on the night. Still, participants in the meetings were left with the expectation that this issue would be reopened at the weekend. In the event, the initial success of the guarantee in reversing flows took the matter off the boil, and nationalisation did not occur until mid-January of the following year, by which stage the top management had been pushed out in disgrace.

Could the threat of a drastic policy step have been used to leverage some degree of burden-sharing with European partners? We will never know for sure. The officials – who in any event did not expect major losses to be incurred – were satisfied that no such possibility existed. It had already been made clear that no collective European solution was available to the emerging bank failures across the continent: each country was to deal with its own banks. Besides, European partners were preoccupied with their own banking fragilities. Anyway, with the Central Bank of Ireland unwilling to buy time by requesting permission from Frankfurt to extend open-ended emergency liquidity support to all of the banks, there was no time for the insistent consultations that would have been required. But, far from endorsing the blanket guarantee as the decisive and calming policy stroke that the Dublin officials imagined it to be, though, the major international partners reacted with alarm. 'Holy cow!'; 'a catastrophe.' The guarantee provided by Ireland's super-safe AAA government unleashed pressure right across Europe to extend guarantees to other vulnerable banks. Rather than being a potential lever for securing burden-sharing, the guarantee had become a political liability vis-à-vis Ireland's European partners. It took all of Brian's personal charm and political skills to contain this political damage and ensure maintenance of good relations.

AFTER THE GUARANTEE

It is hard to deny that had there been better official preparation, greater awareness of the scale of the banking problem and a more intensive engagement with partner countries that also stood to lose from a disorderly bank failure in Ireland, a better overall outcome could have been achieved. But there was no costless way of walking away from the problem. Furthermore, it is hard to attach blame to Brian for this lack of preparedness. He was entitled to take comfort from the fact that top consultants were probing all aspects of the banks and that the Central Bank was fully involved in crisis management. He was right to sense that quick action was needed. He was offered no better alternative. The decision taken, his communication and implementation of it was impressive.

Following the nationalisation of Anglo Irish Bank a few months later (in January 2009), Brian long held on to the hope that the new board and especially the new top management team would be able to create a new business bank from the debris of the old property bank. This seemed unlikely to most observers, bearing in mind the bank's lack of experience or relevant infrastructure in that field, though the new team bought into the idea and developed optimistic recovery plans around it. In the end, Anglo could not shake off the reputational smell that surrounded it and the Government's reluctance to take it out of the market began to poison market perceptions of the Irish banking system. By early September 2010, Brian reluctantly recognised that this particular bird was not a phoenix and, at last, conceded that it should be moved into a wind-down mode.

Meanwhile, the fundamental weaknesses of the other banks – albeit, relatively much less severe than Anglo – became evident also. The need to remove the property loans from their portfolio gave rise to the concept of NAMA, which was at first met with public suspicion that it might serve as a way of covertly saving the shareholders of the banks by over-paying for those developer loans. In the event, the haircuts required by NAMA were too steep to leave any shareholder value and Brian's consistent piloting of the NAMA legislation, in the face of severe opposition, proved to be effective. One by one the directors and top management of the banks also departed, with just a couple of exceptions. While he may have begun with a favourable view of the ability of some of the senior bankers, Brian soon had little compunction about encouraging or in some cases insisting on their departure.

The markets at first largely ignored the possibility that the banking losses would threaten the Irish Government's own creditworthiness, but this was to change, especially given the simultaneous deterioration of the rest of the public finances.

FISCAL ADJUSTMENT
DECISIVE ACTION

The early indications of a financial crisis, both global and domestic, had not been factored-in to the Irish budget of December 2007, which projected continued employment growth at the rate of over 1 per cent per annum for the coming three years – slower than the best years, to be sure, but nothing like the collapse of 14 per cent in job numbers that actually occurred during 2008–10. But by the time Brian had become Minister for Finance, the prospective impact on the budget of the steady fall in house prices and the end of the construction bubble could no longer be ignored. Already, by July 2008, barely two months in the job, Brian was taking an activist role with a mini-budget that cut €1 billion out of annual government expenditure; an early budget was announced for October, and – delivered under huge pressure just a couple of weeks after the guarantee – it would increase tax revenues by about €2 billion. This prompt attempt to get to grips with the looming fiscal crisis before it got out of control exemplified Brian's sense of urgency and decisiveness. Although it was clear that much more would be needed later, at this stage in the crisis Ireland seemed to be determined to keep ahead of changing circumstances.

In the sharp global downturn that accelerated after the Lehman's bankruptcy, national budgets everywhere came under pressure, but Ireland's dependence on boom-related tax revenue had become extreme and its budget was hit worse than anywhere else. By April 2009, despite another tough mini-budget announced in two steps that spring, Brian had to acknowledge that the General Government Deficit was heading for almost 11 per cent of GDP – a level not approached since the crisis days of the mid-1980s. Even without taking any account of the fiscal impact of potential banking losses, Brian announced a schedule of four more tough annual budgets that would have to be implemented by 2013. Even this would not prove to be enough, though it broke the back of the problem. (In the end, between spending cuts and tax increases, budgetary adjustment actually implemented during 2008-13 amounted to about €28 billion on the annual total, just about €8 billion more than Brian's mini-budget of April 2009 had projected, and leaving about €5 billion more to do in 2014–15).

Of course, for Brian, fiscal adjustment was not driven by an ideology of austerity. He knew it was a matter of feasibility. If anyone had any doubt about this, the loss of market access in November 2010 would show just how dependent a small and heavily indebted, albeit prosperous, economy will always be on retaining the confidence of international markets.

But if ensuring market confidence required a clear fiscal adjustment path, ensuring its domestic political acceptance required attention to the distributional and efficiency impacts of the tax and expenditure changes being adopted. There were a few defeats for Brian on this front, perhaps most spectacularly in the matter of means-testing the entitlement of the over-70s to a medical card, granting them extensive healthcare free of charge. Even though this entitlement was relatively recent and the means-testing would affect relatively few, the announcement in October 2008 resulted in a political backlash sufficient to trigger a quick (albeit only partial) retreat.

The biggest single source of fiscal adjustment in 2008-10 was in income tax and related levies. Here Brian's political sense was more finely tuned. A sizable part of the boom-era revenue had been employed, in effect, to reduce income tax rates in the previous decade and Brian realised that much of this lowering would have to be reversed. Tax increases for higher income groups in particular would have to be more onerous. As a result, by 2011, the progressivity of the Irish personal income tax system was judged by the OECD to be among the highest of its three-dozen members – a significant change in just a few years.

Indeed, through tax and spending measures in Brian's budgets, the average fall in real disposable income for the poorest 30 per cent of the population was held to about 5 per cent, while that of the top 30 per cent averaged more than 10 per cent. Minimising the regressivity of the fiscal policy adjustment was a hallmark of his years in the Department of Finance.

Sometimes, the influence of popular perceptions did work against efficiency. The decision, in October 2008, to increase the main rate of

VAT by ½ per cent should not really be blamed for the surge in cross-border shopping around that time, which was more attributable to the sharp fall in the exchange rate of sterling: the cost of a pound sterling in euro fell by 25 per cent between mid-2007 and the end of 2008. Nevertheless, the perennial tendency of Irish commentators to blame their politicians for anything that goes wrong helped fixate Brian on the VAT rate and it became another adjustment which he reversed.

Strikingly courageous was the decision to address public service pay. Rates of pay had drifted up during the boom to unsustainable levels and (with prices actually falling during 2008-10) were not being eroded by inflation. In two steps, during 2009, pay rates in the public service were in effect lowered by an average of over 13 per cent. Furthermore, Brian Lenihan did not favour the Croke Park Agreement of early 2010 which froze further cuts until 2013. While other stressed countries followed suit later, achieving needed adjustment through actual pay cuts was a path-breaking political achievement.

MORE WAS NEEDED

Central banks often have to remind governments of the dangers of letting debt and deficits get out of control. By end-July of 2010, two years of belt-tightening adjustment had managed only to contain the fiscal problem. The promised adjustments had been made, but international and domestic economic conditions were coming out somewhat weaker than had been projected, with the result that the General Government Debt showed no prospect of stabilising on current policies.

As we updated projections of the budgetary position for the coming years in light of the weaker global and domestic prospects, it became clear to the Central Bank during the summer of 2010 that the multi-year budgetary strategy being pursued was not going to be sufficient. The first two years of the strategy (2009-10) had been worked out in a strict and serious manner, but the projections for later years were proving to be quite over-optimistic. I remember one occasion towards the end of August 2010 when, unusually, we met in my office in Dame Street rather than his in Merrion Street, Brian and I discussed the looming growth in government debt. I showed him graphical projections indicating that the ratio of debt to GDP was looking like reaching 100 per cent within months. He vigorously disagreed, having been given different numbers, but I could tell that he realised the writing was on the wall, and that a revised and tougher adjustment programme would have to be negotiated politically and implemented over the coming years. He would need to use the coming three months to build political support for such action (which culminated in a National Plan for Recovery which was not finally published until November 2010, during the negotiations with the Troika).

External forces would not wait, though: markets move faster than politics. By September 2010, the combination of alarm at the emerging scale of banking losses combined with anxiety about the fiscal prospects resulted in Ireland losing access to private funding. As market participants – and indeed official agencies – began to wonder about Ireland's ability to avoid the damaging consequences all round of a default, the risk of having to follow Greece into an external assistance programme was increasing.

THE FINANCIAL RESCUE

Back in mid-April 2010, Ireland had, along with other euro member states, been called to contribute its share of the financial support package for Greece. Brian called me from Brussels to check whether I agreed that it was good for Ireland to chip in. After all, he noted, the interest rate we would get on the loans to Greece were well above the cost of borrowing to Ireland at that time. I agreed that it was sensible to go along, but suggested that the main reason was different: we might be next to need a bailout and it would be wise to be team players. 'Oh no,' he responded, 'we are all right, everyone here is sure that it is Portugal that could be vulnerable, not us.' Indeed, as the euro area crisis surrounding the Greek situation intensified in the following weeks, it was Portugal and Spain that came under European pressure to tighten their fiscal policy.

In their enthusiasm to find an exemplar for Greece and other peripheral countries stumbling into difficulties, official financial

Europe had chosen Ireland as its poster boy. The prompt fiscal correction already put in place by Ireland, especially the public sector pay cuts, which impressed his counterparts across Europe by their audacity, seemed to justify this. But few had paid much attention to the huge banking losses already announced in March 2010 when the Government's debt management agency, NAMA, had completed the first small batch of loan valuations, revealing the haircuts that would be applied to these developer loans when it bought them from the banks. Extrapolating these haircuts to the rest of the portfolio implied losses that would place Ireland's experience among the most costly banking crises ever recorded.

Actually, of external official agencies, only the IMF clearly appreciated the risks at this stage, and their Ireland mission-chief called me ahead of their routine economic appraisal mission (in May 2010) to Ireland to see what I thought of the idea of Ireland applying for one of the IMF's new precautionary programmes – just in case, as it were. Although storm clouds were still only on the horizon, I could see some advantages, but was quickly put in my place by Merrion Street officials, who at that stage regarded any mention of such an idea as anathema; I doubt they even reported the suggestion to Brian with any degree of seriousness. With hindsight, it would surely have been less traumatic to have negotiated a precautionary line while market conditions were still calm.

THE UNFOLDING CRISIS

By late August, though, as the laborious process of NAMA valuations (slowed by EU Commission rules) began to reveal the even larger haircuts required on the rest of the loans it was taking over, not only was the growing scale of prospective banking losses gaining more international attention, but, as mentioned above, the insufficiency of the fiscal adjustment was also becoming undeniable. Lenders in the financial markets were becoming doubtful.

Brian knew well that September 2010 was going to be a testing month for the Irish banks as they would have their work cut out to persuade lenders and depositors to roll-over the large block of bank claims maturing in the last weeks of the original guarantee (which had been for two years only and, therefore, was due to expire at the end of September). All of official Dublin knew that it was highly unlikely that rollover would be successfully accomplished, leaving Anglo and, indeed, potentially other banks dependent on the Central Bank's Emergency Liquidity Assistance. Already at the end of July, I had taken care to make the ECB fully aware of how this situation was shaping up, knowing that they would be uneasy about the prospect, as ELA is supposed to be a short-term facility. Nevertheless, it was the inexorable growth in ELA from the middle of September that would induce ECB staff and Council to press for Ireland's application for a programme of official financial assistance.

For a hammer, every problem is a nail and most external official observers held fiscal hammers and assumed that fiscal tightening was the sole and necessary solution to the emerging Irish problem. By mid-September, Brian acknowledged that more fiscal action was going to be needed, even if it took several more weeks before official Dublin converged on a level of adjustment which would see Government's finances restored to a safe path. But fiscal adjustment was never going to solve the banks' problem if their funding continued to drain away. While Brian fought a rear-guard battle against European fiscal hawks, in particular, resisting their pressure for an early budget, the Central Bank worked to persuade international colleagues to desist from market-destabilising statements that continued to fuel the deposit drain.

At the early-October IMF Annual Meetings, planning for a possible Irish funding application was already under way. At meetings with IMF officials, Brian asked what sort of conditions might a loan application entail and was reassured by the tone conveyed by those on the other side – who would soon form the nucleus of the IMF Troika team for Ireland – and by their message that the existing thrust of announced Irish fiscal and financial policy was broadly consistent with what would likely materialise. Still far from ready to make such an application, it seemed that Brian had mentally crossed a barrier.

In terms of market confidence, the die was cast by the Merkel-Sarkozy announcement on 18 October at Deauville to the effect that the holders of European Government debt would have to contribute to any bailout. As the financial markets absorbed the implications of this new policy, interest rates on all peripheral government debt, but especially Ireland – now clearly seen as next-in-line for a bailout – jumped to insupportable levels. Now Irish companies and individuals joined the external investors in removing their funds from the Irish banking system and the need for the protection of official external assistance became acute. Public and semi-public statements and briefings by senior Eurozone officials to that effect added fuel to the fire.

By Thursday 4 November, as the Government announced the outline of its revised four-year budgetary plan, it was clear to Brian's main official Irish advisers that the game was likely up and it did not take them long to convince Brian that it was time to talk to the Troika. I spoke to the relevant officials at the IMF and ECB and it was suggested that an early meeting be held in Brussels to see what might be available in the way of financial assistance.

By the middle of the following week, Brian had agreed that officials would conduct detailed pre-negotiations on a programme – preferably precautionary in character. The IMF complained that they preferred to have a definite request before embarking on costly and potentially fruitless negotiations, but eventually agreed to proceed as if there had been a formal application. It was decided to hold the discussions in Brussels, as Brian did not at that stage want to have evident teams of negotiators in Dublin. The meeting was set for Sunday, 14 November and almost all of the 17-strong Irish team, led by the Department of Finance, and comprising virtually the entire senior financial policy official cadre of Ireland (no Ministers, though), flew over that morning.

Officials from the three agencies that made up the Troika had pre-negotiated between themselves much of what they had in mind, but their style in these initial negotiations with the Irish side was not to present demands, but instead to lay out what was legally possible in terms of settled policy of their institutions (terms of the loans) and the scale of financing they envisaged. There were no surprises about the priorities. Fixing the banks and guaranteeing the fiscal adjustment were at the core of the Troika's agenda. These were also the priorities of the Irish Government and the Irish side started to draw up a document live at the discussions, reflecting where the Irish officials and the Troika could see more or less eye to eye and highlighting other matters where there were divergences. The scale of the loan envisaged was even higher than we on the Irish side had anticipated, partly because the Troika wanted to provide for the eventuality of a very large capitalisation of the banks to a level which Irish officials thought would threaten debt sustainability of the Sovereign. The Troika insisted, though, on two points: first, discussions could not go much further without a formal application and second the idea of a purely precautionary programme was, in the circumstances, out of the question.

17–18 NOVEMBER 2010

Brian Lenihan was briefed by his officials on the two days of negotiations and was sufficiently convinced to agree that the negotiations should continue in Dublin on Thursday, 18 November. Meanwhile he came under much pressure from alarmed fellow Ministers in the Eurogroup meeting on the Tuesday to make a formal application there and then. I, too, was asked on Wednesday evening to let the Irish Government know that the ECB Governing Council also wanted Ireland to apply in order to steady financial markets. I duly passed on the message by phone, but got a cross response from Brian, who rightly felt that all of the external actors were seeking to bounce him into formally making the application. He said he had no Government approval to do so, but did not at all suggest that he was having second thoughts about the course that he had embarked upon. Instead, I assumed that he wanted to exploit the fact that no formal application had been made as a lever in the negotiations, which were scheduled to begin very visibly the following morning. (Of course, I did not ask him to arrange for a government meeting to be called, though from what he said to others after the call, he might have been contemplating that.)

Noting the bewilderment evidenced in the European official circles, I became increasingly concerned that the financial market pressures, including the huge outflows from the banks[4] would cause lasting damage to the Irish economy. Towards midnight that

Wednesday, as the meeting I was attending broke up, I sounded out Frankfurt colleagues on whether they would support a statement by me indicating that the ECB was standing behind the Irish banking system, but in vain. Already, the following day's editorial in the *Financial Times* had appeared online, speaking of a bank run in Ireland. Things had got to the point where, had it remained silent on the state of play, the Central Bank would have not only failed in its responsibility to use timely communication to steady confidence, but would also have dashed a legitimate public expectation in Ireland that it could be trusted not to deceive through omission.

Fortunately, this could be avoided despite the lack of any application from Ireland for assistance. Thus, though by now all on the Irish side regarded a programme as inevitable and Brian's earlier hope that it could be a merely precautionary arrangement had now all but vanished, I made a point of explicitly leaving these two aspects – whether an application would be made and the possibility of a precautionary-only arrangement – open in the radio interview which I undertook the following morning (Thursday 18 November). The Troika remained in doubt about the Government's intentions and the interview, if anything, improved the negotiating atmosphere somewhat to our advantage. What had not occurred to me was that Brian might not, even by that stage, have communicated to some of his senior ministerial colleagues how far down the road the discussions had already gone. Clearly, the interview was inconvenient for him, but he understood, as he confirmed to me then and later, that my sole aim was to work in the national interest.

Despite all this, the ECB – still not fully convinced that an application would be made – felt it necessary to write to Brian the following day warning that continued emergency lending by the Central Bank to the Irish banks could not be assured unless there were to be an application.

THE PROGRAMME

There was much to dislike about the programme on offer from the Troika. In Dublin, we did not like the proposed rate of interest on the borrowings (they were subsequently much reduced). We were also disappointed by the refusal of the Troika to think outside the box on the banking issue. Instead of demanding that the Government borrow money to recapitalise the banks, they should have been willing to entertain the Irish side's suggestions of some risk-sharing mechanism for the potential banking losses (such as would have been achieved by direct injection by the Troika of capital into the banks). And there was no long-term solution for Anglo Irish Bank's government guaranteed borrowings from the Central Bank (subsequently discussed as the Promissory Note issue).

Above all, negotiators on the other side dangled, but ultimately withdrew support for, the attractive idea of imposing losses on some bondholders (no longer covered by the original guarantee, which had already expired). It was on Friday 26 November that the Troika staff told Brian in categorical terms that burning the bondholders would mean no programme and, accordingly, could not be countenanced. For whatever reason, they waited until after this showdown to inform me of this decision, which had apparently been taken at a very high level teleconference to which no Irish representative was invited.

While he undoubtedly considered it a failure to have had to have recourse to a financial rescue package from international official sources, in fact, Brian deserved considerable credit for pushing ahead with the negotiations without the ineffective grandstanding or attempted blackmail that some other countries have sometimes tried with the IMF. By embarking on the protection of the programme long before he ran out of cash, he enabled the Irish negotiators to settle on what has been a much more gradual path of fiscal correction than that imposed on other peripheral countries.

CONCLUSION

Having been handed the reins of the nation's finances at a moment when the economy and the banking system both hurtled towards a precipice, it was inevitable that Brian's tenure at the Department of Finance would be dramatic and controversial.

In particular, the design of the bank guarantee and the extent to which better options were available will long be debated. In the choices they made, Brian Lenihan and his ministerial colleagues acted in good faith, based on the advice that they were given both by officials and paid experts.

But it bears repeating that by the time he became Finance Minister, most of the damage had been done: no alternative strategy was available to Brian that could have averted all or even most of the economic distress that was to come.

It is a common misconception to suppose that all of the economic stress of the past five years has been attributable to the debts that were incurred from the bailout of bank creditors. Indeed, much of the fiscal adjustment would have been needed over time anyway: the burden assumed by the Government from the banks – huge though it is – has accounted for a smaller part of the total retrenchment of spending and taxation over the subsequent years than is commonly recognised. But the banking failures destabilised both the financial and political equilibrium.

Brian Lenihan inherited economic policy challenges which he handled with vigour and decisiveness as well as considerable charm and persuasiveness. These attributes, along with his quick and agile intelligence, helped protect and even enhance Ireland's standing among his counterparts in the European and international official financial circles. At home, too, the commitment to public service which underpinned his work was recognised at the political level, as exemplified by his retention against the odds of his parliamentary seat in the elections of 2011 despite all that had happened. Importantly, the large fiscal adjustments he launched embodied a crucial degree of concern for progressivity and for alleviating the impact on lower income groups.

By the time he left office, while open issues remained vis-à-vis European partners with regard to the burden of the official debts incurred as a result of the bank failures, the financial affairs of the country, though far from fixed, were set on the right path.

6 A BEACON IN THE DARK NIGHT

CHRISTINE LAGARDE

CRISES AND CHALLENGES ARE defining moments in human history. They tend to foster the emergence of natural born leaders. Economic crises are no different. Once in a while, a true leader emerges from the ashes of economic calamity. Brian was one of those beacons in the dark night of a macroeconomic crisis.

Like many individuals committed to public service, Brian served the Republic of Ireland in different capacities. And like many good leaders, he took on the mantle of leadership and political responsibility out of a sense of commitment to his nation, not out of vanity or interest in personal gain. Brian was pre-disposed to excellence in the service of Ireland. His family's deep involvement in Irish politics meant that the green-white-and-orange flag coursed through his veins from an early age. Indeed, his Irish identity was fundamental in defining Brian. And as the recipient of Trinity College Dublin's Foundation Scholarship, and a First Class Honours, it is safe to say that Brian was one of the brightest of his generation.

Like Brian, I served in two different national ministries prior to being appointed Minister of Economics and Finance. We both were lawyers who were called upon to serve as Ministers of Finance in our respective countries. What first brought me towards Brian was not his love of all things French – although that certainly did not hurt. It was Brian's overwhelming competence, and his strong belief in collegial answers to shared problems. We were both called upon to tackle rapidly deteriorating economic situations. But like any committed individual, Brian was open to outside advice and knowledge. So much so that he pro-actively sought out experts. One anecdote epitomises the degree of Brian's devotion: once the first rumours of gaps in the balance sheets of Irish banks arose, Brian turned up in the middle of the night on the doorstep of a prominent commentator. His gut instinct was that, despite claims to the contrary, the situation was more dire than had been alluded to so far. And he was humbly seeking advice. As a former cabinet member myself, I am well placed to know that such humility in political decision-makers is as rare as a four-leaf clover.

Shortly after Brian's appointment, the global economy went into a tailspin. Within the span of fourteen months, Brian unveiled three government budgets, which must be a record of sorts. Brian and I spoke regularly during those crucial months. He was always honest and open about Ireland's situation. This helped Ireland's partners, and Ireland itself. Now that the situation was being transparently discussed, Ireland's economic partners could develop realistic expectations and propose a pragmatic set of solutions. This act of transparency meant that precious time was not being wasted on discussing fantasist solutions to obscure problems, but rather, when the rubber met the road, Ireland and its partners had a clear vision of the path ahead.

The 2010 Irish Budget, which some referred to as 'the most austere budget in the history of the State,' was a testament to Brian's leadership. It made the fundamental contribution to recovery.

Ireland suffered greatly from global recession, and yet still stands strong. Its economic recovery is gaining momentum, and unemployment has come down, although it is still too high. Ireland has successfully completed the EU-IMF programme – a major milestone. All of this is due to the resilience and determination of its people, and the courage of its political leaders. And like many others, I credit my dear friend Brian for having taken difficult decisions, many of which laid the basis for Ireland's recovery.

But while Ireland was traversing an economic crisis on a massive scale, Brian was going through his own calamity: pancreatic cancer.

When the news first broke out in December 2009, and as it was confirmed in early January 2010, I remember thinking that perhaps Brian would find it hard to carry out the duties of his office. Yet, and true to his own assurances, he continued to work tirelessly for the good of Ireland and Europe. In his last year in office, Brian was as efficient as ever, meeting regularly with his stakeholders and partners, and striving to continue to propel Ireland out of the crisis. Even if at times the affliction Brian was fighting showed, it never stopped him from arguing in favour of and defending Ireland's case. That Ireland's economic situation progressed significantly during the year Brian was fighting his disease is a testament to the work he had accomplished earlier and of his drive during that crucial year.

As I was ready to move to Washington, D.C. to take the helm of the IMF, I learnt the terribly sad news of Brian's passing. Like so many others, I admired him. Like so many others, I relished the opportunities to interact with him and discuss the challenges Europe as a whole was facing. And like many others, I found Brian to be an invaluable source of knowledge.

Antoine de Saint-Exupery once said: 'He who has gone, so we but cherish his memory, abides with us, more potent, nay, more present than the living man.' I often find myself thinking of what Brian would have done. And I find great solace in the knowledge that whatever it would have been, Brian would have given it his all.

When Brian passed, I expressed my confidence in the fact that 'history will be kind' to him. Three years on, Brian is increasingly seen as a model of aptitude, leadership, and pan-European collaboration. In the three years since Brian's passing, tributes to his leadership, competence, and overall person continue to steadily pour in. I am confident that Brian would be proud of this. I know that like so many other of his friends, I am proud for him.

7 FADRADHARC

MARY MCALEESE

ONE MEMORY STANDS OUT in my mind when I am asked to remember Brian Lenihan. It is an image of him as a young student standing in the front square of Trinity College, waiting for the results of the 'Schol' examinations in 1979.

I was lecturing in Criminal Law in Trinity at the time and Brian was one of the Law School's best students. Each year in Trinity College scholarships are awarded to students showing outstanding achievement in a set of non-compulsory exams that are typically taken in second year. Winning a 'Schol' means you get free rooms on campus, your fees are waived and you get in to Commons (dinner!) for free. Above all else, students compete for it because the honour of being a Trinity Scholar is quite a rare phenomenon. The exams, however, are always very difficult. In fact, we would routinely advise students not to attempt the 'Schol' because of the amount of work involved. We encouraged Brian to compete, however, confident in his ability to achieve first class honours.

On Whit Monday, all the candidates for scholarship gather in the front square, as do the staff, friends and family. There's a final meeting of the scholarship committee to decide who gets scholarship and then the Provost walks out on to the plinth in front of the exam hall and he reads out the names. It is absolutely terrifying for the students awaiting the results because it is so public. If you are lucky, you will have a bunch of friends with you to absorb either your mortification or your gratification at being selected. I was there on the day that Brian got his 'Schol.' He was delighted and we were just so proud of him.

Thirty years later, in 2009, I was in that front square of Trinity again, this time with our own daughter, Emma, when the names were called out and she became a scholar. One of the first people to congratulate her was Brian Lenihan. He was so encouraging of her, probably because he himself knew how horrendous it was waiting so publicly for the results in that front square. Brian pointed out to her that every ten years the scholars from the same year in each decade are all called to an anniversary dinner in Trinity. So Emma, as a 2009 scholar, would be at the same dinner as Brian, a 1979 scholar, and he spoke with typical enthusiasm about how he looked forward to these recurring meetings with her. She was invited, of course, to the 2009 dinner and Brian was also there. He chatted to Emma and, as ever, was generous in his encouragement.

Those memories bother me now because it is so poignant to think of the fadradharc, the long sightedness, which Brian had on that day in April 2009, just months before his diagnosis. He had no notion of dying or of his death being in any way imminent.

Brian was an exceptionally bright student. He got a first class honours, which in the Law School in Trinity are as rare as hen's teeth. There was, however, no geeky or academic intensity about him. He brought to his work a very boyish sense of humour and a lovely sweet nature. He embodied that Irish expression about carrying education lightly.

He was a wonderful student. He had one of those brains that not only mastered facts quickly, but was also able to assimilate and analyse those facts. He was also, of course, even then, politically astute and exercised by everything that was going on around him. He probably had three newspapers read before he came to college in the morning. As a student, Brian always gave a sense of being old beyond his years. You could tell he came from a family which had a depth of political insight and wisdom and that he, himself, had from childhood been interested in and involved in adult political and philosophical discourse.

As well as being a very engaging student in the academic sense, Brian had an active student life outside of classes. He did not put everything into academic life, because, quite frankly, he did not need to. He joined college societies. He got involved in college life. He seemed to have a lot of friends, many of them probably political friends and friends from Belvedere College, where he had gone to secondary school.

He was always going to excel, even doing half the work of others. He was also mature in the sense that he really understood his own capacity. Some students fret about their abilities, Brian never did. He was a very humble guy. He took his ability in his stride. He sailed through his courses and exams, but not in an insouciant way. There was an air of calm and solidity about him always.

Brian was active in debating, particularly in the Hist. I remember being at some of these debates. He was, even then, a very passionate debater. On the floor of the debating chamber and in class, he showed an ability to both analyse very quickly and to respond very quickly. He was not the kind of student who would be a nuisance in class, but if he had something to say, you could be absolutely certain that Brian would say it and he would make sure he would be heard too.

The thing which was most impressive about Brian, even as a student, was his powers of analysis. He really was a good problem solver. One of the reasons I think he loved law so much was because you could give him a riddle, a complex legal problem, and he had a great capacity for parcelling it out in a very exact manner that allowed you to see a way of navigating through it to a resolution. That was one of the things that I always liked about his way of working, his powers of parcelling things, getting them lined up like little ducks in a row where other students might struggle to make sense of things.

Shortly after graduating, Brian joined the academic staff of the Law Faculty in Trinity, so having been a student he now became a great colleague. I never sat in a class given by him, but I know he was very popular with the students. He had a lovely manner and he was a good guy to encourage people. He was part of that new generation of young teachers who did not just go in with a set of notes and relay them, but who were interested in interaction. Of course, he was also young and he would have known some of the students he was now teaching as a fellow student a year or two earlier.

Brian had an easy manner as a law lecturer, but this belied his sheer brain power.

His father had a similar kind of hail fellow well met, clap you on the back, come and have a drink type of manner, but he too had a fabulous brain. It used to be said that Brian Senior was the Colombo of Irish politics. Brian Junior did not hide his intelligence, but he did keep the extent of it hidden at times.

In conversation with Brian Junior, you would be impressed by his erudition and the quotations he had. He understood history. He knew the dates of battles. He had a knack for geography. He was a walking encyclopaedia, but he was not one to beat you over the head with his level of knowledge. He would, rather, enrich your conversation.

I lived in Ratoath, County Meath, at this time and would occasionally give him a lift home to Castleknock. I gather that he later told friends that he would often catch me knitting while I was waiting on him.

We had many chats in the car and you could easily disagree with him on things. He would be thinking out loud some of the time and he was always trying to find a way of navigating his argument. One of the things that always struck me about him was that he was a great consensus builder. Brian was someone who always wanted to navigate to the point where he could bring people with him. He was a good synthesiser of arguments. He was never rude in an argument. He never barracked. He was much more diplomatic than that and, I think, that came from his years of experience of listening to frequent political debate at home. I always thought that he would have made a great leader because of his capacity to persuade. He was a persuader and he could build consensus, partly because he used to argue everything in his own head first and then out loud to everybody else.

He was also, of course, wickedly witty and he could be wildly sarcastic. He could occasionally be scathing about someone behind their back. I was always very glad I was not the victim of it, but that was part of the wit of him and there was an acerbity in private conversation with him at times, but in an entertaining way.

While Brian was in college his father was a minister, but, personally, I always assumed Brian Junior would opt for a life in law rather than politics. I expected that he would become a barrister. I always assumed that he had seen his father, his grandfather and his aunt in politics and that he knew how tough political life was. I suppose, I assumed Brian was going to see that life was not for him. I cannot say, however, that I was astonished when he went into politics because of his political history, but part of me thought it was a big decision to make, given the considerable range of attractive options that were open to him.

I should have foreseen that the other side of him would drive him towards politics. He had this sort of Kennedyesque sense of being imbued with public service, which would not allow him to walk away from problems that he saw and which he felt that he could contribute to solving.

He did not choose politics naively. It was all around him growing up. He got to see it close up and he knew how messy it could be. He could see the imposition on family life and the intrusion which politics involves. He could see the media, that gathering swarms of bees or wasps ready to sting you. He also knew the old adage about all political careers ending in failure. He knew all that and yet something in him drove him to it. It was not a desire to make his name or just because it was in his DNA. The answer lies in the realm of service, the idea of giving your best to public service. I do not think anybody can ever take that away from Brian, whatever people may say about the final days and about the dreadful economic circumstances in which his death occurred.

In retrospect, his choice of politics as a career is striking because it shows he clearly was not afraid of failure, which is extraordinary in a fellow who was set for such success. Had he gone into academic life full-time, most assuredly he was set for stardom. Had he continued his career at the Bar, most likely he would have ended up in the Supreme Court at a young age. He could have been a legend in the law, yet he chose politics.

I left Trinity in 1987 and moved to Belfast so we didn't come across each other much over the next decade, but when, in 1997, I decided to seek the Fianna Fáil nomination to contest the presidential election, Brian was an obvious early point of contact. However, he made it clear that he was supporting his Law Library colleague, Michael Kennedy, the former Minister, who was also contesting the nomination. Brian and I parted friends from our discussion. He had been straight about whom he was supporting and wished us well in his usual gentlemanly way.

When I won the Fianna Fáil nomination, Brian was so supportive and so helpful and kind during the subsequent presidential election campaign. He was actually my election agent. It meant a lot to me to have Brian on board for a whole lot of reasons. I trusted him and I trusted his brainpower. I trusted him as a friend. I trusted him also because of the way he handled our initial conversations and how he had been clear about his support for Michael Kennedy.

In a sense the role of an election agent is a prominent one, but not a significant one in the campaign itself. People like Noel Dempsey, who was my director of elections, and Bertie Ahern, who was the then Taoiseach and leader of Fianna Fáil, were actually driving the campaign.

There is one intervention which Brian made in the presidential election campaign which sticks in my mind and for which I will always remember him. It was at a point in the campaign where some supporters of the independent candidate, Derek Nally, had sought to portray me as sympathetic to Sinn Féin and as some kind of ideological fellow-traveller of the IRA. In the middle of all this, the Alliance Party leader, John Alderdice, who the previous year had taken a seat in the House of Lords, issued a statement calling on me to withdraw from the presidential election and suggesting that if I were elected president it would be unhelpful to peace and reconciliation.

Brian Lenihan was one of the people chosen to reply to Alderdice on behalf of our campaign and, in one radio interview, he was particularly robust, even uncharacteristically angry, in response to what Alderdice had said. While Brian could be passionate and argumentative, in public performances he was usually measured and moderate.

In order to understand the intensity of Brian's reaction to Alderdice and the other attacks on me at that time, it is necessary to understand that Brian, unlike many, knew Northern Ireland well and knew my family background. He was, I think, appalled at the suggestion that someone from a nationalist background in Northern Ireland was not entitled to run for President of Ireland.

Brian knew me from the late seventies and he knew my mind on nationalism since then. He knew I was no Provo. He knew I was no Sinn Féin sympathiser. In fact, he was one of the very, very few people in Trinity College who ever asked me about the North or about my experience of growing up there. I could count on one hand those who asked me about Northern Ireland over those years and Brian Lenihan was one of the first.

I recall long chats over tea in the Kilkenny Design Centre across the road from Trinity on Nassau Street, or in the students' commons in Trinity itself. He was full of questions about what it had been like growing up in Belfast during the early years of the Troubles. He was interested in the North, genuinely interested, and so he knew my politics, he knew where I was coming from and he knew me also through my involvement at that time with Fianna Fáil. He also knew that the characterisation of me which John Caden and others were trying to portray was just nonsense. He knew that not only was it nonsensical, it was dangerous talk. Indeed, in the wake of particularly nasty and groundless assertions which were aired on television during the campaign and which were extensively covered in Northern Ireland, my family's security was seriously compromised. We lived at that time, and the three children went to school, close to a Loyalist stronghold. Those comments put them in danger and steps had to be taken to protect them.

Brian Lenihan instinctively knew all this because he was so well read and so interested in Northern Ireland. He, too, would have had a sense of how dangerous it was that these opponents so cynically used something they knew to be untrue in seeking to characterise my candidature in such a way and not having an awareness of, or not caring about, the downstream consequences.

Ultimately, in fairness to Derek Nally, he apologised to me after I let him know in no uncertain terms how dangerous what had been said was and the real impact it had on my family.

Brian knew that the allegations made by Alderdice were also unjust. He would have known also of the consequences of these glib and ill-thought-out assertions and, in the case of Alderdice, they came from someone who should have known better. He too subsequently changed his mind and, of course, was in the front row at my inauguration.

The suggestion that I was a supporter of Sinn Féin or some kind of IRA fellow-traveller was absolutely outrageous. It offended everything I ever stood for. Contrary to the outrageous suggestions made during that campaign, I am an O'Connellite Nationalist and always have been. I was always on the side of saying 'are we so stupid that we always have to play the game of the coloniser by using force.' I have always asked 'are we so stupid that we cannot construct what O'Connell constructed?' He urged constructive dialogue, the constructive power of argument and the power of persuasion. Because we were the first truly educated generation of young Irish people, I knew we could do better than using violence.

It has always struck me that, whatever about past generations, in our generation we had so many other means open to us to assert our rights, to insist on equality and respect for our nationalist traditions. We were the fulfillers of the O'Connellite dream that O'Connell thought died with him in 1847. We, as a generation, had 'intelligences brightened and unmannerly as crowbars,' as Seamus Heaney put it, in 'The Canton of Expectation.' We had the education, we had the skills of articulation and we also had the social sciences. We had the statistics, we could use facts, argument and evidence, and we had the European Union and the Council of Europe. We had places we could go, we had fora outside of ourselves, we could internationalise our disagreement. We had friends in America. We had a diaspora, the global Irish family, all of them with great goodwill. We had international law and international human rights. We had so many resources at our disposal and yet these guys in the IRA and other organisations were using the old 'let's kill them' argument, which had always struck me as just being avidly stupid. Brian Lenihan and I had spent hours in conversations along those lines. He knew with absolute moral certainty where I stood on those things.

On the night that the presidential election result was announced, Fianna Fáil held an impromptu victory party and in my few remarks thanking everyone, including Brian, I said how one consequence of the outcome was that there would now be a Lenihan in the Park. I knew that for him and, indeed, for his aunt, Mary O'Rourke, who had been an early supporter of my campaign to get the nomination, that it was a particularly poignant occasion because of the events of seven years earlier when Brian Lenihan Senior had lost the 1990 presidential election. Although my original surname Lenehan is spelt slightly differently from their Lenihan, we are all from the same Roscommon clan. Indeed, some of my first conversations with Brian were about his name. The difference in spelling means nothing because it is an original Irish name with a litany of different spellings 'as Bearla!'

As President, I watched from a distance as Brian's political career progressed. He chaired the All-Party Committee on the Constitution and he was Minister of State for Children. Our paths would cross reasonably often. He thrived in ministerial office. He was an exceptionally competent and insightful minister, a problem solver. He knew from growing up in a political household more than anybody that as a minister you have to work with what you've got, that there is no point in going in with grand and gigantic crusades on which you cannot deliver. You have to work the space that's available to you.

I do not know what the opinion of the civil servants who worked with him would have been, but I know I worked with him as a colleague and he was an exciting colleague to work with. He was not a person who was firing off all sorts of mad ideas because he was too thoughtful and reflective for that. He was too much the synthesiser. By the time the idea fired from him, it was a gold nugget.

The other thing about him was he was not 'band wagoning.' He was not one of these guys who would knock you out of the way to get his picture in the paper. He was the genuine article when it came to public service. There was a popular regard for Brian because people could see through all the other nonsense of politics. They could see that Brian Lenihan was a guy who was just really genuine and he had other options. He could have done thousands of other things and made a success of a thousand other things and not been bothered with politics, but he had made it his life. It was a commitment to public service, it was a commitment to his country and it was a commitment to a vision for his country – the betterment of his country. Unlike some politicians, for whom the most important thing is the next news story, I do not think Brian ever thought like that. As Minister for Justice, he was brilliant and he was in his element. It gave space and purpose to his high intelligence and to his instinct for problem solving. I have no doubt that it was that capacity which led to him being recruited by Brian Cowen to serve as Minister for Finance. What was needed at that time was someone with Lenihan's steadiness, his coolness and formidable work ethic.

We are, I think, still too close to the events giving rise to and arising from the financial and economic collapse to have any strong analytical sense of what was going on at that time. For me, it is still a very incredibly raw time because it was underpinned by panic.

Many years ago, I remember, I walked out onto a beach somewhere in the Canary Islands. I can swim, but I am not a good swimmer and I literally put my foot in the water and I realised 'Oh, oh, I shouldn't be in here'. I could feel that the undertow was too powerful and I turned to come back and missed the fact that a 30-foot wall of water had just formed. It came over the top of me and the next thing I was about a quarter of a mile out to sea, having been dragged through what appeared to be like an underground rollercoaster. I thought surely I was going to die. I was very lucky two lifeguards on the shore saw me and came out and brought me in. Now, even to this day, what I remember with great clarity about being swept out to sea was the sense of panic. When it was happening, I had no control. There were forces at work that were beyond my control. That was exactly my sense of what was happening, economically and politically, at the time the financial collapse came. It was something similar to that sense I had personally that day of almost drowning.

Many of the things that were happening were not happening in Ireland, they were happening elsewhere, they were happening in America, they were happening in the markets, they were happening in the banks and, frankly, it was impossible to even know what was happening. We now know just how much we didn't know and I am not even sure if we know (or ever will) how much we didn't know at that time.

There was a scarily, blurry period when all the presumptions you make on a daily basis about government, such as that decisions are made with access to the best information, were shaken. We presumed that as a nation we were on an upward trajectory, based on sustainable growth. We assumed that this was underpinned essentially by a strong education system and by globalisation. Then, all of a sudden, it emerged that those presumptions were evidently not solid and we found ourselves caught in that irresistible undertow being dragged away, unsure how it was going to end.

Even now, in 2014, it is probably too early to comprehensively analyse what happened and where we are at in the processes that were unleashed by the onset of the financial crisis because they are not yet fully worked through. In that context, it is probably also too early to fully and fairly analyse Brian Lenihan's part in the rescue effort. If his actions were analysed now, they could be analysed in anger and analysed in cynicism.

Knowing him as I did, I can conclude this much – at the moment that he made decisions, the one thing I would be morally certain of 'til I go to my grave', is that he brought the highest integrity to those decisions and that he would have acted in what he thought was the absolute best interests of the country. He was rock solid in that regard, whether he made the right or wrong decisions. There is an avalanche of information available to us now that was not available to Brian then, that was not even visible to anybody then.

One key factor, I think, and Brian shaped this in part, is that Ireland sought external help relatively quickly and we ran up that flag. Other countries did not. Other countries lived the lie for some time thereafter or certainly lived with a lack of consciousness about the forces that were actually at work in their own economies, until the reality dawned somewhat later in the day. Some people say Ireland got hung out to dry, others say that because we were first up with the flag, seeking help, we would be the first to be able to take the flag of surrender down and put the flag of triumph back up again. Economic historians will argue about that in the years ahead. I do not know, though it is heartening to see the first green shoots of recovery happening in Ireland, for we surely need the hope they bring after the years of depressing disillusionment.

When the crisis first became apparent, I could see that Brian Lenihan was rattled. Every time I met him I could see how rattled. I had a sense that he was under ferocious pressure, in part, because with his brainpower he could absorb the consequences of what was occurring and foresee, at least to some extent, the depth to which things would sink. He could see it in ways, perhaps, others could not. He was processing it and, of course, the prognosis was catastrophic. Undoubtedly, he was very, very disturbed by it all. I think that was a very lonely place for him to be in at that time, an exceptionally lonely place and, of course, as Minister for Finance he had to be the person to make the decisions necessary to tackle the crisis. They were arguably the most important decisions historically and economically that have been made in this country.

Then came the diagnosis of his cancer in Christmas week 2009. I was aware of it very quickly that same afternoon. It was devastating news. As soon as I heard it, I sat down and wrote him a letter and had it hand delivered to him. I probably was the first person to get a letter to him. The purpose of it was to tell him firstly that I had heard and that I knew that the outcome was not likely to be good and so the letter reflected that. I wrote to reassure him that I would be praying for him. In my own life, there have been many times when we faced down a cul-de-sac and I didn't know any other way of navigating out around it except through the power of prayer. The purpose of the letter was to reassure Brian of my friendship and my prayer. He phoned me shortly after he got the letter and thanked me for it and said it meant a lot to him.

A few days later, TV3 published the news that he had been diagnosed with pancreatic cancer. One can try and make all the arguments made at the time about whether it was in the public interest, but there was something just innately unIrish and not decent about it. We are a people who respect old decencies and that for me was an old decency that was shot to pieces. It was horrible, absolutely horrible for his family.

Some time later, we had one of the occasional dinners we used to have in Áras an Uachtaráin where we invited about 50 people from different sectors and areas. Brian and his wife Patricia were among those invited that particular evening. One of the prerogatives of being President is that you get to decide who will sit beside you or at your table, at least, at events in the Áras. Brian was actually assigned the seat opposite me and Patricia was also at our table. Patricia arrived, but, of course, Brian was late, very late. It was one of those days when there was some urgent political or economic development, which he had to deal with. Martin and myself got a chance over dinner to have a conversation with Patricia and it was clear she was devastated by the reality of his terminal diagnosis. After the chat, we were all upset, strangely so in this formal setting. I was on the verge of tears and Patricia was also on the verge of tears. I knew from occasional chats with Brian himself that he had no illusions about the outcome of his illness. His power of analysis forced him to accept that reality, he knew the odds were overwhelmingly stacked against him. He had to accept it, although, of course, he didn't want to.

Brian arrived then at the dinner looking kind of flung together, as he sometimes did. As he sat down at the table opposite me, I caught him looking across at Patricia, appreciating quickly that she had been upset and tears came into his eyes and tears came into her eyes. I almost lost it myself. You could see that they were sharing this precious moment within this public gathering and there were going to be so few precious moments left. Later that night, I took Brian aside and hugged him and just told him that we all loved him and I was just desperately sorry, really, really sorry to see this grand fellow facing death, but also facing, in a sense, into the death of his own reputation.

In all this, it was obvious Brian's reputation was going to take a battering, but I really do not think he gave two hoots about it. What he really cared about was the job he was doing and he cared that he was doing it to the best of his ability. The best people can make the worst of mistakes. I know that, but we are still some way from being able to confidently and accurately judge Brian's ministerial actions of those days.

Some have suggested that he should not have been in the job while he was on medication. Over these months, you would see on occasion a hollowness in his eyes. At times, when I would see his eyes like that, it would dawn on me 'oh my God, he's just spent the weekend on chemo and he's back in the office now.' Mind you, lots of people have to do that. They have to because they are self-employed or have families to care for or for some other reason.

Anyone, however, who would suggest that Brian was in anyway intellectually impaired during his illness clearly didn't know him or didn't know him at that time. I was in relatively close contact with him and he was as sharp as a tack. If I, myself, had thought for one moment that his illness was adversely affecting him in his office, I would have known Brian well enough as a friend of his and somebody who had known him for a very long time that I would have said 'get out of there Brian'.

As well as handling the policy issues, Brian, along with the Attorney-General, Paul Gallagher, was writing some very dramatic legislation, which crossed my desk as President. Gallagher and he were two phenomenal brains, real intellectual peers. As President, of course, I had regard to the quality of the minds working on the legislative task, but, in the end, if I could not satisfy myself as to the constitutionality of the legislation I would have had no difficulty in referring it to the Supreme Court, notwithstanding the emergency circumstances in which some of this legislation was framed. As President, after all the consideration or advice from the Council of State, you still have to ask yourself that one final question: 'Are you happy that the presumption of constitutionality holds in this instance?' If it holds, you sign the Bill because you are under a constitutional obligation to do so. It is as simple as that. I would not have been saying, 'oh it's an emergency, therefore, I must listen to the Minister or the Attorney, therefore, I must sign.' And they would have known perfectly well that would never have been my view.

Ultimately, as we know, there was effectively a political disintegration within the Government. There were occasions when I feared the domestic situation in terms of public anger might spin out of control. One of the things that I have always said since, particularly in discussions with European colleagues, is how the crisis gave all of us an insight into the remarkable solidarity of the Irish people and the cool-headedness of the Irish people, even when they are righteously indignant and angry. We have a phenomenally mature population who are able to analyse things in ways that it strikes me that some other countries have yet to advance to. There is a formidable solidarity among the Irish people that allows us to get through things and that has allowed us actually to get through the worst of these last five or so years without massive social disintegration, in spite of enduring calamitous suffering. That stoical determination and hope and faith in ourselves and this belief in doing things the right way has enabled us to survive. Other countries' leaders have remarked on this phenomenon with admiration and respect. It is no myth. It is real, for we have lived through it, struggled through it and know the effort that went into making the centre hold.

Over the first years of the crisis, it was almost impossible on a 24-hour basis to know what was coming next. All sorts of possibilities were occurring. All sorts of scenarios were commending themselves as possibilities. I was thinking a lot about the situation in my own head and in deliberations with others. It is at times like that that you realise the very limited role of the President under the Irish Constitution. These limitations are paradoxically part of its value. It became very clear to me during the crisis that if in Ireland we had a highly politicalised presidency then that institution too would have been caught up in the vortex of disturbance and might have been collaterally damaged in the disintegration process. The strength of the Irish Presidency is that it operates in a moral space, in a pastoral space and it, in fact, comes into its own in moments like that. In these moments, as President, you just be and do and support and you are not part of, and should not be implicated in, that intimate political decision-making process, but should be standing strong and tall, whether there is good news or bad news, at any particular moment.

I remember sometime during the crisis some commentator or other suggesting that the President should take over the reins of government. You cannot do that. There are other countries where the President can, but that is not the situation in Ireland. This crisis again revealed the wisdom of those who constructed the kind of presidency we have in Ireland and those who developed it into the kind of presidency it embodies. We are very lucky in Ireland that the reach of the Presidency is as it is. It is not possible for the presidency to be entirely detached from political life, but as President you can respond to politics in a way that doesn't drag you into the vortex and perhaps helps to create an anchor.

After the 2011 election, when Brian was out of office, our paths still crossed a few times. I do not think that he was unhappy to be in opposition. He took the fact that Fianna Fáil had done so badly in the election well, as you would expect of someone from a family where there were political highs and lows. The Lenihans know about storms and they know that storms abate. Brian also knew, of course, that he would not be around to catch the next wind if it came. In these months, he was in philosophical form. If there was going to be a political revival for his party, he was not going to be part of it. If Ireland was going to transcend its economic difficulties, he was not going to be here to see it. He was not a bit maudlin, but he was resigned.

When the word of his passing actually came, we were broken, just broken-hearted to hear the news. For me, it felt almost like losing a son. We were not all that far apart in years, but he had been a student of mine and I felt like I would feel losing any student that 'oh God, this is all the wrong way round.' A big light went out because Brian was one of those people who you always felt better for meeting. Somebody once said to me that the world divides into two kinds of people, drains and radiators, and he was the ultimate radiator, he really was. He would radiate a kind of a boyish enthusiasm. Even right up to his death, he still had that boyishness about him. He had a depth to him, a cleverness to him and a wisdom, but he also exuded an engaging youthful love of life and a relish of each day.

My reaction then was, and still is, how it was terrible to lose that lovely human being so young and what a tragedy to lose him from civic and political discourse. I thought back to that bright, tousled-haired young fellow standing in 1979 in Trinity's front square, waiting to know if he would be a Scholar and wondering about what life held for him. I thought of how, from all the paths in life he could have chosen, he chose the most difficult one in going into politics. I thought about how fate conferred on him the toughest of jobs in politics and then the toughest of fatal illnesses in the most exacting personal and political circumstances. So when I think of him now as I often do, what I remember first is his courage.

8 THE POISONED CHALICE

RAY MAC SHARRY

I WAS FIRST ELECTED to Dáil Éireann in 1969. On the day I first took my seat Brian Lenihan Senior was appointed Minister for Transport and Power. He was already a minister of five years standing at this stage and one of Fianna Fáil's rising stars. Brian Lenihan Senior was a central figure during my entire time in Irish politics and he was someone I rated very highly. He was very bright, he had a great way with people and he lived for politics.

I think the highest tribute that I can pay to his son was that not only did he match his distinguished father in ability and skills as a politician, but that in many ways he surpassed him.

Brian Senior was a consummate politician, but he never really got involved in any great depth in economics or financial policy. He had a great brain, there is no question about that, but Brian Junior had an absolutely extraordinary intellect. Brian Junior had huge policy expertise in a wide range of areas, he was brilliant legally and he was a superb communicator. During his time in Finance he also became a very good economist. He had to learn on the job, but he mastered a difficult portfolio extremely rapidly. Like all highly intelligent people, he had an insatiable appetite for knowledge and he was prepared to talk to anybody and everybody that he thought he could learn from.

He was, in his own words, given a poisoned chalice when he

became Minister for Finance. He was regularly in contact with me following his appointment to Finance. I had held the same portfolio on two separate occasions during the 1980s. As he grappled with an unprecedented crisis, I think he found it reassuring to talk to someone who had sat in the hot seat in Finance during a previous crisis and understood, at least, some of the pressures he was facing.

Although Brian's father had been a colleague of mine for many years, I only came across Brian Junior shortly before he was elected to the Dáil in 1996 when he made it clear he wished to be the candidate in the by-election for the seat previously held by his Dad.

From the moment he entered Dáil Éireann, Brian Lenihan's abilities were clear. My early impressions were that he was wasted because he was not being used enough by Fianna Fáil. I viewed this as an absolute disgrace and I said it to Bertie Ahern.

As a backbench TD and subsequently as Minister for Children, Minister for Justice and ultimately as Minister for Finance, Brian Lenihan was the best performer Fianna Fáil had on television. Brian was the one person you could put out to bat with confidence, no matter how difficult the circumstances were for the party. Brian's father had fulfilled this role in different times, but his style was very different. Brian Senior was articulate and he always exuded bonhomie, but people often accused him of bluffing. No one could say that Brian Junior was bluffing. He had an analytical mind and he was always on top of his brief. He was well prepared and he was very well read.

I watched him closely during his first years in the Dáil. At that stage I was chairing the internal Fianna Fáil Constituencies Committee. Bertie Ahern was at those meetings and almost every time I met Ahern I would advise him 'Use Lenihan more, use Lenihan more.' His reply was 'We are using him.' I would say 'Yes, but will you promote him?'

I did get an impression from Brian that he was impatient about his lack of progress. He spoke to me about it on a couple of occasions. Following the 2002 election, Brian asked me to make the case for his promotion to Ahern. I gladly did so. I remember talking to Brian around this time at the launch of a book on Linda Kearns, a founding member of Fianna Fáil from Sligo, who as it happens was a cousin of my mother. I told Brian that I had made the case for him in conversation with Bertie Ahern. Brian told me that he had got word from the Taoiseach that he was in line for promotion. He did not tell me to what office and I did not ask. Of course, I subsequently learned that Brian was appointed Minister for Children, a junior ministerial position. I felt, even at that stage, that Brian was entitled to a Cabinet post.

I did not see a lot of Brian during his tenure as Minister for Children. I was no longer involved in party committees, but I continued to observe his career. Brian was a young man, but he had a great sense of how to conduct himself as a minister and politics was in his DNA. Not only was his father a very canny politician, but his aunt, Mary O'Rourke, was the absolute queen of the grass-roots. Mary always knew what people were thinking on the ground. She never lost contact with ordinary people as some ministers do and Brian's colourful brother, Conor Lenihan, TD, was in constant contact with him. Brian observed this trait and he made it his own. He learned from his aunt, his father, his brother and his grandfather, who had also been a TD, so he was politically savvy from an early age.

I should emphasise that it was to Brian Cowen's credit that Brian Lenihan became the most senior minister in his government. Bertie Ahern had eventually promoted Brian to Cabinet rank as Minister for Justice in 2007, but, in my view, Brian Cowen had a much greater appreciation of Lenihan's talent. Cowen was a team-player and he recognised Lenihan as being his best Minister and he promoted him accordingly. I was delighted to see this happen.

On Lenihan's appointment as Minister for Finance in May 2008, I got in touch with his adviser, Cathy Herbert, and asked her to pass on my congratulations and good wishes. Brian was clearly busy acclimatising to a new department and I did not hear from him for about a fortnight. He rang me and he asked could we meet. It was the beginning of a frequent train of contacts between us which lasted until after the general election in February 2011. I had a sense that Brian was initially cautious about being seen by his officials to be taking outside advice, but that changed radically over the coming months. Brian said he did not want to be seen meeting me in the

Department and we arranged to meet privately in a hotel in Enfield, Co. Meath, and we talked for several hours.

Brian had a great capacity to absorb detail and he seemed to recognise that before he could adequately deal with the situation that then confronted him, he had to fully comprehend how a previous serious crisis in the public finances was resolved from 1987 on. I took Brian through the many decisions we had taken in this period to reduce public expenditure, to cut borrowing and to tackle unemployment levels, which at one stage bordered on close to 20 per cent. This was an extraordinarily difficult period to be Minister for Finance, but I knew – and Brian intuitively grasped – that the challenge that was confronting him was more profound. In 1987, we had in place or had coming on stream a number of positives that were not available to Brian Lenihan in 2008. For example, in 1987, the newly negotiated Programme for National Recovery helped to limit wage increases. In 1987, Ireland was also still in receipt of significant EU structural funds and, thankfully, interest rates began to fall on a weekly basis after we introduced the budget of March 1987. This all helped to create the gold-standard to every economy of confidence. Unfortunately, for Brian, for a variety of reasons, none of these underlying positives were available to him.

I spent a lot of time that day in Enfield talking to Brian about the strategy, the mechanics and the technicalities involved in framing a budget. Outside the parameters of Merrion Street, many people do not realise that there are essentially just three main areas of expenditure, Health, Education and Social Welfare and most of the public pay goes under Education and Health with a further significant element in Justice for the Gardaí and for the Defence Forces.

A big problem for Brian was that because of benchmarking, the public wage bill had gone through the roof. I have always maintained that Charlie McCreevy, as Minister for Finance, was short-sighted in the scale of expenditure he sanctioned. Brian Lenihan was left to pick up the can for the 'when the money's there, we'll spend it' philosophy, which in my view was never strategically sensible. The focus of that Fianna Fáil-PD government was all wrong. They were concentrating on expenditure and where they could most profitably spend money and not enough attention was being paid to the sustainability of the revenue stream. That Government felt that they could afford both massive increases in public pay and huge reductions in income tax because of the enormous revenues that property-related taxes were bringing in. The culture of the time seemed to be to spend this revenue without giving a second thought as to whether this level of revenue would be available the following year. When I suggested this was a mistake, McCreevy was far from happy. In one conversation, he said to me 'I have two billion of a surplus. Do you think I should leave that there?' I replied, 'Yes I do,' but he just laughed at me.

There were up to 90,000 houses being built annually in the country at this time and the extra revenue from this fuelled the benchmarking frenzy. That Government seemed to operate on the basis that it was raining tax revenue, especially from stamp duty. These revenue flows were, however, never going to be sustainable. Ireland, with a population of four and half million, was building almost as many houses as the UK, which has a population of sixty million. It was inevitable that a property bubble of this magnitude was going to burst. When this happened, the Government were left naked for revenue, but they still had huge public pay and other public expenditure bills to cover. At the same time, property was completely overpriced. In good times, our average house-build should be about 30,000 houses per annum and in more straitened times, like today, there should be about 20,000 houses being built.

Brian Lenihan was appointed Minister for Finance in May 2008 as property prices were haemorrhaging across the country. He frankly told a construction industry conference in June 2008 that he had 'the misfortune to become Minister for Finance a few weeks ago as the building boom was coming to a shuddering end.' Brian had known that the job was going to be tough from day one because, as an incoming minister, he would have been handed a detailed brief with the main figures and main projections, but I do not think Brian or anyone else at this stage realised how rough things were going to become. Brian didn't have the full story because nobody knew at that time the seriousness of what was happening in the banks. Initially he looked for a strategy to curb excessive expenditure and shore up falling revenues. On its own, this challenge, though arduous, might have been manageable, but when a banking collapse was thrown into the mix Lenihan was faced with an almost impossible task.

From the outset of his time in Finance, Brian was also battling complacency. There was initially a reluctance across the political system to contemplate the swift and severe measures that were needed to rein in spending. The Government and the civil service had coasted for a long time on the waves of a prolonged boom and they genuinely thought there would be a relatively painless way out. For twelve years, Government's only difficulty was where they could credibly spend the massive amounts of money they had at their disposal. My sense of the first days of the Cowen Government was an administration already badly at sea. The Government was being driven by the Taoiseach, Tánaiste Mary Coughlan, and Brian, as Minister for Finance. Brian Lenihan was still very much a novice Minister reading himself into a complex brief. Brian Cowen had been the previous Finance Minister, but he had served in very good times and it must have been a profound shock to him to find everything collapsing just as he took over the helm as Taoiseach and Mary Coughlan, with her long experience in the Dáil and Government, was also taken by surprise. I think collectively they had a severe case of political stage fright when they looked at the fiscal projections and it was against this backdrop that Brian Lenihan first spoke to me about the poisoned chalice.

My advice to Brian was to level with people straight away, to tell them how bad it was and not to put off making the hard choices. I told him my experience convinced me that no matter how bad the news, the public wanted to know and what they hate most is uncertainty. I told Brian about the time I went on television on the night of the Budget in March 1987 and my message to the people was along the lines of 'listen I am hitting you for 5 to 10 per cent, but if there was a world war tomorrow you'd take 20 per cent and say thankfully we are not in it. So all I am asking you is to make your contribution and we will come out of this.' This message was not popular, but people understood it and they respected it.

Brian, to his credit, was not shy about explaining to the public how difficult the financial situation was and he never went missing when there was a hard message to sell, unlike some of his colleagues. I respected him for that and I think he established a reputation with the public for doing his best. I know that Brian would have liked to have gone further, faster with the scale of fiscal adjustments, but a more cautious view prevailed. He was faced with a general feeling among his Cabinet colleagues and many senior officials that maintained 'ah we'll get out of this, it'll be alright, we saw it all before.' Hindsight now proves that Brian's view of front-loading the most stringent cuts was the sensible option not just economically, but also politically.

The true extent of the banking problems in Ireland only revealed themselves when Lehman's fell. The impact was felt worldwide and the banks here, like everywhere else, began to check their capital assets and assess their value. Of course, our banks were already far overboard on the construction side and these pressures eventually gave rise to the Bank Guarantee in September 2008.

Not many people realise that what Brian Lenihan and Brian Cowen did on the night of the bank guarantee actually saved the euro. I do not think the two Brians comprehended this fully themselves either at that time because they didn't utilise the leverage it gave them. The bank guarantee was about preventing a run on the Irish banks which would have wiped them out, but if the Irish banks had gone under this would have spread to banks in other eurozone countries as well as in the UK. There is no doubt in my mind that if the Irish banks had collapsed in September-October 2008 there would have been a domino effect across Europe and the other European Union countries would have recognised this. The other EU countries were let off the hook that night. They could not allow our banks to fall, no more than we could. It was an incredible mistake on the night of the guarantee not to talk directly to the main EU players – maybe they did, I do not know – and put it up to them by saying 'we are not guaranteeing here unless you do something for us.' The Government could have cut a deal rather than taking on the full responsibility of the guarantee itself. Instead, the Irish Government gave a State guarantee for all deposits and almost all debts of Irish banks, with a total liability of more than €440 billion.

If Brian Lenihan had a political weakness, it was his inexperience at Cabinet level and I think not negotiating with Europe was a missed opportunity. After the guarantee was announced, I said this to Brian at our next meeting. I asked, 'Brian, why didn't you wait and get them to do it.' I appreciate that it was undoubtedly chaotic that evening and it must have been traumatic for a new Taoiseach and a new Minister for Finance to be faced with representatives of the leading financial institutions in the State begging for support to stop them going bust. It was a full blown crisis, but it was, in my opinion, also a time to remind Europe of their responsibilities.

Incidentally, I should add that the current Government is also under-estimating the leverage that our membership of the EU still gives Ireland. I think Ireland should be taking a tougher stance to bring about a write-off on our bank debts. We should not forget that the European Council requires unanimity to effect change in major policy areas. I think that some night that our vote is required we should insist that the price of our vote is a deal on our banking debts. I would make no apologies for taking such a robust stance because Ireland right now is in a position where we will either sink or swim. If Ireland doesn't get a significant deal on our debt we are going to sink because we cannot sustain and service a debt of that magnitude in the longer term.

The other mistake made on the night of the bank guarantee was the failure to bring the Cabinet physically together. The Cabinet should have met, even if it was at some time like 6 a.m. The optics were all wrong that a decision of that magnitude was taken without a Government meeting.

The other hugely controversial element of Brian Lenihan's time in Finance was Ireland's entry into the bailout programme, which was announced in November 2010. The haphazard manner in which this was announced only served to intensify public anger. Most people can vividly recall in the days before the announcement two government ministers standing in the courtyard in Dublin Castle insisting that a bailout was not imminent. I could understand if ministers didn't want to comment on the day or in the days before the Troika came in, but it didn't seem credible to me to deny all knowledge of any bailout negotiations.

Certainly, from my conversations with Brian, it was clear to me, long before November 2010, that there was every likelihood that some kind of bailout was going to be required at some stage. I think the turning point actually occurred in or around the week of his Béal na Bláth oration in late August 2010. Brian had stitched in a rather dreary set of passages at the end of that speech because throughout July and August the scale of the difficulties in the banks had become more apparent. It was becoming clear it was not just liquidity that was the problem.

Brian rang me on his way back from Béal na Bláth and he was in good form. He told me that he had taken great pride in mentioning in his speech that two previous Ministers for Finance – Michael Collins and Ray Mac Sharry – also had to deal with immense difficulties, but that Ireland managed to survive. And so too Ireland will survive as a result of the decisions taken by Brian Lenihan.

Brian's sense, even then, was that by the spring of the following year the question of some kind of facility from Europe and the IMF would emerge. In fact, it happened slightly earlier in November 2010, but that is no criticism of Brian. He was fighting against the inevitable. Increasing bank losses and the consequent increase in state borrowing required to fund their rescue saw serious doubts emerge over Ireland's solvency. Brian was doing his best. It was an impossible situation, but he was courageous and he was tenacious. He knew that we were going to need funding from outside because of the money that was being poured into propping up the banks. On 30 September 2010, Brian told the Dáil that the cost of rescuing the banks would be €50 billion, which would cost Ireland €1.5 billion in interest a year.

Brian rang me several times from Brussels in 2010 and by this stage his illness was becoming more pronounced. He had been diagnosed with pancreatic cancer in December 2009. He used to take time off from meetings to rest, but when he was abroad he would often use this time to ring me from the office of the Permanent Representation in Brussels. I would ask Brian how he was feeling and he would say that he was resting on the couch and then he would launch into a detailed analysis of the euro crisis. In May 2010, the eurozone countries and the IMF had agreed a €110 billion bailout for Greece and there were genuine concerns that both Portugal and Spain would require bailouts, which eventually is what transpired. The EU was much more concerned with these larger economies, but Ireland too was slipping inexorably into bailout territory. At the start of September 2010, Irish borrowing costs had reached new highs. In trying to stem the tide, Brian claimed there was a 'concerted attack' on eurozone members and he appealed to the media to provide more balanced reporting. By October 2010, the cost of government borrowing rose above 8 per cent, a figure that was unsustainably high. On 21 November, the Government announced its intention to request EU-IMF assistance. As Brian later honestly noted in an interview, 'I believed I had fought the good fight and taken every measure possible to delay such an eventuality, and now hell was at the gates.'

Brian had been keen to burn the big bondholders and we discussed this on a number of occasions. One morning I got a call about a quarter past eight and it was Brian. He told me that he was able to burn the bondholders and he was very happy because the European Central Bank President, Jean-Claude Trichet, had told him he could do it. This would have improved Ireland's position significantly and it was going to be a big story, but later that day a now despondent Brian rang me back. He said Trichet had changed his mind because he realised that the main casualty if the bondholders were burnt would be big German and French banks. This was a disgraceful decision because the ECB is supposed to represent the interests of Europe generally, but they were clearly under the sway of the German and French banks. Even today, I still would not have much confidence in the ECB and until Europe gets a totally independent entity to defend its currency, the euro will remain a fragile currency.

I do not think that the ECB behaved even-handedly towards Ireland or Brian Lenihan. I know that Brian said in an interview with BBC Radio 4 shortly prior to his death that the ECB had threatened him both verbally and by correspondence about what would happen if Ireland refused to accept the bailout without burning bondholders. Mr Trichet has said that these letters should not be made public, but undoubtedly they will have to be considered by the banking inquiry and I suspect they will make for very interesting reading. People may then appreciate the uphill battle that Brian Lenihan had to fight.

In October 2010, Brian told me that while he was visiting Washington to meet the IMF, he had gone to see a top medical consultant. The advice Brian got was that his cancer was inoperable. Brian knew he was a dying man, but he was stoic about it and he was determined to keep working hard on behalf of the Irish people for as long as he could.

I know there has been a lot of speculation about how Brian got on with Brian Cowen, but my sense of their relationship was that it was good. Of course, they didn't always agree on everything, but that is natural in governmental relationships. I remember on the eve of my budget in 1982 having a stand-up row with Charlie Haughey about the re-introduction of vehicle tax. I know that Brian Lenihan and Brian Cowen had opposing views on social partnership and the extent to which the public service pay bill could be cut, however, they respected each other and they never fell out.

My biggest concern was that an election would be averted. I believed that Fianna Fáil needed at least a year to avert the worst electoral effects of what had been announced in the Budget in December 2010.

At this time, I pleaded with Lenihan to go and get a deal with the Greens to stay on for at least another year to put some distance between a very harsh budget and an election. Lenihan did try to broker such a deal, but by this stage relations between the parties had irreversibly broken down. Lenihan himself had a good relationship with Eamon Ryan and he was never one to hold a grudge in politics, but he was angry about the manner in which the Greens left Government.

The election ended up being held in February 2011 and, while canvassers were at the doorsteps, people were opening their post with their pay-cheques and realising they were down on average €70 a week. The universal social charge deductions had just come into effect. As a result, Fianna Fáil reaped an electoral whirlwind. The party would have suffered serious losses in any case, but this calamity in timing only served to compound matters.

The great irony of the situation was that had the Government not delayed and taken the stringent, but necessary steps to get wages under control, to increase income tax revenues and to rein in spending in earlier budgets, especially the Budget in 2008, as Lenihan had advocated, economic renewal would have happened quicker and Fianna Fáil and the Greens would probably have saved more seats in the 2011 election.

Brian had the right temperament for politics. He did not take things personally and he did not let criticism get to him. In one of our earlier meetings after he became Minister for Finance in 2008, I told him he should prepare himself to become the most hated man in Ireland. Brian, I think, was slightly amused by this. I had taken a lot of personal abuse in the 1980s for some of the budgetary measures I had introduced, but I think Brian was actually placed in a more difficult position because the correction he had to implement was coming after the 'Celtic Tiger' boom. It was harder for Brian because people had more to lose when the crisis hit in 2008, but even though he was taking money out of people's pockets, he still managed to retain public respect and affection. People understood that the crisis was not a mess of Brian Lenihan's making, but he was doing his damndest to put it right, irrespective of his own health.

Brian worked extraordinary long hours and this comes with the territory of being at the helm in the Department of Finance. I know that Brian Lenihan continued to work long hours, even after his diagnosis. As well as contending with Budgets and supplementary Budgets, Brian, as Minister for Finance, brought in twenty pieces of legislation.

The pressures he faced were far greater than those that any Irish Finance Minister has had to contend. Brian had to try to steer Ireland through the worst global financial crisis since the Wall Street Crash in 1929, while, at the same time, trying to deal with the seismic fall-out of the implosion of a domestic property-bubble, which brought the very future of the Irish banking sector to the edge of the cliff. It was a full-on economic tsunami, but Brian Lenihan never flinched. He didn't get everything right, but he did an outstanding job.

On 15 December 2013, Ireland exited the €85 billion EU-IMF bailout programme. While a variety of Fine Gael and Labour politicians took to the airwaves to take credit for this progress, my thoughts turned to Brian Lenihan. Sadly, Brian didn't live to see the day, but he more than anyone else was responsible for Ireland's swift exit of the bailout programme. Most of the heavy-lifting of financial adjustment had been carried out on Brian's watch and the austerity plan Enda Kenny's Government followed on assuming office was essentially Brian Lenihan's plan. Given the nature of our adversarial politics, it was hardly surprising that Brian's contribution went unacknowledged by the current government. Politics is an ungrateful business and it moves on very quickly, but history will not and should not forget Brian Lenihan's strong contribution.

9 BRIAN LENIHAN: A PROFILE IN COURAGE

Martin Mansergh

BRIAN LENIHAN EPITOMISED THE courageous politician. He battled to maintain the State's viability in a ferocious financial crisis, while latterly fighting a deadly disease. Vital to confidence, he carried the struggle to a point, from which, provided his successors stuck to the path, Ireland would emerge battered, but intact. Party considerations were subordinated to the public interest. His battles recall a book by John F. Kennedy. Brian Lenihan identified with the Kennedy family, and approved refurbishment of the Kennedy homestead near New Ross through the Office of Public Works.

John F. Kennedy, while a Senator, wrote *Profiles in Courage,* with the theme 'the courage of men of integrity caught in a net of adverse circumstances.' In any Irish study, Brian Lenihan would be a prime candidate for inclusion. So would Michael Collins, about whom Brian Lenihan spoke in August 2010, as the first Fianna Fáil Minister invited to give the Béal na Bláth oration.

During a confidence motion on 15 June 2010, Brian Lenihan defined political courage:

> The ultimate test of any government is its ability to take decisive and courageous action, react rapidly in changing times, hold its nerve in the face of enormous domestic and international pressures and say 'No' to sectional interests. Such a government should have a

determination to make difficult and unpopular but fair decisions in the teeth of opposition, should be able to communicate successfully the need for such decisions and should have the ability to lead citizens towards the common good.

Many democracies witness political involvement of members of particular families through several generations. In Ireland, many political families began with the independence struggle, but others, like the Lenihans, developed a tradition of political service later. Brian Lenihan Senior and his sister Mary O'Rourke held important cabinet posts. The younger Brian Lenihan, elected to the Dáil in a 1996 Dublin by-election following his father's death, had great ability of his own.

While awaiting appointment to Cabinet, he was an excellent Chairman of the Oireachtas Committee on the Constitution and junior Minister for Children. He only served 11 months as Justice Minister in 2007–8 with the change of leadership.

Brian Cowen became Taoiseach on 7 May 2008, having been Minister for Finance from late 2004 during the frenzy of the late 'Celtic Tiger'. In 2006, he was hailed by the *Economist* as the most successful EU Finance Minister. Growth was strong; the fundamentals looked sound. As Brian Lenihan observed to European colleagues and then to the Dáil on 28 October 2010, Irish public finance fully complied with the European Growth and Stability Pact, while the property bubble was brewing. One crisis outcome is stronger budgetary rules restricting structural deficits.

Brian Lenihan was appointed Minister for Finance, in recognition of the strength his ability would bring to the new administration. Indeed, he became its key figure, bearing much of the heaviest ministerial burden.

Brian Lenihan acknowledged ruefully that his tenure would be different from his predecessors. From 1989, Finance Ministers had been able to announce tax reductions and breaks and significant increases in public investment and welfare expenditure. Social partnership agreements provided increasingly generous remuneration, particularly at higher levels, for a public sector that grew in numbers by 50 per cent between 2000 and 2008.

Ireland was persuaded that it had found the philosopher's stone regarding economic management. Pressures on government were pushing for less restraint. The Left argued Ireland was the second richest country in the EU, and awash with money; social spending should be further expanded. They did question the prolongation of property breaks. Though the Right argued for better value for money and against public sector benchmarking, Opposition motions demanded lower taxes and charges or increased public spending. An EU Commission call in 2001 for restraint was brushed aside. Critics denied economic success had anything to do with the Government; the credit belonged to the people. Consequent economic disaster, however, was down to government mismanagement and unhealthy closeness to bankers and developers.

It was long axiomatic that the best investments were property and banks. Not just cheap credit from abroad, but higher disposable income from wage and salary increases and tax cuts, as well as glossy advertising, persuaded many people to invest surplus cash in property, and use their assets to leverage large loans. Independent Ireland never experienced a property crash to act as a warning. Such events abroad were dismissed as not applicable. Yet, as in the Great Depression of the 1870s, a crash typically follows long periods of growth that end in a bubble.

When Ireland joined the euro, a political decision that was a logical extension of its pro-European policy since accession in 1973 and ERM membership since 1979, it should have involved budgetary discipline. The early years seemed to demonstrate otherwise. Interest rates fell sharply. Markets assumed that the risk of holding Irish bonds and German ones were virtually the same. Capital flowed to the periphery, where accelerated development was happening, oblivious to the massive overshoot taking place with State support. If there was imprudent borrowing, there must have been imprudent lending, but subsequently the correction was borne by countries, whose private sector had over-borrowed.

The soundness of the Irish banking system was taken for granted. Light regulation became the new orthodoxy, and competition seen as good for the consumer. Prudential rules were bypassed, as 100 per cent plus mortgages were granted. A few expressed unease. Financial institutions entering the Irish market aggressively sought market share, with long-established ones fighting to defend theirs. Gushing revenues from stamp duty made the Exchequer a prisoner of the boom, and nervous of doing anything which would trigger a slide, including a rapid withdrawal of property incentives.

Fianna Fáil, under Bertie Ahern, developed budgetary alignment with the electoral cycle into a fine art. Largesse accelerated approaching a general election, with brakes sharply applied afterwards. Policies were set to mature at election time. Manifestos were partly based on opinion research. The electorate welcomed competing offers and parties putting themselves on hooks which provided useful leverage afterwards. Caution was brushed aside by the imperatives of auction politics. Few had any inkling that the carpet of flowers that promised a soft landing and quick recovery covered the abyss.

Following the 2007 General Election, as the Taoiseach's difficulties increased, everything was concentrated on ensuring a smooth succession. The budgetary brakes, which caused anger in 2002-3, were not applied. This exacerbated subsequent difficulties. Brian Lenihan summed up the disaster in a Dáil statement on 28 October 2010:

> A major crisis was created by the extraordinary property bubble, which was fuelled by and large by the availability of cheap credit after Ireland's admission to the Eurozone. It was not just a question of the banks, however. The property bubble made increased tax receipts available to successive Governments. These moneys were used to finance expenditures which were unsustainable.

One overhang that immediately hobbled the Cowen administration was the loss in June 2008 of the Lisbon I Treaty referendum on a low turn-out. The result manifested the hubris of the late 'Celtic Tiger' era: Ireland could tell the EU where to get off, and veto a WTO deal, if it threatened farm interests. There was a sense of invincibility.

Ireland had to face into an unprecedented crisis, with doubts over its continuing EU status, until the Lisbon II referendum was convincingly passed in October 2009, after careful opinion-sounding and diplomacy.

In his first Dáil speech as Finance Minister on 14 May 2008, Brian Lenihan looked back over an astonishing economic performance since the mid-1990s. Referring to the ESRI medium-term outlook, he noted with satisfaction that 'the ESRI acknowledges our sound economic and financial fundamentals. It points to our ability to absorb shocks in an efficient manner, to limit the economic fall-out and to return to the trend rate of growth fairly rapidly'.

Six days later, he took up a constant theme, public service reform. He expressed dissatisfaction with the proliferation of quangos: 'We have gone too far right across government in handing over specific functions to agencies. In doing so, we are abdicating our responsibilities as the elected government of the people'. Economic conditions were 'challenging'. The outlook was less benign with more uncertainty and a liquidity squeeze.

When the 2008 half-year Exchequer returns were published, a rapid deterioration in the public finances was evident. There was deep gloom in the Department of Finance. Everything was beginning to fall apart. Long paraded as a star performer, Ireland suddenly looked vulnerable. Brian Lenihan did not wait for things to become worse. Notwithstanding social partnership negotiations, the Government introduced a mini-budget with expenditure savings of €440 million for 2008 and €1 billion in a full year.

Decentralisation was suspended, where projects were not sufficiently advanced or contractually committed. The premise that rents and site costs were much lower in provincial towns and that the State could profit from selling city centre locations, worth astronomical prices in the boom, no longer applied in a sinking market. Public Private Partnerships (PPPs) stalled, as developers faced huge financial problems. As a Dublin Deputy, Brian Lenihan knew that decentralisation was not popular with his constituents or the Dublin-based public service.

He set about cutting the public service pay bill by 3 per cent by end-2009. He shelved pay rises recommended by the Review Body on Higher Remuneration in the Public Service, which for years tried to match it to lower level boardroom pay. Though the pay of politicians tended to be highlighted, secretaries-general could retire, before 65, with lump sums up to half a million euro and six-figure pensions. Public resentment grew, as the economy deteriorated. Public procurement was to be rationalised. The development aid budget was trimmed. Priority areas in the capital budget were protected, notably the motorway network, completed in 2010.

In September 2008, the chickens came home to roost. While a new social partnership agreement was concluded, involving modest pay rises and social commitments, it was rapidly bypassed by events. Social partnership had become over-ambitious and over-extended. The Department of Finance, central to pay control, had less control over wider Government commitments coordinated by the Taoiseach's Department. The Dáil felt sidelined by the process. Brian Lenihan was not a devotee, and this caused some tensions in Government Buildings.

Financial tremors were felt in February 2008, when an English bank, Northern Rock, was hastily nationalised with an immediate State bailout of £24 billion. Veteran Labour politician Tony Benn, somewhat conflicted, wrote in his diary: 'I mean, if Northern Rock had gone bankrupt, there would have been a complete run on all the banks, so they did the right thing' (18 February). This was followed end-September by nationalisation of Bradford & Bingley, which involved taking liability for toxic mortgage debt initially estimated at £150 billion.

In March 2008, New York investment bank, Bear Stearns, heavily into sub-prime mortgages, was taken over at a fraction of recent market value. A seismic event occurred in mid-September, when Lehman Brothers was allowed to collapse without any bailout. Brian Lenihan described this in the Seanad on 1 October as a 'default by the US authorities.' It put under intense pressure weak links in banking everywhere. According to *Der Spiegel* (39/2008), world financial markets ran the danger of core meltdown. The American authorities hurriedly devised a bailout package for toxic sub-prime securities, still the subject of Congressional wrangles at the end of September, adding to international instability. While the *Financial Times* (29 September) lamented 'how bail-outs poison a free market recipe for the world,' when devastation is to be averted, pragmatism trumps ideology. Previously, the message from the authorities was that Irish financial institutions were sound and not exposed to the US sub-prime market. On 30 September, the Minister acknowledged in the Dáil that it was only a matter of time before the effects of the US turmoil visited our shores.

The fall-out also hit the German bank Hypo Real Estate. It had taken over Depfa in the International Financial Services Centre in Dublin, which had engaged in high-risk hedge fund activities. Its liquidity severely squeezed after the collapse of Lehman Brothers, it sought German Government support. Chancellor Merkel and Finance Minister Steinbrück played hardball to force German bank participation in the bailout, all sides knowing that, if Hypo Real were to fail, the German banking system would be at risk. State support ballooned from €20 billion to over €100 billion, and the bank was nationalised. The German deposit guarantees were political, not legal, statements. The episode gave Merkel expensive experience of Irish light regulation. While Germany had greater flexibility, its hardball approach did not ultimately spare German taxpayers.

The collapse of Lehman Brothers triggered a crisis of confidence in the Irish banking system. To prevent a run, the Government issued on 20 September a scheme to protect bank deposits up to €100,000. Anglo Irish Bank, which had focused on the speculative property market, remained under heavy pressure, and faced collapse, bringing down the Irish banking system, if market assumptions that the State would stand behind systemic banks proved wrong. On the night of 29 September, after flurried consultations, the Government decided to guarantee all deposits and bondholders. The guarantee involved no upfront payment, but required belief it would never be called in.

Despite heavy criticism in hindsight, no plausible alternative has been proposed. The bank guarantee was a disaster, because bank lending had gone completely out of control and because there was no better choice. As Brian Lenihan said in a Dáil debate on 4 November

2009, 'the reputational damage to Ireland was done long before the night of the guarantee.' He added:

> The idea that the collapse of such an institution by a Government would have no implications for the rest of the banking sector or for the financing of the State, guarantee or no guarantee, is utterly fallacious.

In a later Dáil banking debate on 30 March 2010, Brian Lenihan again strongly defended the guarantee:

> The detailed information that has emerged from the banks in the course of the NAMA process is truly shocking. At every hand's turn our worst fears have been surpassed. Some institutions were worse than others but our banking system, to a greater or lesser extent, engaged in reckless property development lending. In far too many cases there were also shoddy banking practices. The banks played fast and loose with the economic interests of this country. Our previous regulatory system failed abysmally . . .
>
> Anglo Irish Bank was much larger relative to the Irish economy than Lehman Brothers was to the US economy. The disorderly failure of Lehman Brothers brought the global financial system to its knees. The disorderly failure of Anglo Irish Bank two weeks later would have had the same effect on the entire Irish banking system.

Even when Ireland had to suspend raising money on the international markets, Brian Lenihan remained emphatic, when introducing legislation to extend the guarantee (excluding subordinated bond holders) on 29 September 2010:

> It is a source of bewilderment that the brave decision to introduce the original guarantee, supported by the vast majority in the house, is now being characterised by some as the root of all our problems. Let me be clear: had that guarantee not been introduced, we would not

now have an economy, never mind a banking system. On that night two years ago, our banking system was perched on a precipice. Funding had all but dried up and the banks faced closure within days.

Brian Lenihan never resiled from that defence. The then Head of the European Central Bank (ECB), Jean-Claude Trichet, told the European Parliament on 14 January 2014 that the Irish Government's decision at the time was 'justifiable given the situation it found itself in.'

Government alone bears responsibility for the consequences of its crisis decisions. As Brian Lenihan said in the Dáil, it was 'a lonely place' the Taoiseach, himself and the Attorney General found themselves in. No government wants to run a high risk of massively disrupting the lives of its citizens, by decisions that cause large-scale panic or disorder or a major breach with its international partners. The priority, he said on 17 October, was to protect the real economy from the effects of severe financial disruption. Neither the Argentinian default nor the experience of the small population of Iceland offered Ireland a plausible alternative. Iceland has little attraction for investors, and is still legally pursued for losses to depositors. *The Economist* (15 February 2014) cites Argentina as a parable to be avoided.

The decision taken did not benefit directors of Anglo Irish Bank. The Anglo tapes reveal the deep frustration of senior executives that they could not lay hands on State money, the first injection coming after the chairman and chief executive officer had resigned in December 2008. A month later, it was nationalised. Brian Lenihan did not give them 'the moolah'.

Bankers and developers did not escape. Owners of banks, the shareholders, were wiped out. Share options to part-remunerate executives and board members became worthless. Many developers lost control of assets, went bankrupt, or are being pursued by creditors. Some face court charges. Careers were terminated, reputations destroyed. None suggested receipt of favours from Brian Lenihan.

Criticism that most Government members were out of the

loop ignores the reality of modern government. Financial crisis management always involves a tight group at political leadership level and a few key officials. (The present Government formalised this, by establishing an economic committee of four cabinet members.) Other ministers might be asked to ratify decisions. Some ex-ministers have since complained; one fulsomely praised the guarantee at the time.

The inclusion of subordinated debt holders was criticised. After the two-year guarantee expired, when they had to accept heavy write-downs, Brian Lenihan defended their inclusion at the time:

> However, on the night of 29 September, there simply was too much at stake to discriminate between different types of bondholders, and in the end those whom the Governor felt should not have been covered accounted for just 3 per cent of the covered liabilities.

Bank nationalisation would not have diminished obligations on the State, which needed time to clarify the real situation. On 20 January 2009, Brian Lenihan told the Dáil that bank nationalisation that night would have led to a systemic run on the banks. In the NAMA bill debate on 16 September 2009, he quoted President Obama's statement: 'Pre-emptive government takeovers are likely to end up costing taxpayers even more in the end and are more likely to undermine than create confidence.'

On 28 April 2010, Brian Lenihan argued that blanket nationalisation would have deprived Bank of Ireland of access to private funds.

The bank guarantee had short-lived popularity. Its main effect was to protect the economy from immediate massive disruption. There were complaints from EU partners and the UK, which feared an outflow of deposits to Ireland, but there was no short-term EU crisis management mechanism to meet market emergencies. Fence-mending was done afterwards. October's Credit Institutions (Financial Support Scheme) Bill had prior EU Commission approval.

The 2009 Budget was brought forward to mid-October showing Government will to tackle the yawning gulf in the public finances.

The era of benign budgets was over. Brian Lenihan acknowledged in a debate on 29 January 2009: 'Perhaps as a Government we were over-ambitious in trying to meet the understandable demands of our people for new and better public services when the resources were available'.

Now, the Government had the daunting task of turning round public expectations. The 2009 Budget introduced a progressive income levy, raised the standard rate of VAT by 0.5 per cent to 21.5 per cent, increased excise duties, and brought in an air travel tax as well as a tax on non-principal private residences. Education cuts, together with the travel tax, remained contested, along with the wider gap in the UK and Irish VAT rates, exacerbating a cross-border shopping exodus more due to sterling depreciation.

A political earthquake was caused by withdrawal of free medical cards for the over-70s, introduced following a 2002 election commitment. Expensive to implement, it had been a bridge too far. Without being worked out in detail, the cutback seemed draconian. Pensioners angrily protested on the streets and filled the airwaves with individual tales. The older population were a core element in party support. A backbench revolt loomed; a deputy resigned. The Government had to retreat and soften its proposals, so that only the substantially better off would be affected.

The comfortable classes complained the budget did not go far enough. Few appreciated Ireland was facing a deep and prolonged recession, and would have to pace remedial action at a rate of adjustment that the public would bear. With a further drastic fall in revenues, the Minister went back to the well with the public service pension levy in winter 2009 and a supplementary budget in April. He was always conscious of the need to maintain Ireland's attractiveness to investors. He commissioned a comprehensive report from a Special Group on Public Service Numbers and Expenditure Programmes led by economist Colm McCarthy to provide a menu of budget cuts, and established a new Commission on Taxation.

There was intense debate over whether the Government was pursuing the right budgetary policy, and whether austerity, in other words the overriding emphasis on bringing the deficit back within eurozone limits, would work. The alternative was a Keynesian-style stimulus and to raise more taxes from the better off. Given most western economies had been hit, the State had to take a grip of its finances, to continue borrowing from financial markets. The wider eurozone, especially its strongest country Germany, like the United States, had broader choices, but retrenchment remained the norm with a cumulative depressive effect. The nineteenth-century motto 'Am deutschen Wesen soll die Welt genesen' ('the world should recover the German way') prevailed. Experience in the 1980s and since, in Ireland and France, show that unilateral attempts to swim against the tide only make matters worse.

Ireland's opening situation in 2008 had mitigating features; low public debt; substantial reserves in the National Pension Reserve Fund; and a strong export-oriented multinational sector underpinned by low corporation tax. Ireland was too vulnerable to engage in counter-cyclical experiments.

There was also an alternative of defaulting and leaving the euro, requiring an immediate expenditure cut across the board of 30-40 per cent, and the near-certainty of becoming an investment pariah.

The Government opted for battening down the hatches and trying to ride out the storm. Job losses were heavy and hardship widespread. The Government parties comforted themselves that there was still time after some tough years to emerge from the crisis ahead of a 2012 general election.

Governments and the Department of Finance had long experience in dealing with budgetary crises and correcting deficits. There was no familiarity with banking crises. Prudential bank supervision fell to the Central Bank; the Financial Regulator was most focused on consumer protection. There was one crisis in 1985, when Allied Irish Banks was jeopardised by imprudent management of its Insurance Corporation of Ireland subsidiary. The Government provided a bailout in excess of £100 million. In reality, it was a bail-in of the industry and its customers, with the sum recouped by an insurance levy.

Following the breathing space of the bank guarantee, Brian Lenihan was in no rush to recapitalise the banks, but it became increasingly evident that their problems went far beyond an externally induced temporary liquidity squeeze. The banks were not upfront about their problems, and probably harboured lingering hopes of an early property recovery. The worth of their loans depended on assumptions about this. The situation in Anglo Irish Bank, specialist in property lending, was hopeless.

Previously, bank nationalisation was advocated only on the Left. In 1992, the Labour Party advocated a third banking force, but dropped it in government. Ideology aside, nationalisation only occurs when the private sector cannot guarantee a vital public service. Early in 2009, Brian Lenihan had to introduce legislation nationalising Anglo Irish Bank, citing the uncovering of unacceptable practices, such as concealment of loans to directors. A Fine Gael predecessor, Alan Dukes, was asked to chair it. Past investigation was referred to the Office of the Director of Corporate Enforcement. The trial of three former directors commenced in February 2014. One was acquitted.

Recapitalising the banks started to get underway. In the case of AIB, recapitalisation eventually involved virtual outright nationalisation with a State shareholding of 99.5 per cent. Bank of Ireland managed to retain partial independence, with the State taking a substantial minority shareholding. While originally the plan was to make Anglo Irish Bank viable again, it was later wound down, with its remaining assets transferred by Minister for Finance Michael Noonan to the Irish Bank Resolution Corporation (IBRC).

Successive recapitalisations, as the assessment of the banks' situation worsened, which eventually amounted to €80 billion by March 2011, proved the Achilles heel that led to the Troika bailout, as markets lost faith in the country's ability to manage the situation independently.

Much of Brian Lenihan's time was taken up in 2009 and 2010 with the fall-out of the banking crisis. There was an on-going problem of getting the banks to undertake normal commercial lending, while trying to salvage their own balance sheets. A lot of mortgage-holders were in negative equity. With job losses and the income squeeze, many found it difficult to keep up repayments. The Government with its stake in the banks and public interest directors was expected to direct them to behave sympathetically. Some assurances on lending were obtained, and home repossessions were put off. Brian Lenihan also tackled excessive remuneration of bank directors and senior staff and the elimination of bonuses offensive to taxpayers saddled with having to bailout the banks.

With new bank lending virtually frozen and consequences for employment and the economy, the separating out of impaired loans by creating a 'bad' bank, as had worked abroad, was advocated. A plan was drawn up by economic consultant Peter Bacon. The establishment of the National Assets Management Agency (NAMA), under former Chairman of the Revenue Commissioners, Frank Daly, was strongly contested politically, on the grounds that NAMA would pay too much for the assets, gifting a soft bailout at taxpayers' expense for bankers and developers. Instead of €54 billion mooted for the acquisition of loans nominally totalling €70 billion, NAMA paid only €32 billion. On 11 October 2010 in the Dáil, Brian Lenihan explained that the three reasons for the discount being much larger than anticipated were the poor level of security in respect of assets, the reckless optimism behind the loans, and the roll-up of interest into the capital sum. He promised that 'a far more rigorous approach will be taken with regard to developers than was taken by many of the financial institutions.'

Court challenges so far have proved almost uniformly unsuccessful. In recent times, Michael Noonan has said that he is very happy with NAMA, even though Fine Gael in opposition was very unhappy with it.

Poor January 2009 Exchequer returns, confirming a revenue implosion, combined with €8 billion to recapitalise the banks, meant that further action to counter the ballooning deficit was required. The public sector could not be insulated, while there was a haemorrhage of private sector jobs, a fall in private sector incomes, and growing deficits in private pension schemes, especially defined benefit ones. This contrasted with public service job security, substantial earlier gains from benchmarking, and solid pensions requiring only modest contributions. A widespread reaction from public servants was that they had nothing to do with a crisis caused by bankers and developers.

The Government needed a public expenditure reduction

amounting to €2 billion, the main element being a public service pension levy averaging 7.5 per cent but progressive. Protracted trade union negotiations were abortive. Their mood precluded a social partnership agreement. The leadership would not share responsibility for tough decisions adversely affecting the incomes of their members. This marked the end of a 22-year-old process, which saw employment double to over 2 million, and real incomes substantially improve through a combination of wage rises and tax cuts, together with many welfare improvements, against a background of industrial peace. Social partnership unfortunately fell short at the challenge of taking necessary and painful action to secure the continued viability of the State and its services.

A full supplementary Budget was introduced in April. A high-profile issue, the incomes, allowances and pensions paid to politicians, was addressed, with ministerial pensions abolished for sitting politicians. Ministers of State were reduced from 20 to 15. The Christmas bonus was suspended. Social welfare rates were untouched, despite an anticipated 4 per cent drop in inflation. The main tax measures were doubling of the income and health levies and curtailment of mortgage interest relief.

The process of adjustment amounted to a form of internal devaluation, necessary to restore Ireland's competitiveness. As Martin Wolf commented in the *Financial Times* (23 March 2010), Irish policy-makers 'really do seem to understand the implications of being in a monetary union'.

The Government had three hurdles to overcome in autumn 2009; to pass the Lisbon II referendum; to renegotiate the Programme for Government with the Greens; and to pass a stringent budget for 2010. To the surprise of commentators, the Government succeeded in all three.

The Budget involved a further adjustment of €4 billion. Desperate efforts were made by trade unions to avoid public service pay cuts by taking additional unpaid leave, but, not providing the required savings, this was ridiculed in the media and by Government backbenchers. This budget, consisting mainly of expenditure cuts, cut public service pay by 5–8 per cent (more at high levels), child benefit, unemployment and carer's benefit, while imposing a small prescription charge. A carbon tax in keeping with the green agenda was introduced.

The public was oblivious to the support provided by the ECB to the Irish banking system, which was unable to borrow on the markets. In his budget speech, Brian Lenihan reminded people of the underlying realities:

> The single currency has provided huge protection and support to Ireland in the current crisis. It has prevented speculative attacks on our currency and provided funding to the banking system ... However, membership of monetary union also means devaluation is not an option. Therefore, the adjustment process must be made by way of reductions in wages, prices, profits and rents.

With regard to speculative attack, the markets were about to commence a sustained onslaught.

On St. Stephen's Day 2009, TV3 controversially reported that Brian Lenihan had been diagnosed with a serious illness. He reassured people that he could continue to carry out core ministerial functions, while receiving treatment. Over the following 15 months, he was as good as his word. Less essential tasks were delegated. In spring 2010, a second Minister of State was appointed. His successors in 2011 were two Cabinet Ministers, for Finance and for Public Reform and Expenditure, sharing the heavy workload.

Brian Lenihan introduced some twenty pieces of legislation. Most weeks, there were debates on the crisis, whereas, previously, the economy was a subject opposition parties preferred to avoid. There were constant EU Finance Ministers' meetings.

Entering 2010, there was cautious optimism that the worst might be over. The Minister's tasks involved progressing impartial inquiries into causes of the disaster and appointment of a regulator, Matthew Elderfield, whose office was tied into the Central Bank. Lenihan was scathing about the past, saying that 'the banks played fast and loose with the interests of this country', and that senior banking figures had made 'appalling lending decisions that will cost the taxpayer dearly for years to come' (Dáil Éireann, 30 March 2010). Earlier, he stated

1. Handing in his father's nomination papers for the 1989 General Election. (pic: Independent News and Media)

2. Canvassing in Ballyfermot during the 1996 Dublin West by-election (pic: Jack McManus, *Irish Times*)

3. At Dublin West by-election count 3 April 1996 with (seated) Sean Sherwin, National Organiser Fianna Fáil, and (standing l/r) Noel Dempsey TD, Director of Elections; Mary O' Rourke TD, Deputy Leader of Fianna Fáil; Marty Whelan, Fianna Fáil Press Office and Joan Keating, Fianna Fáil HQ (pic: RollingNews.ie)

4. Launching a report, as Minister for Children, at Government Buildings, November 2006 (pic: Tom Burke, Independent News and Media)

5. Receiving the seal of office as Minister for Justice from President McAleese with Taoiseach Bertie Ahern, 14 June 2007 (pic: Albert Gonzalez, RollingNews.ie)

6. Congratulating new Garda recruits, as Minister for Justice, at Templemore College July 2007 (pic: Eamonn Farrell, RollingNews.ie)

7. With Mary O'Rourke TD and Conor Lenihan TD at Fianna Fáil Parliamentary Party conference, Druid Glen, September 2007 (pic: Independent News and Media)

8. Shopper watches as the Minister for Finance delivers his first Budget 14 October 2008 (pic: Martin Nolan, Independent News and Media)

9. With Taoiseach Brian Cowen at Annual Fianna Fáil Wolfe Tone commemoration, Bodenstown, 18 October 2009 (pic: Donal Doherty, Lensmen/Irish Photo Archive)

10. Visiting the Mountainview Resource Centre, Blanchardstown, in his own constituency of Dublin West (pic: Frank McGrath, Independent News and Media).

11. Minister for Finance Brian Lenihan arriving at the Treasury Building, July 2009 (pic: Cyril Byrne, *Irish Times*)

12. Giving a briefing on the legislation to establish NAMA, November 2009 (pic: Brenda Fitzsimons, *Irish Times*)

13. At a media briefing with Eamon Ryan, Minister for Communications, Energy and Natural Resources, Government Buildings February 2010 (pic: Sasko Lazarov, RollingNews.ie)

14. Speaking at the Annual Michael Collins commemoration, Béal na Bláth, Co. Cork, August 2010 (pic: Eamonn Farrell, RollingNews.ie)

15. Making a point to Christine Lagarde, the French Finance Minister, EU Finance Ministers meeting, Brussels, January 2011 (pic: © Peter Cavanagh, www.irishphoto.com)

16. Waiting for the General Election result in Dublin West with supporters, including Mel Kelleher, Mary D'Arcy, and Margaret Kenny, Coolmine Leisure Centre, 26 February 2011 (pic: Damien Eagers, Damien Eagers Photography)

that 'the previous regulatory system failed spectacularly to prevent what we now know to have been grossly excessive and irresponsible lending to the property sector' (Dáil Éireann, 28 March). At this point, he introduced the funding device of promissory notes to cover an extra €32 billion required to recapitalise the banks. Because of European statistical rules, this caused a once-off spike in the 2010 General Government Deficit to 32 per cent of GDP, which shocked European Finance Ministers at a July ECOFIN meeting.

The skies darkened again. Growth had not materialised. The Greek situation developed into a full-scale crisis. Partners now knew that Greek public accounts had been falsified to gain euro entry. Austerity decisions were violently contested on the streets of Athens. It was an open question whether Greece would leave the eurozone. When Germany concluded that this was not in their interests, the Greek Government still had to be persuaded to implement the necessary reforms in return for new tranches of funding. 'Ireland is not Greece' was the mantra, but the markets looked around for other vulnerable countries. They betted on disintegration of the eurozone, disliked in many Anglo-American financial circles, but ignored strong political commitment to the euro. The stand-off was only defused when new ECB President Mario Draghi promised to do whatever it took to defend it in mid-2012.

Potential widespread strikes were averted by the Croke Park Agreement with public service unions, which, in return for a four-year commitment not to cut further pay and pensions nor impose compulsory redundancies, demanded greater workplace flexibility. Given the parlous State finances, this was a substantial Government concession.

By early autumn, it became apparent that the banks required still more capital, and that a fiscal adjustment of €15 billion was needed to reduce Ireland's deficit to 3 per cent of GDP by 2014. Ireland could no longer borrow at under 7 per cent on international markets, despite funding to mid-2011. A bond auction was cancelled.

Political and market pressure was mounting, with no light at the end of the tunnel. The Government's Dáil majority had eroded. The Green Party privately debated continuing in government. Fianna Fáil backbenchers were mutinous, and looking to change leader, even though this meant an election. When they were quoted by name in the *Frankfurter Allgemeine Zeitung* or *International Herald Tribune*, this compounded the impression of a government falling apart. Brian Lenihan tried to hold support together, adding to the many strains upon him. He told the Dáil on 30 September: 'The public is understandably and rightly angry about what has happened in our banking system in recent years. I share that anger, but anger is not a policy'.

A meeting at Deauville on 18 October between President Sarkozy and Chancellor Merkel was the catalyst for an intensification of the crisis, which within a month forced Ireland to adopt a Troika programme. Grappling with ways to avoid future crises, they envisaged that from 2013 private bondholders would participate in solving them. While in Ireland there was much support for burning bondholders, timing meant that within three years countries that had not regained market confidence would be forced to impose 'haircuts' on their creditors. This happened subsequently with unmanageable Greek debt, and savagely with Cypriot debt. Brian Lenihan acknowledged in the Dáil on 15 December that 'Chancellor Merkel's intervention played a large part in the escalation of our bond prices last autumn'.

Under increasing pressure from the ECB, Brian Lenihan announced on 27 October 2010 that the Government would be bringing forward a four-year plan to bring the Irish public finances back within the 3 per cent deficit limit, front loaded with a €6 billion cut in the 2011 Budget. Whilst they must protect the vulnerable, everyone must make a contribution. Regarding a Greek-style programme, 'the whole purpose of what we are engaged in is to ensure that we do not need one.' Borrowing to bridge a deficit of €19 billion could not continue. He stated:

> The difficulty for the State is that we cannot rely indefinitely on this stimulus. It has brought too much pressure to bear on us in the financial markets and exposed the unsustainable character of our expenditure and taxation base.

Time was running out. Confidence faded in Ireland's ability to emerge unaided from a combination of colossal bank debts, large budget deficits, and escalating sovereign debt. Like Portugal in 2011, a reluctant Government faced intense pressure to adopt a formal programme, which would bind an incumbent government and its successors to a closely supervised programme under the Troika of the IMF, the EU Commission and the ECB. Ireland tried to play poker with few cards. For the ECB, it was not just Ireland's position at stake, but the whole eurozone's. A couple of Ministers became blindsided in public, unaware exploratory discussions were underway. Brian Lenihan justified the secrecy, on the basis that alerting the public would have weakened the country's diplomatic hand. The Central Bank Governor decided that the charade had gone on long enough. Then it was a matter of terms and conditions.

The Minister explained to the Dáil on 1 December that Ireland had sought external assistance, 'because the problems in our banking sector simply became too large for the State to bear on its own'. During his budget speech on 7 December he said there was no way the country could unilaterally renege on senior bondholders without their consent and without the consent of international institutions. His successor Michael Noonan was told the same thing in March 2011. Privately, as he revealed in a Dan O'Brien interview on 24 April 2011, Brian Lenihan was devastated. He had fought two-and-a-half years to avoid a situation, where he had to do what no Irish minister had ever had to do before. 'The European Central Bank appeared to have arrived at a view at governing council level that Ireland needed to be totally nailed down.' Yet the UK under Labour Governments twice sought IMF assistance, and, though it was politically damaging, soon recovered. Was the forced Irish recourse to external assistance and supervision necessarily such a bad thing? Certainly it was devastating to the reputation of the parties in Government. In regard to Sinn Féin, Brian Lenihan privately mused whether it would be a 1918 landslide all over again. Neither the general nor presidential elections of 2011 bore that out. A mid-term advance came in 2014.

Politically, it was over. The Green Party announced withdrawal from Government, once the budget and Finance Bill had been passed. With defections and unreliable independents, the Government retained only a tiny, conditional majority. A general election was announced for the spring. The public recriminations were savage. Ireland's lost sovereignty, already much modified like other member States', was lamented. To past failures and present hardships was added the charge, however unfair, of deceiving the people.

There was still important work to be done, publication of the four-year plan, embedding it in the Troika programme, and passing a budget. The opposition could have defeated the budget, but it was not in their interest to begin government making a €6 billion adjustment. The Finance Bill had an expedited passage in January 2011 so as not to delay the election.

EU Finance Ministers were in a tough and not particularly forgiving frame of mind when setting the loan interest rate at 5.8 per cent. Later developments in the euro crisis, involving Portugal and Spain, led to some softening subsequently.

The Plan and the Programme contained significant long-resisted reforms, such as property tax and water charges. To implement these, the succeeding government had to expend some political capital. The universal social charge, while a killer on election doorsteps, meant that, a low income exemption threshold aside, everyone would contribute something. No bonuses would be paid to senior executives in State-owned banks, a position adhered to by Brian Lenihan's successor Michael Noonan. Since Noonan's return as Fine Gael Finance Spokesperson in mid-2010, the two had a constructive relationship that facilitated continuity in the handover, notwithstanding Dáil clashes.

The last month was chaotic, with a failed party challenge to Brian Cowen's leadership, followed by a botched reshuffle involving coordinated ministerial resignations but no replacements, culminating in Cowen's resignation as party leader and then a leadership election. Brian Lenihan was one of four candidates, but Mícheál Martin was elected. The messy political collapse masked the fact that the economic course to be pursued had firm parameters. The people of Dublin West re-elected Brian Lenihan as sole Fianna Fáil TD left in Dublin, amongst 20 returned to the Dáil. People expressed their anger constructively through the ballot box. Democracy worked.

There was a postscript. Despite deteriorating health, Brian Lenihan spoke in the Dáil from opposition in March and April 2011. On 30 March, describing himself as a social democrat, he emphasised the importance of a viable tax base, which had been eroded to an unsustainable degree. Taxation was fundamental to the ordering of society. Everyone must contribute according to their means, and no one can be left where they would contribute nothing at all.

Commentators highlight the comparative fairness of Brian Lenihan's budgets.

On 31 March, he expressed scepticism about abolishing the Seanad:

> If we are sharing the function of legislation with another
> House and we also need to supervise a Government that
> is highly centralised, we need some assistance in the
> legislative role.

He poured cold water on claims about the election outcome: 'The people voted at the ballot box not for a revolution but for a profound change'.

On 6 April, he chided the new public relations approach:

> Of course, the Government finds it necessary to insert
> a narrative into its political discourse on the subject,
> which suggests this is a radical new policy different to
> the mistakes of its predecessors. In fact, it is the same
> policy and is the correct one. It will be implemented, and
> I wish the Minister well in its implementation.

About €20 billion of a total €32 billion adjustment was carried out under Brian Lenihan. He played a big part in retrieving a catastrophe not of his making, even if he eventually had to accept outside help. He courageously led down a path he would never have chosen. Like Michael Collins, the first Minister for Finance, people may wonder what he might have achieved, given a longer life.

10 BRIAN LENIHAN AND EUROPE
– MEMORIES FROM TRINITY AND BRUSSELS

RORY MONTGOMERY

BRIAN LENIHAN AND I first met in October 1977 outside the Trinity Exam Hall, as we registered as first year students of Legal Science and History respectively. Our last meeting was on 3 June 2011, one week before he died, when I called on him at his home in the Strawberry Beds. At that stage, I had been based for two years in Brussels as Ireland's Permanent Representative to the European Union. Until the change of government in March 2011, I had worked very closely with Brian as Minister for Finance during his increasingly difficult and dramatic visits to Brussels. I heard of his death when attending a Justice and Home Affairs Council, a formation he attended from 2007 to 2008.

Rather than trying to tell the full story of a thirty-four-year friendship, I have chosen to recall and reflect a little on Brian's views and experiences of Europe over that period, as this was the context of the last period of that friendship. But I hope to be forgiven a short preliminary meander through our Trinity days.

Going back to October 1977, we were introduced by Tom Doorley, who was to be my classmate but had gone to Belvedere with Brian. As often happens at that age – we were both eighteen – and in the enclosed world of university Brian and I very rapidly, over the course of just a few weeks, became close friends. We were also both part of a wider group made up mostly of law students, but with a few historians thrown in.

True friendship is a mystery and a blessing. It is never possible to explain exactly why you hit it off with some people when with others, apparently as compatible in terms of interests and personality, a pleasant acquaintanceship does not go further. Brian and I had a number of things in common – including a fascination with history and politics, a love of gossip and conversation, preferably in one of the pubs near Trinity like O'Neill's or the Stag's Head, and a serious, but not monomaniacal approach to our studies. We were both responsible eldest children and had been selected by our school authorities as sufficiently worthy and conformist to serve as head prefects.

But we were also very different in many ways. Brian was at that time quite a serious, though never fully orthodox, Catholic and I was from a (non-practising) Ulster Presbyterian background. I did not share his immersion in Fianna Fáil, though, of course, I found his profound knowledge of its lore and culture fascinating – at that point his father had just returned to the Dáil from the Dublin West constituency and had once again become a Minister. Brian was quite scornful of party politics at university – though a member of the FF cumann he preferred to develop his skills in Dublin West. Brian had very little interest in sport and almost none in fiction – history, philosophy and the law were his staples, and some poetry – one of his party pieces was a lengthy (allegedly 500-line) recitation from *Paradise Lost*. Nor, unlike some other good friends, did he much care for the cinema – though we did sometimes go to the theatre.

However, our friendship blossomed. In that first year, we devoted much time to debating at the Hist. (neither of us was a particularly successful competitive speaker, though Brian could on occasion be brilliant) and even more time to its internal machinations. We were both elected as officers at the end of that year, in part thanks to attaching ourselves rather cynically to the successful Auditorial candidate. I became a bit fed up with the Hist. in my second year and did not bother too much with debating thereafter, but Brian came back in his last year as Treasurer and as a major backer of the successful candidate for Auditor, Bill Maguire, in a hotly-contested election. Bill could not have imagined at that time that he would fly back from New York for Brian's funeral.

In our second years at Trinity we both succeeded in the optional Scholarship ('Schol') examinations, which allowed us free rooms in College for the remainder of our time there. We chose to share a large but spartan set, no. 26.3.1, in the Rubrics, the oldest building in Trinity: a large sitting room and two bedrooms, the whole heated by a single gas fire; a toilet at the bottom of the stairs; and a shower some distance away across the cobbles. 26.3.1 became a centre of social life for the next two years, our staple lunchtime offering to visitors being Campbell's soup, bread and cheese.

Most evenings, we availed of dinner ('Commons'), which was free to Scholars and Fellows. This was a mixed blessing gastronomically (though the old-fashioned puddings were generally good). But the excellent company from across faculties and departments, the free small glasses of Guinness and the chance to recite the Latin grace from a pulpit for a fee of £10 annually were all excellent compensations. Commons was, understandably in retrospect, viewed by the Students' Union as elitist and inegalitarian and there was a long but in the end fruitless period of picketing of the Dining Hall led by the SU President, Joe Duffy, and his deputy, Alex White. Brian, as a well-known figure, was often singled out for particular abuse. At the time, most of us felt aggrieved that the free meals won by our hard work were under threat.

On Saturdays, we fended for ourselves (nearly always spaghetti bolognese, my own standard dish which became Brian's) and, on Sundays, we normally went to our homes.

In our third and fourth years, we carried on studying steadily, though our techniques were rather different: I did not follow Brian's pre-examination practice of strewing vast numbers of books, papers etc. all over the sitting-room floor. I also got involved in writing for and editing a magazine and managing a particularly mediocre cricket team, neither of which interested Brian in the slightest. But then he, unlike me, now had a steady girlfriend. However, in the summer of 1979, we started walking in the Dublin and Wicklow mountains – and hill-walking quickly became a real enthusiasm for us both and one which lasted through the years right to the end (with our great mutual friend and fellow-walker, David Lowe, we climbed Lugnaquilla the summer before Brian died). Brian's excellent sense of direction led to his being christened Sherpa: a title of which he was quite proud.

After Trinity we both went to Cambridge for a year (Brian to Oliver Cromwell's old college) and, thereafter, headed towards the Bar and the Department of Foreign Affairs. Our friendship remained very close and our meetings very frequent in those early post-college days with Brian being best man at my wedding and my wife, Gerardine, and I welcoming him and his bride, Patricia, to our apartment in Rome during their honeymoon. Inevitably, there were periods over the following years and decades when family responsibilities, my postings abroad or duties at home, or Brian's increasing political involvement, on his father's behalf and then his own, led to gaps or hesitations in our contacts. But the moment I saw him or heard his voice on the phone my spirits would lift, knowing that his charm and charisma would light up any situation. At times, this meant accepting a role as audience or sounding board. He often developed his thinking by advancing an exaggerated or even unreasonable argument, which he was quite prepared to be persuaded to modify or abandon at the end of a conversation.

I was, of course, happy when he won election to the Dáil in 1996, following his father's death. His election posters showed him in a blue blazer and Trinity tie – the latter, he told me, was a visual assurance to the Protestants of Castleknock that he was 'a respectable type of Fianna Fáiler.' The count, in which Fine Gael transfers narrowly got him past Joe Higgins, coincided with an Anglo-Irish meeting between Dick Spring and Patrick Mayhew, with Spring describing Brian as 'coming from one of our most respected political families' – an indication of the general esteem in which Brian and his family were held across the system.

I occasionally saw him in operation in the Dáil, most memorably when he made a brilliant off-the-cuff speech on the constitutional background to and implications of the Good Friday Agreement – helping the Minister, David Andrews, address a number of recondite points raised by John Bruton.

But mostly our professional paths did not cross and our meetings were largely confined to the mountains and the pub afterwards. Like others, I wondered why he was not promoted more quickly and, as a friend, was delighted when he eventually was. And then we began to see each other a great deal more often once again – above all in relation to European issues.

Brian's interest in Europe was first and foremost cultural and historical. He really enjoyed classical music, including the great choral works. He could play the piano and his tenor voice was not at all bad, in short bursts: he was very proud of sharing his Athlone roots with Count John McCormack, whom we talked about at our two last meetings. And he used to sing with great gusto and exaggeratedly over-articulated diction a parody called 'I'm an Irish Tenor.' He was remarkably well-versed in history and philosophy (in his family home was a leather-bound set of canonical works of which he had certainly read several) and his wonderful memory allowed him to deploy arguments, anecdotes and facts to superb effect. I think his Jesuit education made him feel connected to a wider European intellectual Catholic tradition and he spoke of modern Catholic thinkers, like Jacques Maritain.

This is not to suggest that he, any more than the rest of us, was immune to some of the follies and pretensions of students through the ages. Nor were his arguments or anecdotes always well-grounded – his rhetoric sometimes outran the facts. But these peccadilloes were far outweighed by his sparkling intelligence, warm humour and justified self-confidence.

Brian was fascinated by Irish history, but was by no means parochial. He knew a great deal about Europe's past too. And sometimes he would display his knowledge at unexpected times. For example, I remember once flying with him on the Government jet from Baldonnel to Brussels, along with a team of Finance officials. It was a fine day, which first allowed him to identify all of the Wicklow mountains we were flying over. And then later, as we flew above Northern France and Belgium, he compared and contrasted in detail the lines of the German advances in World Wars 1 and 2. During Christmas 2009, just two days after his pancreatic cancer had been abruptly reported to the world, he called in to my home. In his usual open, calm and knowledgable way he spoke to my wife and me for a quarter of an hour about his condition and how it had emerged. Then, clearly feeling that he had said all he wanted to say on that subject, he spotted a book about the Italian front in World War 1 and began to talk in detail (accurate detail, I checked later) about the experiences of the young Rommel. And so we headed off for another hour or so of chat.

During our time in Trinity, I can remember very little discussion about Europe and its institutions or future. At the time, the era of 70s stagflation and the oil crises, the European Economic Community was very much in the doldrums, politically and economically: this was some years before the great advances of the Single European Act and the Maastricht Treaty and the controversy they generated in Ireland and elsewhere. Europe was clearly important for Ireland in a pragmatic way, above all as a source of funding for agriculture, but it did not generate much interest or passion. And there were many other fascinating issues to talk about: above all, the tragedy of Northern Ireland, which gave rise to the most passionate debates in our circle; the emergence of Charles Haughey as Taoiseach (Brian was always loyal but never fulsomely so) and his duels with Garret FitzGerald; the elections of Margaret Thatcher and Ronald Reagan; renewed superpower tensions over Afghanistan and missile deployment.

I do not think Brian as a student was ever particularly idealistic about the European project. This was not affected by a short stint in early autumn 1979, at the end of our second year at Trinity, when he was an intern in the Gaullist/Fianna Fáil group in the European Parliament. He appreciated the classic Gaullism of the group's leader, a French ex-Minister called Christian de La Malène, and would enjoy imitating his sonorous cadences (Brian's French was certainly good, though not maybe on a level with Christine Lagarde's English, as he liked to imply). General de Gaulle was, indeed, one of Brian's heroes; he read a number of books about him over the years and, after my wife and I visited Colombey-Les-Deux Eglises over

Easter 2011 (six weeks before Brian's death), he was able to engage over the phone in spirited debate about the great man, with detail about his origins in Lille. Brian's admiration for General de Gaulle was not confined to his sense of political theatre, his triumphs over adversity, or his eloquence: he also used to cite approvingly the idea of a 'Europe des Patries.'

Just after Brian's period in the European Parliament, we went to Paris for a week with another very close friend, Damian Collins. Brian was critical of an excessive dependence on guidebooks (he accused me of a condition he christened 'Baedekeritis'), but we visited the tomb of another great hero, Napoleon, in the Invalides. And drawing on his Shannon side experience, he rowed Damian and myself around the ornamental lake at Versailles. During that time, he also read Duff Cooper's biography of Talleyrand: and ever after prized Napoleon's description of Talleyrand and, indeed, diplomats in general as 'shits in silk stockings.'

Brian had no particular interest in, or reason to be interested in, European issues during the early years of his political career. He did argue to me in early 2001 that a referendum on the Nice Treaty, which most people at the time saw as a sure winner, was not, in fact, constitutionally necessary and should be avoided. Subsequent events certainly showed he had a case.

The focus of his work as Minister for Children was overwhelmingly domestic. On his appointment as Minister for Justice in 2007, which involved attendance at EU Justice and Home Affairs Councils, he joined the Cabinet Committee on European Affairs, to which I sometimes went to accompany the Minister for Foreign Affairs, but so far as I recall he was not especially active – until later on in 2008 when the legal and constitutional issues around the Treaty of Lisbon came to the fore. Once, however, he had to stand in for the Taoiseach, Bertie Ahern, as host of a lunch for the visiting Icelandic PM. After much comparing of notes on our two countries' economic successes (this was 2007…), PM Geir Haarde apologised, but said he had to raise for the record a rather technical issue about Iceland's claim to part of the continental shelf. To general surprise, Brian responded with a most fluent disquisition on the evolution of the law of the sea and its application to this case. My Icelandic counterpart said he had never seen a politician from another country who could do more than repeat a couple of speaking points. I asked Brian later about the source of his knowledge: 'Ah, I just remembered a couple of international law lectures in second year.'

Of course, everything was to change soon after his appointment as Minister for Finance in May 2008. The EU became central to the preoccupations of his Department and of the Government and the consequences of its decisions and actions were of enormous importance for Ireland.

I was not in Brussels at the time of the bank guarantee in September 2008 and, though I was around for the November 2010 bailout, others are much better placed than me to tell the detail of the story. What I can offer are some personal recollections and reflections.

Brian would normally travel to Brussels or Luxembourg for Finance Ministers' meetings once a month, though the frequency of his visits increased sharply in autumn 2010. The full meeting of the ECOFIN Council of 27 Ministers would usually take place on a Tuesday and would be preceded on Monday evening by a meeting of the more restricted Eurogroup, chaired permanently at that time by Jean-Claude Juncker. The crucial business from an Irish viewpoint was mostly done in and around the Eurogroup. Such were the enormous pressures on Ireland that Brian clearly focussed his efforts on what was vital nationally. He spoke eloquently and forcefully on issues he felt were relevant, but usually eschewed (like many colleagues) more general debate, or discussion on new financial services legislation, which took place mostly at ECOFIN.

During 2009, there was a general feeling in Europe that the economic downturn, while hugely severe, was above all 'made in America' and that the necessary corrective action was being taken. While very stringent budgetary measures were taken at home, the major issue in our dealings with the Commission was the restructuring of our banks, on which the Directorate-General for Competition played a leading part. The full scale of the banking disaster that had taken place in Ireland was not yet clear and nor were its longer-term political, fiscal and economic consequences.

The eurozone crisis began in February 2010 with a spiralling of Greek bond rates and the beginning of the still-unfinished debate on how to explain and resolve the crisis. But in the first half of 2010, Ireland was not particularly in the spotlight – indeed there was some praise for the tough corrective measures that had been taken. Discussions with the Commission were still largely about individual banks, though, of course, the need for significant further budgetary adjustment was also emphasised.

Soon after I arrived in April 2009, Brian started to stay with me on his visits to Brussels. He would generally come back from a Eurogroup meeting late on a Monday evening eager to unwind. He would talk – often starting with an account of the meeting, but moving on to Irish affairs and then to whatever caught his fancy. (I remember a great account of his grandfather Paddy's career and unavailing pursuit of a public service pension). He would drink red wine. And, knowing his tastes well, I always provided plenty of cheese. None was ever left over.

This pattern continued for the rest of his time as Minister. I think he enjoyed being able to relax away from the EU quarter of Brussels and to bounce his thoughts and ideas off an old friend. On his visits to Brussels, he depended heavily on the support and professionalism of a small group of travelling officials from Finance: his private secretary, Dermot Moylan, his press officer, Eoin Dorgan, and Second Secretary, Jim O'Brien, who helped prepare, and attended, meetings of the Eurogroup. But his relationship with me perhaps allowed him to be a bit more free.

Perhaps, his stays with me became particularly valuable once he was diagnosed with his illness. He would tell me about his treatment in a factual way, without self-pity: otherwise nothing much changed in our conversations. He started asking for wine made from the Pinot Noir grape, which he had heard had special health-giving properties, but was not exclusive in his tastes.

His illness and its treatment both took a physical toll on him. But he insisted that they had also narrowed his focus to what was really important. And his intellectual bite and zest remained unaltered. Sometimes he looked a bit better, sometimes alarmingly worse. He needed more rest and sometimes chose to go later to the Tuesday

ECOFIN – leaving me as Permanent Representative to sit in the chair until he arrived. But, on other occasions, he would not heed his own instructions. Once he had arranged to have lunch with Commissioner Geoghegan-Quinn – but I was told he must finish by a certain time to allow for a short nap before his next meeting. At the appointed hour, I entered the restaurant and beckoned to him – to be waved away. I came back half-an-hour later. 'Ah Rory, can you not see we're having a good chat?' No nap was had. Very near the end of the Government's life, I was asked if I could vacate my office to allow him to stretch out on a sofa for a while. But even as I left the room he was starting a call about the Fianna Fáil leadership contest which was about to take place. And the same – or a similar – call was going on when I returned some time later.

There was, at times, some gallows humour. He found one Finance Minister colleague who was due to chair the Council a couple of years later very tedious. 'But by the time he's in the Presidency it's most unlikely Fianna Fáil will be in office; and even if they are I won't be around.'

The summer of 2010 was a good one for Brian. His treatment had been halted and he regained some strength and energy. He took a family holiday, climbed a couple of mountains and was delighted to accept the invitation to speak at the Béal na Bláth commemoration. But then everything quickly started to go very wrong. Irish bond yields began to rise sharply as the full scale of the banks' capital needs emerged. In early September, he was atypically gloomy, saying to me that in some circumstances an international rescue of some kind could not be ruled out – though he did not repeat this afterwards and cheered up as the evening proceeded. He learned that autumn that his illness could not be cured. There were also quite considerable tensions within Fianna Fáil and the Government, which were much on his mind. He would talk about various scenarios involving himself and others, but it was never clear that in the country's and his own circumstances this was more than speculation.

As I said earlier, it is not for me to describe or analyse the process which led to the bailout. But I have some vivid memories of Brian during that period. He was dismayed and angered by the Deauville statement by France and Germany, which threatened the burning of

145

bond holders and further pushed up interest rates. Having always been quite fascinated by and indulgent towards Jean-Claude Trichet's urbanity and ambiguity, he grew increasingly exasperated by what he saw as the ill-founded dogmatism of the ECB. This came to a head with the Frankfurt leaks which precipitated the final phase of the November 2010 crisis. Brian was late arriving at the first Eurogroup meeting thereafter, because of fog and had to rush into a meeting already in session. I remember him after the meeting explaining the pressure he had come under to announce an application for a bailout that evening, though some colleagues were understanding of his position; and France and Germany had sought to pressurise him on our corporate tax rate as a quid pro quo for support. On neither point could he or would he move. Brian was in the impossible position of, in effect, having to start to negotiate with partners while, pending a Government decision, denying that actual negotiations were under way. He spoke to the *Morning Ireland* radio programme from my kitchen the following morning and moved somewhat away from a blanket denial. But the stark reality was clarified not long afterwards by Governor Honohan.

Negotiations on the detail of the Troika Programme took place mostly in Dublin over the next few days, but then had to be signed off by Finance Ministers in Brussels at a special Sunday meeting (and simultaneously announced in Ireland by the Taoiseach). Brian described vividly a few months later how he felt departing snowy Baldonnel, as if he were at the gates of hell. I met him at Brussels airport. He was exhausted, downcast, looking pale and very sick. But he somehow rallied himself to take part in the meeting and to speak clearly and fluently to RTÉ afterwards. And he had not lost his self-deprecating wit: chatting to me, he compared himself to the Spanish warrior El Cid, who even when dead was propped up on his horse to give hope to his own side and to confuse the enemy.

During this period, we never talked philosophically about the European Union. It was more a matter of getting from one day to the next. However, Brian had always had an acute sense of the diverse histories of European countries, including his own. He was a proud Irishman and a patriot of a broadly ecumenical type; he could also see the advantages of pragmatic European co-operation for Ireland and for others, but, in my view, he never, from his student days onwards, saw integration, or ever-closer union, as ends in themselves. He was certainly not hostile to the EU as it developed, nor a Eurosceptic, and supported the various Treaties which were negotiated over the years. But he was pragmatic, not romantic. Ireland and Irish politics remained very much at the centre of his thoughts and Irish interests were paramount. His interest in and respect for other countries and cultures meant that he expected their approaches to be similar. I think he remained attracted to the Gaullist notion of a *Europe des Patries* – allowing for all the steps forward by the EU which had taken place over the previous half-century.

Therefore, I doubt if Brian was surprised by how the various actors lined up with the position of each determined by its own interests and interpretation of the crisis. He did not believe that larger Member States or the EU institutions had any special wisdom, but they had more power than the smaller members to insist on their own views. And he also recognised that this was a time of unprecedented crisis in Europe with no rulebook to guide those who had to make decisions, often at breakneck speed. Other than the occasional outburst born of frustration, I found him remarkably resilient and determined to continue to play the hand he had been given – knowing that his room for manoeuvre was limited in the extreme and the choices hugely unpalatable.

He generally enjoyed dealing with his European counterparts, with whom he was as friendly and sociable as he was with everyone else. And even when under what he saw as unfair pressure from some, he did not hold it against them personally. He apppreciated both Christine Lagarde and Wolfgang Schäuble, and admired the political savvy of Joaquín Almunia and the straight-forwardness of Olli Rehn. People had their appointed roles to play in the drama and if this led them to take positions unhelpful to Ireland, he would strongly argue against them as a politician, but with no ill-will.

His last visit to Brussels was in February 2011, just before the general election. His further physical decline was apparent, but we had as lively a conversation as ever – for once, after his meeting we went out to a restaurant near my house, which was full of happy couples who must have been surprised by the arrival of two middle-aged men in rumpled suits: we had forgotten it was St Valentine's Day.

Brian had very much wanted to bring his son Tom to Brussels and environs to see the historic sights, especially Waterloo. He was never able to do so, but I was honoured to welcome Patricia, Tom and Claire some months after his death and we made the pilgrimage to the battlefield.

Having had the good luck to enjoy Brian's friendship for over thirty years has been one of the great blessings of my life. What began in carefree student days came to an end in extraordinarily difficult circumstances for him, personally and as a Minister. But if indeed courage can be defined as 'grace under pressure,' as Hemingway said, then it was indeed an honour to know someone whose remarkable courage was matched by his charm and brilliance.

11 LIME TREES ON THE LEFT

JOHN MULLEN

I FIRST GOT TO know Brian Lenihan in 1999, while working as a researcher for the Fianna Fáil Parliamentary Party on the fourth floor of Leinster House. The Fianna Fáil Press and Research Office was at this stage situated on the same corridor as Brian's Dáil office and he was a regular, often daily, visitor to our office. Brian would drop in to say hello, to shoot the breeze and chat about political developments. He would often ask us to check a statistic or to elicit information from a government department on matters that he was working on.

As a backbench TD, Brian was a solid media performer on any issue that was dominating the news agenda and the Fianna Fáil Press Director, Tom Reddy, and the Government Press Secretary, Joe Lennon, would regularly put Brian forward to articulate the Government position on radio and television. Brian welcomed any opportunity to involve himself in public debates on and off the airwaves. He was also a very useful resource to staff in the Research Office. He was extraordinarily well-read and he was always a good sounding board on research projects that we would be tasked with, such as providing historic views on Fianna Fáil, developing new policies and preparing briefings on various legislative, constitutional and political issues.

Brian was undoubtedly intellectually gifted, though this has sometimes obscured the fact that he was a very capable political organiser and a great campaign tactician. I was lucky enough to see Brian's skills in this regard at first-hand when we worked closely together in a by-election in Tipperary South in the summer of 2001.

The context to this by-election was the highly unusual circumstances of a second by-election in that constituency in the space of a year. Tipperary South was a three-seat constituency and at the previous general election in 1997 it had returned one Fianna Fáil TD, Noel Davern, one Fine Gael TD, Theresa Ahearn, and one Labour TD, Michael Ferris. Seamus Healy, a key figure in the Clonmel based Workers and Unemployed Action Group, had run Ferris close for the final seat. Cllr Michael Maguire had been Davern's Fianna Fáil running mate and had polled respectably without ever being in contention for a seat. In the aftermath of the general election, Davern had been appointed a Minister of State in the new Fianna Fáil-Progressive Democrat Government.

The first Tipperary South by-election was caused by the sudden death of Michael Ferris in March 2000 and voting would ultimately take place three months later on 22 June. Fianna Fáil had selected as its candidate a young county councillor from Cahir, Barry O'Brien. As was the regular practice, Noel Davern, as the local Minister, was appointed as Fianna Fáil's Director of Elections. By-elections are usually not very good platforms for government parties, but this was a horrendously difficult campaign. A fortnight before the writ had been moved, the Government had appointed the former Supreme Court Judge, Hugh O'Flaherty, to the plum position of Vice-President of the European Investment Bank. This decision provoked public outcry. O'Flaherty had resigned from the judiciary a year previously in the course of a controversy relating to the early release from prison of a drink-driver. Public disquiet with O'Flaherty's appointment was a significant factor in a disastrous by-election performance for Fianna Fáil. Seamus Healy was comfortably elected and O'Brien was beaten back into third place. This was the party's worst ever by-election performance in its history.

Before the bad memories of that by-election could even begin to fade, another by-election in 'Tipp South' tragically appeared on the horizon. In September 2000, the popular Fine Gael TD, Theresa Ahearn, lost her long battle with cancer. The by-election to fill this vacancy ultimately took place on 30 June 2001 and Brian Lenihan would be a central figure in the Fianna Fáil campaign.

By-elections are not necessarily a barometer of national opinion, but two by-elections in the same constituency in such a short period of time was a subject of some concern to senior Fianna Fáil strategists. There was a definite fear that another bad performance might develop a worrying trend in the build-up to the 2002 General Election. As such, it was viewed as imperative that Fianna Fáil achieve a better result so as to alleviate pressure on the coalition government and to ensure preparations for the next General Election were not derailed.

Steadying the ship was very much the thinking behind Brian Lenihan's appointment as Fianna Fáil's Director of Elections in the second Tipperary by-election. The disastrous outcome in the previous by-election had resulted in the thinking that new less 'biased' leadership of the party campaign was required. Though Noel Davern was a local Minister of State and he outranked Brian, (a deputy from a Dublin constituency), in the parliamentary party hierarchy, Bertie Ahern ultimately opted for Lenihan as the Fianna Fáil Director of Elections. Brian's appointment over the head of Davern was a surprise in the constituency, but, in reality, Fianna Fáil had used 'outside' directors of elections to great effect in the past, particularly in the 1960s and 70s. Brian Lenihan's father, along with Neil Blaney and Kevin Boland, were instrumental in by-elections during those times and they helped to elect candidates deemed by many as 'unelectable,' including the election of Desmond O'Malley in the neighbouring Limerick East constituency in 1968.

Though Brian Lenihan was still a backbencher when he arrived in Tipperary South, he enjoyed a higher national profile than some cabinet ministers. In some respects, the fact that Brian had not attained ministerial rank was an advantage to the campaign. Cabinet ministers and their highly visible Mercs had been a noted negative factor during the previous by-election.

Lenihan's appointment was also popular with the party rank and file. He was the son of a beloved Fianna Fáil figure, he was a great speaker in his own right and he had a love of meeting the members of the organisation, who quickly embraced him as a rising star and one of their own.

Another advantage which Lenihan brought to the table as Director of Elections was born out of his savant's knowledge of Irish political history. This enabled him to comprehend both the electoral intricacies of Tipperary South and the mind-set of the local party organisation. Brian knew that County Tipperary had been a hotbed of Republican activity during the War of Independence and the Civil War. He also understood that the Fianna Fáil tradition in 'Tipp South' was immersed in this proud history. The Cahir electoral area was traditionally the strongest base for the party with up to 60 per cent support and it was no coincidence that this was also one of the last hold-outs of republican anti-treaty activity.

Despite being a Dublin TD, Lenihan fitted in well to 'Tipp South' because he possessed a genuine 'grá' for rural issues and the character of large rural towns, such as Clonmel, Cahir, Tipperary, Carrick on Suir, and Cashel. Brian had grown up in Athlone and he seemed to instinctively understand the particular nature of rural and provincial town politics.

He also brought determination to the task in hand. He chose to live in the constituency for the entire four-week campaign in June 2001, which was a massive commitment for any politician to give to another constituency, never mind the family sacrifice involved.

The second 'Tipp South' by-election also meant an extended return trip to Tipperary for me. In by-elections, Fianna Fáil would usually send at least two HQ and press office staffers, along with some administrative personnel, to the constituency in question to run the local campaign office. I had taken up the position of Fianna Fáil's Deputy National Organiser shortly before the first 'Tipp South' by-election and I had been seconded to the campaign office in Clonmel for most of June 2000. During this period, I built up a close working relationship with the local organisation and public representatives. As such, it was appropriate (and inevitable) that I would fulfil this role again in 2001.

The HQ personnel or the 'crowd from Dublin,' as we were sometimes un-affectionately referred to, had the onerous task of providing a professional campaign back-up. The tasks of providing postering and canvass schedules, organising campaign events and media opportunities, and helping to co-ordinate the members of Parliamentary Party and their supporters, who would arrive at the weekends and at evenings to canvass, went hand-in-hand with the knowledge that, however strong our efforts, 'the crowd from Dublin' were not always going to be flavour of the month with local elected representatives and organisational figures.

Diplomatic relations need to be maintained to drive the campaign forward and there is always a delicate balance to be struck between trying to get the best out of local volunteers and deploying professional staff to deliver modern campaigning requirements under a pressurised time-frame.

By-elections are also notorious for local Fianna Fáil reps arriving with 'wish-lists' of 'crucial issues' that if only resolved would turn the tide for the party. Whether they would help turn the tide of the election for the by-election candidate or might only serve to benefit the local rep was always the question to be decided.

Weekends are usually the busiest time in by-elections. Outside media and politicians would arrive in the constituency to respectively cover events or canvass. Preparations for this could take a number of days.

It is important that the staff have a good relationship with the Director of Elections so I was delighted with Brian's appointment. From my time in the Research Office, I had an excellent working relationship and friendship with him. We both shared a love of the grassroots Fianna Fáil organisation matched with a necessary cynicism of the inflated parish pump nature of elections, especially in a rural constituency.

Brian Lenihan thrived on elections. On his appointment, he conducted a meticulous study of the electoral history of the 'Tipp South' constituency. He then proceeded to talk to as many members of the local organisation as he could about their ideas and the appropriate strategies to use in particular areas. His keen political antennae swiftly allowed him to sort those who 'flattered to deceive' from more down to earth honest appraisals of the situation.

Brian was a realist. He knew winning the by-election was never really an option. Tom Hayes, the Fine Gael candidate, had a strong foundation from the previous by-election in which he had polled strongly and finished second. Political momentum would also be with the Fine Gael campaign, given that the vacancy had been created by the death of a hard-working and respected party colleague.

Michael Maguire replaced Barry O'Brien as the Fianna Fáil standard bearer for this second by-election. The big challenge that Brian Lenihan was set as Director of Elections was to improve dramatically on the previous result with an older candidate from the lowest populated part of the constituency.

Brian loved being 'the DOE' – it's a very different role from being a candidate and it brought back memories for him of organising his father's campaigns. In Fianna Fáil terms, the Director of Elections is like a General on a battlefield. Brian had to get the best out of the local organisation and ensure they knitted efficiently with the outside help. Most, importantly, he needed to secure the maximum help possible from the sitting TD's core supporters, who naturally would be wary of 'giving too much away' in the run-up to a general election. The maxim 'to thine own seat be true' was understood by Brian from the outset. It was, therefore, his priority to impress upon the Davern camp the need for as much activity as possible. And by this, I mean activity in favour of the candidate!

The numerous meetings with the local party organisation in the function rooms of pubs and halls (sometimes, three or four a night) would be a nightmare for many a Dublin TD, but Lenihan loved it and always 'sent them home sweatin'!' He liked to finish meetings with a rousing motivational speech, but even when the formal proceedings were over I noticed that many members would wait around to shake his hand or regale him with a story of having once met his father or aunt. Invariably, Brian would stay until the last person had been spoken to and he could often be persuaded to adjourn for a sociable pint.

Brian's friendly manner was a real asset in the tricky process of maintaining relations with the sitting TD. The relationship between Davern's supporters and HQ had deteriorated badly in the blame game that had followed the previous by-election. And certainly the view from HQ when a second by-election became a reality was that co-operation from the Davern camp would not be 100 per cent to say the least. Lenihan, however, proved to be perfect in the role of bridge-builder. He, himself, was no fan of an over-centralised Fianna Fáil headquarters clumsily walking over the local organisation and throwing their weight around. His long years of campaigning experience also made him very wary of the type of HQ mandarin who obsessed about focus group reports and ideal campaign strategies with little reference to the volunteers on the ground.

Noel Davern was much older than Brian and he had served with and been friendly with Brian's father. This undoubtedly helped keep things on an even keel. It was also clear that Noel respected Brian's abilities, but both TDs were initially very wary of each other. Brian, however, put a lot of his time into ensuring that Davern's input was listened to and not just tolerated. This, in turn, convinced Noel that Lenihan was not working behind his back or out to do a demolition job. Brian also went out of his way to ensure that Noel Davern's key supporters were treated with real respect, which was crucial as they had felt isolated in the previous campaign.

Staying in the constituency for the duration of the entire campaign was a huge commitment, but it allowed Lenihan the time to visit the kitchens and living-rooms of key members of the local party organisation. The members of Fianna Fáil in a rural constituency are organised through cumainn and local electoral areas and their level of activity during a by-election can often be the difference between a good result and a bad one. Lenihan believed this and he would attend numerous one-on-one meetings in the back-office of the campaign centre or on house visits to win the trust of local members. He did not just listen passively though. He could be assertive when he felt an element of the organisation was not playing its part or where unrealistic demands were being made. In particular, he saw his relationship with all the local councillors as key to his strategy. He felt every councillor should be capable of delivering between 500 to 1,000 votes. Negotiating, cajoling and encouraging some councillors to act selflessly on behalf of the party candidate required constant work by Lenihan, yet he managed to never lose his cool with the exasperating demands of some.

Brian knew winning was not possible, but, in order to radically improve the result, he worked hard to get everyone in Fianna Fáil pulling together in a rural constituency where internal local rivalries had often been raw. In regard to the media element of the campaign, Lenihan was confident that he could communicate with a cynical national media, who would sometimes treat rural by-elections as some sort of safari into the wild. In this case also, many had written the election off as a no-brainer with the only story being how bad the result would be for Fianna Fáil. Lenihan wanted this campaign to be kept as low on the radar as possible.

He wanted to minimise the negative aspects of being a government party in a by-election. He was wary of constant streams of ministers and their entourages arriving like celebrities. He saw only political negativity in this. A line of ministerial Mercs might go down well in certain parts of South Dublin, but in rural towns it reeked of arrogance.

Brian established a solid working relationship with our candidate, Michael Maguire and this developed into a friendship. Michael was a rural politician of the old school, steeped in agriculture and GAA traditions. He and Lenihan knew each other's strengths and weaknesses. Maguire's easy going manner worked well with Lenihan's sometimes manic intensity. Lenihan also got on very well with Michael's family, as he could empathise with the stress of a pressurised campaign for family members.

In the end, as was predicted, Tom Hayes, who had been beaten by only 500 votes in the first by-election, comfortably won the seat. Michael Maguire managed to increase the Fianna Fáil vote by four per cent on the previous by-election, but Brian was annoyed that a controversial TG4 opinion poll, broadcast late in the campaign, on the supposed position of the candidates had cost Fianna Fáil another four per cent. Maguire had doubled his vote on his previous Dáil electoral outing in 1997 and he secured over 1,500 more first preference votes than Barry O'Brien had obtained twelve months previously. More disappointingly, although Maguire had obtained 560 more first preference votes than Phil Prendergast, the Workers and Unemployed Action Group candidate, he was narrowly edged out of second spot on transfers.

The Fianna Fáil performance was in truth mixed, but Brian had played an important role in ensuring another probable disaster was averted. Looking back on the by-election, it is clear that Brian learned from the experience and it contributed to his political development as a national figure. The political animal that he was revelled in being the Director of Elections and his commitment to the party's candidate was highly impressive and could be, at times, all-consuming.

Brian and I shared an apartment during the four-week election period and even the few hours down-time accorded to both of us would inevitably turn back towards the election. Constituency maps would be studied until the wee hours of the mornings and he had a habit of giving strange code names to important elements of the campaign that were a constant worry. On the few occasions where he did try to switch off, he would read an Irish Bible in order to improve his grasp of the language. In some cases, this would be read aloud to the consternation of his tired flatmate!

Possibly, most remarkable of all, was the respect and affection Lenihan enjoyed from people of all political colours in Tipperary. He had not even achieved junior ministerial rank at this stage, yet walking to lunch in Clonmel, Brian would constantly be stopped by people out and about doing their daily routine – housewives doing their shopping; retired gentlemen slipping in for an early afternoon pint; opposition politicians about to hit the canvass trail; army personnel from nearby Kickham barracks; barristers on their way to court – all would want a chat with Brian. He had a good manner and he treated everyone with true respect and a spirit of camaraderie.

What I remember most about him was his sense of fun. Lenihan, knowing my left of centre republican leanings, once deliberately rankled me on a trip around rural Tipperary. He had been invited by an old Law Library colleague to call for lunch. Lenihan asked me to join him, jokingly remarking that we had to learn about all the elements of Tipperary South's electorate.

Bewildered, I wondered what all this was about until Lenihan got me to phone our host for directions. The grand English-accented gentleman told us to follow the road until we saw rows of lime trees which would be the start of his estate! 'Lime trees on the left,' as I nicknamed him, lived in a grand Anglo-Irish mansion of which there were quite a few in South Tipp. After a very fine lunch, as I was shown the Cromwellian charter which gave this gentleman's ancestors a chunk of rural Tipperary, I could see the mischievous glint in Lenihan's eye as he observed my stiff, but polite responses.

Lenihan could discuss the finer points of the Cromwellian settlement of Munster with a descendant of the ascendancy and later that night be singing a ballad about General Liam Lynch in the bosom of the Knockmealdown mountains. He truly was a man for all seasons!

12 THE TRANSFER GOSPEL, ACCORDING TO BERTIE

BRIAN MURPHY

ON 30 JANUARY 1996, in Washington, President Clinton urged the IMF to grant a $9 billion loan to Russia. In London, Prime Minister John Major and Chancellor of the Exchequer Kenneth Clarke were at odds over the need to dramatically reduce public spending. In Belfast, the murder of the INLA Chief of Staff raised fears that the deadlocked peace talks could lead to renewed all-out conflict. Meanwhile, in the function room of a small Dublin hotel, though it received far less media attention, Brian Lenihan took the first steps in a political career that a decade and half later would see him become not just the most talked about politician in Ireland, but also a major focus of attention for international economists and global political leaders.

In the West County Hotel three candidates met to contest the Fianna Fáil convention to choose a candidate to contest the Dublin West by-election. On the first count, Brian Lenihan, whose father's death the previous November gave rise to the need for a by-election, received 24 votes, Cllr Finbarr Hanrahan received 14 votes and Senator Marian McGennis received 14 votes. McGennis was eliminated after a run-off ballot to separate her and Hanrahan was decisively won by the Lucan based councillor by a margin of 24 votes. Hanrahan then announced his withdrawal from the contest in support of Lenihan securing the nomination.

In his acceptance speech, Brian Lenihan paid tribute to his father's eighteen years of service to the people of Dublin West in Dáil Éireann. He said: 'I hope that I can in my time and generation serve the people half as well as he did in his.' Touching on a theme which he would frequently return to throughout his career, that those seeking public office should be responsible and realistic in their election pledges, Lenihan said: 'Politicians should not promise the moon and the stars. But it is important to tackle long-term and youth unemployment in a serious and comprehensive manner – and not just to win a few headlines in the run-up to the budget.' At this time, unemployment stood at 12 per cent, with over half of those registered as long-term unemployed. Debate on Ruairi Quinn's second budget, which had taken place a week earlier, largely focused on whether the Rainbow Government was doing enough to tackle the jobs crisis. Lenihan also signalled that law and order would top his campaign priorities. Ireland was experiencing a rapid and disturbing rise in drug related crime, which was identified as being responsible for 80 per cent of all indictable offences. Lenihan told delegates: 'Throughout Ireland at present daily life is blighted by crime and the fear of crime.' These comments were in tune with a populist and hard-line approach to crime which Fianna Fáil pursued in opposition and would ultimately evolve into the controversial 'Zero Tolerance' policy document.

Not long after this convention, Brian Lenihan asked me to participate in his campaign. He told me that had he not been selected at the convention, he would have gone back to work as a barrister and that he could have a less stressful and more lucrative career outside of politics. Brian said that public service was his passion and that he wanted to use the talents at his disposal for the betterment of our local community. He stressed that there was no family pressure on him to contest the by-election and that he had sought the nomination because of his own commitment to politics. I distinctly recall him saying that though he was intensely proud of what his father had achieved, he was his own man and that he was going to do things his own way. It was inspiring stuff and though I had been more prominently associated with the Kevin Barry Cumann in UCD and locally with Finbarr Hanrahan, who had taught in my old school, I assured Brian I would help him in any way I could.

For me, as a young postgraduate student, the by-election was a great opportunity to experience a political campaign at first-hand. For Brian, as a first-time candidate, it was an intense battle to secure a political future and, in a sprawling, largely urban constituency, he would face stiff competition. Ultimately thirteen candidates would go before the public. Brian brought many qualities to the field. He was highly intelligent, extremely articulate and he had already amassed a lot of political experience. He had been immersed in local politics since his teenage days and he had first acted, in his own words, as his father's 'permanent escort' during a local election campaign for Dublin County Council in 1974. Brian had actually been thrust centre-stage in the 1989 General Election, when he effectively acted as a proxy-candidate because illness ensured that his father was absent from the campaign trail in the Mayo Clinic, Minnesota. In 1990, Brian had worked closely with his father during his unsuccessful campaign for the Presidency. Brian told me how much he learnt about human nature during that campaign, which was a difficult election for his family. In 1991, Brian was elected secretary of the Fianna Fáil Dublin West Comhairle Dáil Ceanntair, the party's local constituency executive, and he was a respected figure in his own right within the Fianna Fáil organisation.

Despite his experience, Brian was initially slightly awkward as a candidate. He was quite academic and he sometimes found it difficult to engage with people. He was certainly uncomfortable about selling himself or pointing out his own abilities. Brian was also a notoriously bad time-keeper and this caused him, on one or two occasions, to miss residents' meetings or to leave his own canvassers waiting indefinitely for him to turn up. He was, however, very knowledgeable about the issues and he much preferred to talk to people about local concerns than himself. Sometimes, to the frustration of his canvassers who wanted him to cover as much ground as possible, he would spend far too long on a doorstep where an issue that interested him was raised. I remember one instance where Brian had to be literally dragged away by his canvassing team from an entertaining and good-natured, but lengthy debate with an older resident, who was clearly a Fine Gael supporter, on de Valera's policy towards large farmers during the Economic War!

Brian had to learn quickly as a candidate, but from the outset he was a supreme strategist and a great reader of electoral trends. Brian knew that to be elected, he had to keep voters onside in his father's political backyard of Castleknock, a middle-class suburb, where turn-out was traditionally high. Voters in Castleknock were especially worried that Fianna Fáil on return to government would facilitate the redevelopment of the Phoenix Park Racecourse by the introduction of legislation which would licence a casino on the site. This proposed development, which would also have included a conference centre and a large hotel, had a lot of support in other parts of Dublin West and, indeed, through the city because of its potential to generate jobs. However, in Castleknock local residents were concerned that a casino would be a beacon for anti-social behaviour and that such a large-scale development would create traffic logjam. Brian raised the issue with Bertie Ahern, the Fianna Fáil leader, and he insisted that he could only mount a credible election campaign on the basis that Fianna Fáil robustly opposed the development of a casino at the Phoenix Park Racecourse site. Tactically, this was the right call. Brian's strong support for the right of local residents not to have a casino in their area helped to secure a solid vote for him in Castleknock and this was to prove telling in a tight election.

At the same time, Brian was making himself proficient in a variety of other local issues, including the future of James Connolly Memorial Hospital, the difficulties being experienced by Dublin 15 commuters and other key local issues, including the establishment of a Regional Technology College in Blanchardstown and even the matter of wandering horses, which in the mid-to-late 1990s was actually a big local issue in parts of Dublin West.

Brian grew in confidence as he performed competently at public meetings and residents' association gatherings. Occasionally, Brian would ask me to research issues or provide him with extra detail for meetings he had to attend. He had a lawyer's respect for the facts. He insisted on accurate information and up-to-date statistics and he never wanted the facts massaged or spun in briefing material to suit his case. This was probably because Brian was a natural orator and, at once, he had the salient points he could fashion these into a far better argument than anyone else could. Brian's skills as a persuasive communicator, undoubtedly honed by years of court room experience, stood him in good stead in media interviews and in public meetings during his first campaign. Throughout the by-election, Brian had to contend with the charge that his candidacy was largely based on an appeal for sympathy votes. Even the Taoiseach, John Bruton, who campaigned vigorously for the Fine Gael candidate, Cllr Tom Morrissey, suggested that it would be 'difficult for a Fianna Fáil candidate without any track report of his own to win the by-election on the strength of his family name.' However, the more the voters saw and heard of Brian, the more it became apparent that he was a genuine candidate of substance and a person of immense abilities.

Brian played to his strengths. A lot of candidates in Brian's position might have been tempted to concentrate on door-to-door canvassing and ask a more experienced elected representative from their own party to fill in for them at large meetings. Brian, however, knew that he had the talent to acquit himself well in public debate and that these events were important to show constituents that he was not just 'a name' and that he was up to the job. Brian also knew that he was good in the media and so he readily made himself available to journalists. This approach was readily endorsed by the Fianna Fáil Director of Elections. Noel Dempsey recalled:

> Brian was a good candidate in that he was bright, intelligent and articulate. He really surprised me when he did his first radio interview which was with a local community radio station. Not only was he articulate but he knew the issues in great detail, despite the fact that he would not have been actively involved in them previously. My thoughts after that were 'wow, this candidate can be let on to any radio or television programme.'

The campaign had the assistance of Marty Whelan, a colourful press officer provided by Fianna Fáil headquarters, and the advice of Brian's brother, Conor, who had worked for a number of media organisations. It was a source of great amusement to Brian that Marty, in his student days, had been a member of the Communist Party of Ireland. On one occasion, as we travelled in Brian's battered car, which had originally been white, to meet a reporter in Palmerstown, I rather intensely tried to focus Brian's mind on some mundane point of Fianna Fáil policy, which I thought he could usefully raise in the interview. Brian, however, was much more interested in interrogating Marty on his knowledge of the finer points of Marxism, Leninism and Trotskyism!

Brian's two greatest resources in the by-election were Marian Quinlan and Maura Cosgrove. As soon as he was selected as a candidate, Brian opened an election office in Laurel Lodge, which he once compared to Athlone because it was strategically located in the centre of the constituency. Brian asked Marian to manage the office and she was a fantastic choice. Marian was sociable and affable and she was almost universally popular with the Fianna Fáil membership in Dublin West, which was quite an achievement in an organisation that was factioned into supporters of Lenihan, Lawlor, Hanrahan and McGennis. Marian Quinlan had a great ability to cajole people into canvassing and dropping leaflets, who otherwise might have sat out the by-election. Her logistical skills in co-ordinating canvasses in a vast constituency and her political antennae were huge assets to Brian. As the Dublin West constituency at this stage straddled both sides of the Liffey, Brian also established a campaign office in Palmerstown. He entrusted the running of this office to Maura Cosgrove, who had previously worked as his father's secretary in the Oireachtas. Maura was extremely efficient and organised, which was a good thing because Brian could be slightly chaotic. She also had experience and common-sense, a real handle on local issues and Brian rightly put great stock on her judgement. He trusted Maura implicitly to get things done. She did much of the unglamorous, but invaluable work to a candidate of following up on constituents' representations. Not surprisingly, Brian viewed both Maura and Marian as indispensable and, though they had signed up with Brian for the couple of weeks' duration of the by-election, they both ended up working closely with him for the next fifteen years.

Noel Dempsey was an unexpected, but shrewd, choice as Brian's Director of Elections. Noel was only a couple of years older than

Brian, but he had a lot more first-hand political experience. Noel arrived in Dublin West having already successfully contested three General Elections in the neighbouring constituency of Meath, topping the poll in 1992, and having garnered experience at the cabinet table, as Albert Reynolds's Chief Whip. Eighteen years on from his appointment, Noel Dempsey admits to having been somewhat taken aback at being asked to run the Dublin West campaign. He recorded:

> I was surprised to be asked and don't know what happened behind the scenes before I was asked. Pat Farrell [the Fianna Fáil General Secretary] did the initial 'sounding' and when I agreed I met Bertie. He emphasised how important it was for the party to get a good result. He said it would take a lot of hard work and organisation and he 'trusted me to do it.' He made it clear I had 'carte blanche' as Director of Elections. I presume the fact that I was recognised by Bertie as someone as committed to the organisation as he was, that I worked closely with Bertie on negotiations for a number of Programmes for Government and at the time was travelling around the country reorganising our county and town councillors gave Bertie the confidence that I would do the job well. It was also mischievously suggested that some people, who felt that I needed 'my wings clipped,' thought it a good idea to push for me as Director of Elections in what they regarded as an impossible task. The reasons for my appointment were probably a combination of all these. Whatever the reasons at the Convention to select Brian Lenihan both Bertie and Michael Woods gave me a ringing endorsement as Director of Elections.

Noel Dempsey rapidly gained the trust of most of Brian's supporters. He was politically astute, he was organisationally meticulous and he had a necessary toughness. One of the worst mistakes an election candidate can make is to try to single-handedly run their own campaign. This can result in serious misjudgements because it is hard to be impartial or dispassionate about one's own candidacy. With

Noel Dempsey at the helm, there was no danger of this happening to the Fianna Fáil campaign in Dublin West. Brian respected the fact that Noel had carved a seat out of nowhere in Meath and he accepted that Noel had real political 'know-how,' but this did not stop Brian from being very opinionated. Noel was always open to taking on board good ideas from Brian or anyone else, but he had to be fully convinced of their merits. It was, in fact, at Dempsey's insistence that Brian actually campaigned under the name of 'Brian Lenihan.' Noel Dempsey recalled:

> Brian was known as 'Breen' before the election. I had to spend some time convincing him of the benefit of becoming plain old Brian, like his father! He wanted to get elected on his own merits and not 'on his father's name or coat tails.' I found out how difficult it was to match him in debate at that early stage and eventually I concluded the discussion by saying: 'Brian next time round you can get elected on your own merits and in any name you like. This time I have to get you elected and you are Brian.' 'Fair enough,' he replied. It was typical of the various debates and discussions we had on points of policy or organisation during the campaign. He won some of the arguments and I won some or just pulled rank as director of elections. Either way once the decision was taken, it was taken as far as he was concerned and there was no more debate.

For Fianna Fáil, securing the right timing for the by-election was another important tactical question. Political tradition maintained that the party who lost a TD moved the writ to call the by-election, however, the Government would still have the numbers to vote down any writ that did not suit them. A by-election was also pending in Donegal North East, as Neil Blaney had died just one week after Brian Lenihan Senior. In this instance, given that there was no other Independent Fianna Fáil TD in the Dáil, the prerogative for moving the writ in this constituency fell to the Government. Easter Sunday in 1996 was 7 April and, for some months, government sources had made it clear to political correspondents that they did not envisage any writ being passed until after Easter with a view to a May polling date. Though I did not know it at the time and I suspect Brian didn't either, this time frame probably didn't distress Bertie Ahern unduly because of his preference for summer elections.

Brian was impatient to get on with things. Some Fianna Fáil strategists sought to assuage Brian's frustrations with the argument that a longer lead in would allow him to consolidate his position on the ground, but Brian didn't buy into this. He may have been focussed on standing as his own man, but everything Brian instinctively knew about elections told him that the affection the people of Dublin West had for his father gave him a distinct advantage. Brian's blunt concern was that the further away the by-election might be, the more likely it was that any sympathy vote would dissipate. On securing the Fianna Fáil nomination at the end of January, Brian discussed this with Bertie Ahern, but he recognised the logic in the Fianna Fáil's leader's argument that there was little to be gained at this stage in moving a writ that the Government would simply vote down.

Noel Dempsey shared Brian's anxieties about not delaying. He recalled:

> My strategy from the time I was asked to take on the job, on 30 January 1996, was to have the election as early as possible. I believed that the quicker we had the election the better to capitalise on the name factor (hence the debate with Brian) and because I felt that the longer it was delayed the more momentum Joe Higgins would have. I was frustrated when Bertie delayed the decision on the date because we needed to finalise the Donegal arrangements.

Dempsey's persistence brought the issue to a head at a meeting on 6 March 1996 with Bertie Ahern; the Dublin West TD, Liam Lawlor; and Donegal TDs, Pat the Cope Gallagher and Jim McDaid. Dempsey recalled:

The reluctance to go ahead in Donegal because our candidate was a newcomer, I argued, was not a good reason to delay as Donegal was a virtual certainty and we needed to move fast in Dublin to maintain any advantage we had there. Two days later Bertie agreed to move both writs the following Tuesday.

The Government was unlikely to acquiesce to the Fianna Fáil writ, but Dempsey had factored this into his calculations. As a former whip, he had realised that the Government could be defeated in the Dáil as a result of the annual exodus of ministers abroad for St. Patrick's Day. This plan had the added bonus of the campaign commencing while ministerial heavyweights were abroad and would be absent from the hustings in some cases for well over a week. It would also mean that Fianna Fáil would be dispensing with the parliamentary courtesy of pairing ministers engaged in State business abroad for Dáil votes.

Dempsey's plan was discussed with Dermot Ahern, the then Fianna Fáil Whip, and Bertie Ahern, who, of course, had been Charles Haughey's Chief Whip. They had an instinctive feel for parliamentary numbers and knew that the Government could be defeated. The big question for Bertie Ahern, as leader of Fianna Fáil, was would this be advantageous to his party? His party's candidate, like a thoroughbred racehorse, was chomping at the bit to get the race started, but what seems to have convinced Bertie were reports that the Government had plans in train to fund a number of community projects in Dublin West. He subsequently explained to Alison O'Connor of *The Irish Times* that Fianna Fáil had moved the writ because he understood that the Government was going to 'give out money all over the place over Easter.'

A problem for Bertie Ahern was that though he was now in favour of taking advantage of the travels abroad of Government ministers to force through the writ, both he and his deputy leader, Mary O'Rourke, also had commitments in the United States at the same time. O'Rourke, however, readily agreed to stay behind to politically manage Fianna Fáil's effort to spring a by-election.

On 12 March, *The Irish Times* reported that Fianna Fáil would later that day move the writ for the Dublin West by-election to take place on 2 April. This news story undoubtedly sent alarm bells ringing in Government Buildings because that morning, as Mary O'Rourke chaired a meeting of the Fianna Fáil front bench, she received a phone call from the Taoiseach. John Bruton said to Mary that the by-election should be deferred until May and he requested Fianna Fáil not to proceed with moving the writ. Mary immediately declined this request and the Taoiseach told her that the Government would oppose the Fianna Fáil move on the Dublin West by-election. However, Mary O'Rourke had held her trump card to the end. She told the Taoiseach if the Government insisted on opposing the Dublin West writ that Fianna Fáil would withdraw all pairing arrangements in the Dáil. In *The Irish Times* the following day, Denis Coghlan observed:

> Over-confident in the strength of their Dáil majority, the coalition parties had operated for months on the basis that they would hold the by-elections in May... Bertie Ahern's absence in the United States may have prompted a sense of false security or the Coalition may have depended too much on old-style parliamentary niceties. Whatever the reason, when Fianna Fáil delivered its ultimatum they were in no position to fight back. Mary O'Rourke's message was simple and clear: the by-elections would be held in the shortest possible time allowed under the Constitution. And polling day would be April 2nd. If the Government parties demurred, she told John Bruton, then Fianna Fáil would cancel its Dáil 'pairing' arrangements and vote the writs through. With up to 20 ministers and Government deputies absent or abroad on various duties, the outcome was assured. Rather than open their campaigns with a Dáil defeat, John Bruton, Dick Spring and Proinsias De Rossa bowed to the inevitable. Within hours Fianna Fáil posters were going up in Dublin West.

The fact that Lenihan posters hit the lamp-posts in Dublin West so quickly helped to create an immediate impression that the Fianna Fáil campaign was fine-tuned and well prepared. Dempsey recalled:

> Posters with Brian Lenihan's name were on the poles before anyone else could move. The basic strategy was get the name out and re-emphasise it over and over again, hence posters were just Brian Lenihan name strips at the beginning with more conventional picture posters later.

Brian was delighted that the campaign had at last begun. Fianna Fáil's success in forcing the Government into a by-election at a time not of their choosing gave Brian's campaign momentum and it gave it confidence. Brian, however, was astute enough to recognise that a parliamentary victory meant little to voters on the ground and that there was a lot of work to do. The next twenty-one days were days of frenetic activity. My thesis went on the back-burner, as I spent my days and evenings either canvassing with Brian or other party members, researching material that Brian requested for public meetings or helping out in the office in Laurel Lodge. Brian was everywhere trying to cover as much ground as possible in a constituency that had experienced rapid housing growth in the previous five years and was described by *The Irish Times* as 'the highest mortgage-holding constituency in the State.'

Brian's campaign was bolstered by members of the Fianna Fáil Parliamentary Party who were assigned individual areas of the constituency to canvass. I quickly learnt that this was a task that different individuals took to with different degrees of enthusiasm. I will always associate the Dublin West by-election with a horse called Rough Quest and not just because its name aptly described the battle that Brian Lenihan faced to win his father's seat. On the Saturday before polling day, I had helped to coordinate a canvass in North Clondalkin which was led by a visiting member of the Fianna Fáil Parliamentary Party, though not a member of the frontbench. The canvass was only in its infancy when our public representative insisted on an adjournment to a local pub so he could watch the

Aintree Grand National. I can still vividly see him roaring on the horse he had backed – Rough Quest – to victory and punching the air in triumph afterwards. He then generously bought a celebratory round of drinks for our team of canvassers and when these were completed he insisted on buying us another one. Somebody else then produced a further round and, at that stage, the canvass was aborted and a lengthy session ensued. I do not know whether our visiting public representative had actually won big in his bet, but his drinks bill that day was certainly not small. It was some years before I shared that particular story with Brian Lenihan.

On the other end of the scale of professionalism was Ray Burke. He did Trojan work for Brian in this by-election and it was something that Brian never forgot. Burke had been good friends with Brian's father and he was determined that Fianna Fáil would not lose his seat. Ray did a huge amount of canvassing and a lot of his supporters from Dublin North were also very active in the campaign. Every Sunday evening, a group of us from Dublin West would meet Ray and some of his local team outside Blanchardstown church to canvass mass-goers. Ray Burke was always early and he exuded enthusiasm. Brian himself had suggested that Burke be deployed in Blanchardstown because he felt his presence would be popular with older residents. Ray's father, Paddy, had once represented this area and he must have been a very popular and hardworking TD because I was struck by the amount of elderly people who remembered him with affection or told Ray some story about him helping them. Burke's sobriquet in the party was 'Rambo' and though I did hear reports of him berating errant TDs who had neglected their canvassing responsibilities, I found him to be warm and kind-hearted.

One Sunday, it was so wet and cold that only a few hardy volunteers turned up for duty at Blanchardstown church. Burke, as always, was there. After we had given leaflets to people going into mass, there was time to kill before we would repeat the exercise with people leaving church. I was shaking from the cold weather and Burke threw me the keys of his car and instructed me and two of his local supporters to get in. He disappeared, but returned shortly afterwards with bags of chips and cans of coke for us all. I had just finished reading *The Boss*, a riveting book about Charles Haughey's leadership by Joe Joyce and Peter Murtagh, and, as I munched my chips, I quizzed Ray on the heaves in Fianna Fáil in the 1980s. Burke was happy to indulge my interest in this tumultuous period in the party's history and I could see that he was enjoying himself, but it didn't stop him from ordering us all out of the car when he spotted the first mass-goer exit the church. In later years, it was rare to hear Ray Burke's name mentioned in Fianna Fáil circles without some degree of criticism attached, but I never heard Brian Lenihan speak anything but fondly of him and the work he did in that by-election. Brian was always unlikely to kick people when they were down and I admired that about him greatly.

Dermot Ahern was another TD who worked very hard during that by-election. As the Fianna Fáil Whip, he had to juggle business in the Dáil – and especially the need to ensure sporadic high attendances of Fianna Fáil deputies for parliamentary votes, so as to keep Rainbow TDs pinned down in Leinster House – with a heavy canvassing schedule. One evening after a late vote in the Dáil, Dermot, showing true commitment, decided to drive out to Dublin West to join the tail-end of a canvass rather than take the rest of the evening off. He parked his car at the edge of a housing estate in Mulhuddart, but a short time later he was confronted with the shocking sight of his own vehicle speeding away in the possession of young joyriders. The crime epidemic that almost all of the parties were pledging to crack down on in their leaflets was not scaremongering by politicians hungry for votes, but a grim reality of daily life in Dublin 15. Noel Dempsey has a strong recollection of the sense of social exclusion that was prevalent in many communities in Dublin West. He noted:

> The abiding memory that I have of the constituency is thinking for the first time ever in my political career 'I can understand now why people would say there is no point in voting.' The levels of poverty and deprivation in areas of the constituency shocked me, particularly when contrasted with other areas of the constituency which were affluent.

I had a few brief conversations with Bertie Ahern during this by-election, but he was constantly on the move. I think our longest exchange concerned a goal that Eric Cantona scored against Tottenham to put Manchester United top of the league. Bertie was splitting his time between Dublin West and the other by-election in Donegal North-East and he was also back and forth between his offices in Leinster House and Drumcondra. Even then, it was clear to me that Bertie Ahern was somebody who put work above almost everything else. He had a huge network of supporters in the neighbouring constituency of Dublin Central and they decamped en masse in Dublin West for the duration of the by-election. They knew that this by-election was being viewed as an important measure of Bertie's leadership and they were intensely committed to getting Brian over the line. Brian used to refer to them as a 'machine' and he was particularly impressed with the work ethic of Chris Wall, one of Bertie's closest political allies, who had been raised in Blanchardstown and seemed to know everyone.

At a party rally in the Clonsilla Inn not long after the writ was moved, Bertie was at pains to stress in his remarks that if a voter said he or she was committed to another candidate that we should try to nail down their second preference and if this was not available to seek their third preference and so on. During the campaign, Brian, in conversation with me, would sometimes irreverently refer to Bertie Ahern's speech as 'a reading from the transfer gospel, according to Bertie.' Brian had not been impressed that the Fianna Fáil leader had relied on a prepared script that night, but, at the same time, he totally bought into the speech's message. This emphasis on picking up transfers was also reflected in the party's campaign leaflets. Noel Dempsey noted:

> We produced a series of short sharp Q&A cards as election literature and the last one actually conceded that not everyone would give us their No.1 and asked them to consider us for a 2,3,4, or any preference. I believe the general approach and this leaflet in particular had a significant effect on the result.

Fine Gael also understood the value of transfers. Their campaign was confident of success and the Taoiseach was spending long hours on the doorsteps of Dublin West. Jim Mitchell, Tom Morrissey's exuberant Director of Elections, had taken to referring to his candidate's constituency office as 'the winner's enclosure.' Mitchell reminded reporters that the combined Fine Gael and Labour vote was 37 per cent in Dublin West at the previous general election, compared with 31 per cent for Fianna Fáil. He also pointed out that Fine Gael was 'much better at getting transfers.' Mitchell knew the constituency well, having formerly represented Dublin West. He had also spectacularly masterminded Liam Skelly's victory the last time there had been a by-election in Dublin West, following Charles Haughey's appointment of Dick Burke to the European Commission in 1982. Mitchell had a wily talent for electioneering, but we were clear that the message from the doorsteps was that while Morrissey would poll well, the Fine Gael candidate would not be in the final shake-up.

Our canvassing returns quickly identified Joe Higgins as the main danger to Brian. The Militant Labour councillor had received just 1,400 votes in the 1992 General Election, but he had worked assiduously since then at building his base. Higgins's performance in the 1996 by-election was nothing short of phenomenal. He did not have a fraction of the resources or personnel that Fianna Fáil had, but yet he managed to come very close to edging Brian Lenihan out of the seat. Higgins had captured the public mood in large tracts of the constituency through his vigorous campaign against water charges and he was vehement in his contention that 'the establishment parties' had let people down. It is fair to say that Brian and Joe Higgins were never close, but Brian respected him greatly and never under-estimated him. Joe was a fine public speaker, he was intellectually sharp and he was ideologically driven. Their styles were very different, but Joe was one of the few people in Irish politics who could match Brian Lenihan in debate. I think it was apparent to all of us who observed Joe Higgins in that by-election – whether we agreed with him politically or not – that he had what it takes to be an excellent TD and so it has been proved.

The powerful impact of Higgins's campaign in 1996 was disconcerting for the main parties and it resulted in a surprise suspension of outright hostilities between the Fianna Fáil and Fine Gael camps, which was the usual fare at elections. At the time, I had no idea that there were informal contacts between Noel Dempsey and the Fine Gael Director of Elections, however, Dempsey has now confirmed:

> Half way through the campaign I had a discussion with Jim Mitchell following incidents where our posters were being torn down by Fine Gael activists. We compared notes and both of us claimed (naturally) that our candidate was ahead. More seriously, we agreed that it was in both our interests as parties to ensure that either one of our candidates won so we should quietly look for preferences for each other.

Prior to polling day, Geraldine Kennedy noted in *The Irish Times* that the collective wisdom from canvassers across all parties in Dublin West was that Brian Lenihan would need to increase the Fianna Fáil vote to 35 per cent at least to stave off the challenge from Joe Higgins. Kennedy's assessment was very much in line with what the thinking was within Fianna Fáil on the ground in the constituency. Deep down, despite the major emphasis Brian, Noel Dempsey and Bertie Ahern had placed on seeking transfers, I certainly felt that the ingrained pattern in Irish politics of Fianna Fáil versus the rest, born out of the party's strident rejection of coalition until recent times, meant that Fianna Fáil would attract fewer preferential votes and that Brian would need to be well clear of Higgins on the first count.

The bookmakers, who rarely get it wrong in by-elections, had installed Higgins as the favourite. This was particularly agitating Fianna Fáil strategists because when a number of Dublin radio stations referred to the by-election in their news bulletins, they invariably referred to Joe Higgins as 'the bookies' favourite.' The fear was that undecided voters might throw in their lot with Higgins if it looked like he was going to win. One night in the latter stages of the campaign, I was in the West County Hotel enjoying an end-of-day pint with Brian and a large contingent of Fianna Fáil supporters. There were whisperings that a wealthy Fianna Fáil Senator had placed a very substantial bet on Brian to cut his odds and ensure that he would assume the status of favourite. I never established the veracity of this rumour, but if it was true the strategy did not work. On the day before polling, the *Irish Independent* reported that betting in Dublin West had Joe Higgins as the even money favourite, Brian was trailing at 5/4 and Tomas Mac Giolla was available at 5/2.

In hindsight, it is not surprising that the Fianna Fáil candidate was not the bookies' favourite. The party's record in by-elections around this time had been abysmal. There had already been five by-elections in the lifetime of the Twenty-Seventh Dáil and Fianna Fáil had lost the lot. The most recent by-election had been in Wicklow the previous summer and it was Bertie Ahern's first electoral test as party leader. Fianna Fáil had performed poorly and an Independent, Mildred Fox, won a surprise victory. The votes in Dublin West and Donegal North East were being billed by political pundits as an important indicator as to whether Bertie Ahern could electorally cut the mustard. Of the two by-elections, Dublin West was viewed as the most significant to the Fianna Fáil leader because the case for his leadership had been partly rooted in the need for a Dubliner as a way to increase the party's vote in the capital. If Bertie was under pressure, he did not let it show. He remained the smiling leader and he continued to work hard, but he boxed cautiously. Two days before polling, an *Irish Times* reporter joined Bertie on the canvass trail in Lohunda and noted:

> Mr Bertie Ahern's pronouncements are not those of a confident man. 'We haven't done that well in by-elections over the years. Of course, it would be nice to win. But if we lose it won't put me down hugely or put me up if we win.' He does not, he says, believe it will be damaging to him as leader if the candidate fails to be elected.

The *Irish Times* suggested that Ahern was deliberately playing 'down the importance of a victory' and that his comments were 'a pre-emptive strike to ensure that he won't carry the full can' should Brian

Lenihan be defeated. On 1 April, 1996, the day prior to polling, the front-page headline in the *Irish Independent* read 'Election Challenge Crucial for Ahern' and the story cast serious doubts on Brian's prospects. It stated:

> Although party strategists maintain Brian Lenihan junior is faring well, there is concern that his vote may prove 'patchy' and growing worry about Fianna Fáil's capacity to attract sufficient transfers from other candidates if this transpires. Failure to win the seat in Dublin, particularly from the Opposition benches, would not just be a serious blow for the party but would damage Mr Ahern and his attempts to rebuild Fianna Fáil in the capital.

On that same day, Brian asked me to canvass with him in the Strawberry Beds and Porterstown. We were accompanied by Nora Comiskey, a long-time Fianna Fáil activist, a neighbour of Brian's and one of his favourite people. Despite the newspaper coverage, Brian was in great form and he was hugely optimistic that he would win. In Porterstown, Brian canvassed the mother of good friends of mine. I knew she was a Fine Gael supporter. She immediately told Brian that she was voting for Morrissey, but that she would give him 'the number two.' As we walked back up the driveway, Brian made the stunning prediction that he would be elected on heavy Fine Gael transfers. I thought he had taken leave of his senses and told him so! Brian, however, was adamant. He told me that what had happened at the previous doorstep was far from an isolated incident and that many Fine Gael supporters he had encountered over the past few days were telling him that they would transfer to him to stop Higgins. Brian's reasoning for this was that Fine Gael supporters were conservative and mostly well-off and that they were frightened by Higgins's radical socialism. Brian told me of Fine Gael voters who had expressed concerns that Higgins might support a stringent wealth tax or even wish to nationalise the banks. Had I known then that a dozen or so years later Brian Lenihan would be the Minister for Finance who would effectively nationalise the entire Irish banking system, I would have been even more bemused.

The prospect of Brian being any sort of a minister or even a TD seemed fairly remote on the morning of 3 April 1996. Not long after the boxes had opened in the Lucan Community Centre, the tallymen were pronouncing with chilling certainty 'Lenihan's fucked.' It was clear that Brian's first preference vote was going to fall far short of the magic number of 35 per cent. In fact, Brian's first preference vote would ultimately prove to be 7 per cent down on Fianna Fáil's percentage in Dublin West at the last election. It seemed impossible on those numbers that he could win. Brian was at home resting after a hard campaign. I am not sure if it was Des Kelly or possibly Oliver Leahy who rang Brian with the news, but the word came back that he was not in the slightest bit perturbed. In contrast, all around the count centre I saw people wearing Lenihan stickers and desolate faces. At some point, as the tallymen continued with their dismal science, I ran into a positively beaming Sean Sherwin, Fianna Fáil's National Organiser. Sean was utterly convinced Brian Lenihan would prevail. With characteristic kindness, he bought me a cup of coffee and, in intricate detail, he brought me through his analysis of how the votes would end up breaking down from each polling district. Like Brian, he was sure that Morrissey would put us over the top. I now clung to this analysis like a life-raft, even when one Fianna Fáil TD told me it was 'absolute horse-shite!'

I might have felt more reassured had I known that Noel Dempsey had taken to the airwaves steadfastly refusing to admit defeat, although his viewpoint was given little credence. Dempsey recalled:

I predicted a narrow win on the RTÉ programme at around 11 am. I was in a minority of one, as the pundits and, much to my annoyance, Charlie McCreevy predicted otherwise on *the News at One*.

When the first count was declared, Brian had polled 6,995 number ones, but he was only a disappointing 252 votes ahead of Higgins. At lunchtime, Charlie McCreevy had said Fianna Fáil would need the kind of transfers the party 'hadn't got for decades' to win. Almost incredibly, this is what proceeded to happen. As the counts progressed, Brian was holding his own in accumulating transfers and, as the tallymen worked their way down through later preferences, word was seeping out that a miracle might be on. The mood among the Fianna Fáil members in the count centre became increasingly giddy and, of course, with a victory now possibly in the offing our numbers expanded rapidly. Back in Dáil Éireann, as Geraldine Kennedy subsequently reported, 'Fianna Fáil frontbenchers roamed the corridors of Leinster House scarcely believing that they could be the victors. Most of them had conceded defeat when the first-count tallies came in at lunchtime.'

Later in the afternoon, Brian arrived at the count centre and, for the first time, he looked nervous. He declined to answer media queries and he immediately went into a huddle with some of the Fianna Fáil tallymen. On the tenth count, following the distribution of the votes of the former leader of the Workers' Party, Tomás Mac Giolla, Joe Higgins went ahead of Brian Lenihan for the first time. The margin was 140 votes as Tom Morrissey was now eliminated. On the eleventh count, Brian received 2,084 votes from the Fine Gael candidate and Joe Higgins received 1,574 votes. It meant that Brian Lenihan was elected to the Twenty-Seventh Dáil by a slim margin of 370 votes.

The moment that Brian was declared elected was an exhilarating one, but a sense of sheer relief was also palpable in the hall. With his supporters prepared to cheer his every word, Brian might have been forgiven if he made a raucous acceptance speech, however, he was dignity personified. He praised his party leader as an electoral asset and said 'Bertie Ahern crosses class boundaries in Dublin and put up a fantastic show in Dublin West.' He thanked the party workers, 'particularly Director of Elections, Noel Dempsey, who delivered when it mattered.' Brian said that he had conducted his campaign throughout the entire constituency on 'bread and butter' issues and he maintained his composure when acknowledging the public's 'goodwill' towards his father. Outside, it was a different story. Brian was surrounded by a media scrum and when a reporter asked him if his father would have been proud, Brian just about managed to answer in the affirmative before beginning to cry. Looking on, Conor too was in tears.

Brian's victory was Fianna Fáil's first by-election win since 1984 when Brian Cowen had been elected in Laois-Offaly. News was coming through that Cecilia Keaveney was going to be elected in Donegal, thus, ensuring Fianna Fáil's first by-election double since 1967. The political correspondents at the Lucan count were fascinated by the retreat of the 'Spring tide.' Labour's vote in Dublin West had dropped from 22.6 per cent to 3.7 per cent and their campaign had not been helped by a fundraising controversy involving the Minister for Arts, Culture and the Gaeltacht, Michael D. Higgins. The greatest sensation though was the unprecedented number of preferences Brian Lenihan had received from Fine Gael voters. Austin Deasy, the former Fine Gael Minister for Agriculture, put it well when he remarked: 'Since the advent of Civil War politics, there had never been such a crossing of party lines in vote transfers.' Right from the beginning, Brian Lenihan was breaking moulds.

In the car park of the Lucan Community Centre, I watched contentedly as a group of Fianna Fáil TDs and Senators jostled to get into the camera shot alongside Brian Lenihan and Bertie Ahern. I realised Mary O'Rourke, who had done more canvassing for Brian than probably anyone else, was missing from this happy throng. I spotted her on the other side of the car park thanking two elderly women who had been supporters of Brian's dad. A journalist asked Brian another question. Would his election mean big changes in his life? Brian paused, he smiled and then he remarked: 'I don't suppose I can expect much peace in my life from now on.' How right he was.

13 ATHLONE BACKGROUND

HARMAN MURTAGH

BRIAN LENIHAN LIVED IN Athlone for the first twelve years of his life between 1959 and 1971. Throughout that time, his Christian name was pronounced 'Breen' in the Irish form, reverting to Brian only after he had moved to Dublin. It is impossible to measure with precision the full impact that growing up in Athlone had on the formation of his personality and character, but there is plenty of anecdotal and circumstantial evidence to show that it was substantial. In later life, his recollections of Athlone were extremely vivid, and he retained an abiding, deep and genuine – if understandably nostalgic – affection for the town and companions of his childhood. When he enrolled in Belvedere College, the famous Dublin north-city Jesuit school, his classmates teased him as 'the farmer Lenihan' on account of his provincial accent. Certainly the flat-A vowel sounds and other characteristics of Athlone speech were noticeable features of his enunciation that he never lost or adjusted.

The Lenihan family had settled in Athlone in the 1930s, when Brian's grandfather, P.J. Lenihan (1902-70), a native of Clare, was seconded from the civil service at the behest of Sean Lemass, then minister for industry and commerce, to be company secretary of General Textiles Ltd, the newly-established cotton factory in Athlone. Five years later, P.J. became the general manager. The industry was a commercial success, and it became a major factor in the economy of the town, with a workforce of more than 700. Gentex was notable for its community spirit, with workers' councils, trade-union recognition and a medical service, together with active in-house sporting, cultural and social activities. All this was very much in line with P.J.'s advanced social thinking. Both he and his wife, Annie, were graduates of University College Galway (now NUIG); he read widely and kept abreast of modern thought and ideas. In 1957, he retired from Gentex to run a small hotel he had established in a Georgian house on the west shore of Lough Ree at Hodson Bay, again with considerable commercial success.

In personality, P.J. was warm, enthusiastic, quick-minded, witty and gregarious. These qualities, allied to his paternalistic management of Gentex and interest in public affairs, pointed to a political role. His background was Free State rather than Fianna Fáil, and he was first elected to Athlone Urban District Council in 1942 as an independent. He soon transferred to Fianna Fáil, probably out of loyalty to Lemass, whose commercial policies he greatly admired, and possibly even at his suggestion. And in Fianna Fáil he remained, to be followed in time by his family, although his second son, Pádraig, a Roscommon county councillor, later reverted to 'independence'. Further election success followed: P.J. became chairman of Westmeath County Council and was eventually elected to the Dáil for Longford-Westmeath in 1965.

By then, his eldest son, Brian Lenihan Senior (1930-95), was already a TD, having been first elected for Roscommon in 1961. Brian Senior had grown up in Athlone, where he attended the Marist College secondary school before studying economics at UCD. He was called to the bar in 1952, and practised for a time on the midland circuit. However, doubtless because of his father's formative influence, he was attracted by politics, first contesting a Dáil seat in 1954 and becoming a senator in 1957. He was part of a new wave of young professionals to enter Irish politics at that time, especially through Fianna Fáil, and on arriving in the Dáil he was immediately appointed a parliamentary secretary (as junior ministers were then entitled), before joining the Cabinet as Minister for Justice in 1964.

Although more polished than his father, Brian Senior possessed much of the former's genial bonhomie, which rather masked his shrewd judgement and intellectual depth. Intellectuals at that time were generally suspect, especially in politics, so this was possibly to his electoral benefit. Universally well-liked, Brian Senior was a leading figure in Irish public life for thirty years, holding a greater variety of cabinet portfolios than any other minister in Irish modern history. He was resilient in the face of the inevitable disappointments and setbacks of political life. After losing his seat in the volatile Roscommon-Leitrim constituency in the general election of 1973, he was elected for the Dublin West constituency (then Dublin County West). He held his seat there until his death in 1995 and was succeeded by his son, Brian Junior, who won the subsequent by-election. In 1982 Brian Senior's sister, Mary O'Rourke, was elected to the Dáil for her father's old constituency of Longford-Westmeath, and subsequently served with her brother in cabinet.

Neither P.J. or Brian Senior were imbued with civil war bitterness, nor did they ever choose to adopt or feign that stance. They liked to get on with everyone, even political opponents, both nationally and locally. When Sean MacEoin, the War of Independence veteran and Fine Gael elder, was defeated in the 1965 election, which returned P.J. to the Dáil after a marathon count, the Lenihan family declined to hold a victory celebration. Brian Senior emphasised their respect for MacEoin and correctly stressed – contrary to popular perception at the time, and since – that it was not *his* seat that P.J. had taken, but rather one of the two outgoing Fianna Fáil seats in the Longford-Westmeath constituency that he had held. The Lenihans were not ideologues: their politics were 'pragmatic' (to quote Brian Senior), but this did not mean that they were without conviction. They were strongly committed to economic development and social improvement, taking the view with Lemass that the latter very much depended on the former. Brian Senior saw himself as a social democrat, and he advocated a closer relationship between Fianna Fáil and Labour. His viewpoint was probably not dissimilar to that of his British contemporary, the Labour politician Tony Crosland, a Keynsian moderate, whose book *The Future of Socialism* was widely influential in the 1960s and which he must have read.

While he lived in Athlone, Brian Senior was frequently invited to open premises and events or to speak at local functions, such as the annual dinner of the Marist Brothers Past Pupils' Union, of which he was sometime president. Young Brian later recalled the crowds of people in his parents' kitchen and a virtual traffic jam outside the gate of their house in Retreat, when his father was at home. These were constituents and other local people seeking his father's assistance or advice, or supporters discussing electoral strategy or giving him their views. Young Brian sometimes accompanied his mother – an enthusiastic canvasser – in her Mini-Minor during election campaigns. While he always disliked being described as a member of a political dynasty, he was certainly introduced to grassroots political life in Athlone. As he grew older, he must have been alert to the political discussion between his father and his grandfather at the regular family Sunday lunch in the Hodson Bay Hotel. Another influence from an early age was law: his father, after all, was a barrister, his grandfather a Garda superintendent and his uncle, Dermot ('Derry') Devine, a solicitor (and later a law professor), as was the father of his close friend, Harry Walker. Not surprisingly, Brian Junior (and three of his siblings) later chose law as a career.

Brian Lenihan Senior married Ann Devine in 1958. She was the only daughter of the then Athlone Garda superintendent and IRA veteran, Joe Devine, and his wife, Ita, a medical doctor. Ann gave up her dental studies when they decided to get married. They lived on the east side of Athlone, first in a small semi-detached house in St Mary's Place, moving after three years to a detached villa on Retreat Road. They had six children, of whom the eldest three were born while they lived in Athlone. Annual holidays were generally spent in Connemara. The family suffered a tragedy when Brian Junior's next sibling Mark, with whom he shared a bedroom, fell ill and died of leukemia at the age of five. Brian Junior bottled up his emotions at the time, possibly not fully comprehending what had happened, but in later life his on-going grief at the loss of his brother came to the surface. 'Pop' and Granny Devine lived near the Lenihans' house in Retreat and Brian Junior grew extremely close to his grandparents and remained very fond of them, sometimes accompanying them on holiday. He was an adult when they died, but still loved them both greatly and found their deaths very hard to accept.

Brian Junior's early education was with the La Sainte Union sisters at the Fair Green infant school in Athlone. The new class started after Easter in 1963 in the converted school shed and Brian Junior and the others were present a month or so later at the opening of the new Marist Brothers national school nearby, to which he transferred after making his first communion in 1966. From the outset he loved school. He was fortunate in the quality of his teachers, such as Sister Mel and Eithne Madigan, who were both in the infant school; and in the Marist school notably Brother Seamus Walsh, who taught Brian's class for three years. Brother Seamus was young, energetic and with the gift of enthusing his students. Brian Junior was recognised by his classmates as being outstandingly gifted amongst a group that included several other able students, such as Martin Hanevy, currently assistant secretary of the Department of Education, and Harry Walker, who has become a leading classical scholar in the USA. Brother Seamus was committed to the revival of Irish and in the opinion of the primary schools inspector his class had the best spoken Irish in the midlands. He brought the class to the Gaeltacht, where they had the adventure of crossing to the Aran Islands in a rickety turf boat. In later life, Seamus Walsh left the Marist congregation, married and became a taxi driver. Brian Junior, then a minister, having discovered his whereabouts, made a point of looking him up. After her retirement, he entertained Sister Mel in Leinster House. He was never slow to recognise old friends or schoolmates.

The Brothers made much of Brian Senior's appointment as Minister for Education on the death of Donogh O'Malley in 1968, somewhat to Brian Junior's embarrassment, as he mixed well with his schoolmates and disliked being singled out for praise, at least on account of his father's importance. Nevertheless, he was intensely proud of his father and his achievements. He took piano lessons after school at the Bower Convent, and when he won a silver medal for his performance at a *feis* in Sligo his success was publicly acknowledged in his school. However, as he ruefully confided to his classmates, the truth was that there had been only two in the competition! He recalled later in life the Brothers' liberal use of the cane, although he cannot often have been at the receiving end himself, as he was studious, steady and seldom in trouble. He was inquisitive and loved learning new things. He was a serious-minded boy, not perhaps with a great sense of humour – although this developed in time – but certainly out-going and gregarious, with plenty of friends beyond his immediate family.

Harry Walker, one of his schoolmates, was his 'intellectual' friend. He recalls Brian Junior as very lively and cheerful. Together, they discussed articles in *Look and Learn*, the British weekly educational magazine for children, collected stamps – examining 'approvals' from a firm in England and investing their pocket money in purchasing what appealed to them – played board games, such as 'Cluedo' and 'Risk' and maintained a keen interest in the Second World War through magazines, Biggles stories, Airfix models and toy soldiers. Brian Junior read popular comics such as *The Beano* and *The Dandy*, graduating later to *The Rover* and *The Hotspur* that were rich in war and football stories. He particularly liked history. He was quite religious, serving as an altar boy in St Mary's Church and was a member of the school choir that sang the Latin mass at funerals. The streets were relatively safe and it was easy for young people to move around on foot or – as in Brian Junior's case – by bicycle. Athlone in the 1960s was a good place to grow up.

The River Shannon defines Athlone. The *raison d'être* of the town's existence is its location at a point where the river shallows to break through an esker ridge, facilitating the passage across the water initially via the ford, which gives Athlone its name, and later by a succession of bridges. The esker enabled traders, travellers, soldiers and livestock to converge on the crossing, clear of the bogs and wetlands of the midland plain. Anglo-Normans and Elizabethans identified Athlone as the key gateway to Connacht. A castle was constructed, followed by town-wall fortifications, a famous stone bridge and a large army barracks. Houses of brick and stone 'after the English fashion' were built within the town core, with mud cabins for the poorer inhabitants in extra-mural Irishtowns. The town has a strong sense of its own history. Every schoolboy knew the story of Sergeant Custume's courageous defence of the bridge against the Williamites in 1691. Later, Athlone became an important railway centre, served by four lines that focussed on an impressive iron railway viaduct. Inns and hotels served travellers' needs. A substantial textile industry developed. Housing, especially for the poorer sections of the community, greatly improved in the twentieth century, although in general the town was not architecturally distinguished.

Administratively, from 1899, Athlone on both sides of the river was included in Westmeath. But in many respects the Shannon divided the town. Each half lay in a different diocese, so that there were two parishes, each with its own leadership, church, suite of schools and services structure. Each side had its own commercial core: Church Street, the east town's 'golden half mile', had the largest and most modern shops, whereas west-town businesses, chiefly located in Connaught Street and the Market Square, tended to be smaller, many retaining the traditional arrangement of groceries in the front and a bar to the rear. Professionals were mainly located in the adjoining Edwardian terraces of Garden Vale and Pearse Street. Nevertheless, despite Athlone's binary character, in 1968, there was widespread opposition to a proposal to divide it between Westmeath and Roscommon for electoral purposes.

The population in the 1960s was about 10,000 and gradually rising. Suburban sprawl was in its infancy, with most 'townies' living inside the urban district council boundary and clearly distinguishable, even in appearance, from their rural neighbours, 'the country people.' Most residents knew each other at least by sight; perhaps less so when they crossed the river. Athlone was a market and service town; but a poor agricultural hinterland made its economy heavily dependent on the army barracks, the textile industry and tourism. Surplus labour moved to Dublin or migrated, chiefly to England.

The Lemass years were vibrant, modernising, prosperous and optimistic. The 1960s opened in an atmosphere of tradition and continuity, but the impulse for change was everywhere soon felt and by the end of the decade had clearly gained the ascendancy. In Athlone, the army, challenged by the Congo and subsequent UN peacekeeping operations, overcame its post-Emergency stagnation and modernised. Its personnel returned to Custume Barracks experienced in the cultures of the wider world. As the town's textile industry declined, early difficulties in replacing it were overcome: by 1971, an Anglo-Chinese apparel manufacturer was established in the empty woollen-mills premises, a plastics firm was operating in the former Gentex spinning shed and a Swedish company was completing a purpose-built plant to manufacture cable and wire at a factory in Bliary. Telecommunications-hardware and pharmaceuticals followed in later years. The choice of Athlone as a centre for one of the new regional technical colleges was strongly promoted by the Lenihans at local and political level. Brian Senior, an advocate of 'scientific education,' foresaw it as 'ensuring that Athlone would be the centre of future development in the midland and western region.'

Commercial and business life were also changing. In 1960, Brian Senior opened 'a modern self-selection showroom' at Burgess's, the town's largest drapery shop. Annual fashion shows, featuring some of Dublin's top models, introduced the haute couture of the 'swinging sixties.' At the end of the decade, Dunnes Stores opened its first Athlone branch, a development that marked the beginning of the end for much of the town's traditional family-owned trade. Hotels, including P.J. Lenihan's Hodson Bay, were improved, extended or even re-built. There was much emphasis on Athlone's tourism potential, as boating and angling developed on the Shannon. The development of a riverside promenade greatly improved the town's appearance. The river was 'the key to midland development' in the opinion of P.J. Lenihan. Street fairs which – as Brian Junior remembered – obliged his school to close were eventually banished to the Fair Green, before disappearing entirely. On the roads delivery vans and 'lurries' – the local pronunciation – supplanted horse-drawn drays and messenger bicycles, although Broderick's Bakery for long continued to use horse-drawn vans, brightly painted in the firm's red and yellow livery. Car ownership grew and with it traffic congestion. Planners – a new profession viewed with considerable suspicion – advocated a by-pass road and a new bridge. Amid the Fords, Hillmans, and Volkswagens – some *very* second-hand – the black ministerial Mercedes of Brian Senior still turned heads. On the railways, diesels had already replaced steam trains.

The dominant organisation was still the Catholic Church. Its powerful position was symbolised in the west town by the splendid riverside church of Saints Peter and Paul, often mistaken for a cathedral. In the east town the parish church was the dignified gothic-revival St Mary's, executed in grey local limestone. It was there that Brian Junior, prepared by Sister Mel, made his first communion, and where he was later confirmed by Bishop (later Cardinal) Cahal Daly. He was brought to the ceremony by his Devine grandparents, due to the death at the time of his grandfather, P.J. Lenihan. Brian Junior later recalled the large number of priests, brothers and nuns in Athlone and the atmosphere of intense religiosity that pervaded the town. Sunday masses were packed, sodalities thrived, thousands walked in Corpus Christi processions and Bishops' pastorals were serialised (if perhaps not widely read) in the *Westmeath Independent*. A 'teenage crusade' was organised by a local friar as 'a bulwark against the modern spirit of liberalism.' Priests were held in high respect and their influence and leadership role extended far beyond the realms of worship, education and social concern. They were conservative upholders of a traditional faith that seemed strong and unchallenged. The Second Vatican Council took Irish churchmen by surprise, although the octogenarian Bishop McNamee of Ardagh and Clonmacnoise (who never missed a council session) perceptively told his flock: 'the little fresh air spoken of by Pope John has become a mighty rushing wind.' From 1965, mass was in English; sometimes in Irish.

A more fundamental change, as Brian Junior later recollected, was the questioning of ideas. The old order exerted its power with the banning in 1961 of *The Pilgrimage*, a novel depicting sexual need in 1950s Ireland, by the local writer and critic, John Broderick, who was a friend of P.J. Lenihan. Together, in 1963, under the auspices of Athlone Arts Council, of which P.J. characteristically was chairman, they brought Kate O'Brien, another banned author and outspoken critic of conservatism, to speak in the town. Brian Junior's uncle, Derry Devine, was the driving force in Athlone of *Tuairim*, the

1960s questioning 'think tank.' The organisation was viewed with suspicion by the Catholic Church, who countered it with meetings of the Legion of Mary's Patrician Society. The first woman was co-opted to Westmeath County Council and, in 1965, Athlone UDC had a woman as town clerk, albeit temporarily.

Much wider – and more revolutionary – in its impact was the arrival of Irish television, which brought the challenge to established authority and conventional mores into every home, particularly on Gay Byrne's Saturday-night *Late Late Show*. The reaction the programme aroused amongst appalled conservatives is exemplified by a resolution of Athlone Urban District Council, which declared it to be 'slanted against everything the Irish people hold dear ... would-be intellectuals telling us our way of life, the glorious traditions handed down to us by our forefathers – in fact our purpose in life – is all wrong ... [It is] a platform for heresies that decent people abhor ...' But there could be no returning the genie to the bottle: Kilkenny Corporation dismissed the Athlone resolution as 'codology' and it was reported to have evoked widespread hilarity as far away as Carrickmacross. Other stimulants for change were the cinemas, although heavily censored and showing somewhat dated films and the local library, where in 1961 – somewhat surprisingly – Graham Greene's *A Burnt-Out Case* and Hugh Thomas's *The Spanish Civil War* were amongst the most popular books. Nowhere was the impact of the new more widely felt than in popular music. In the dance halls, showbands, such as the Royal and the Clipper Carlton, were eclipsing céiles and Glenn Miller-style orchestras alike. A correspondent to the *Westmeath Independent* complained that young men had no time for girls unable or unwilling to Rock'n Roll or Twist and the new-music craze was blamed for declining attendances at VEC night-classes.

Athlone has a rich musical tradition, exemplified in the 1960s by the very active musical society, the army band, visits by the Irish National Opera Company and a gramophone society that brought to the town musicians of the calibre of the O'Grady sisters and the pianist Charles Lynch. John McCormack was, of course, the most famous of all Athlone musicians. In 1970, a memorial to his memory was erected on the new riverside promenade in the form of a bronze head by the Cork sculptor, Seamus Murphy. Brian Junior had a lifelong love of music and was quite an accomplished pianist. He acknowledged the root of this interest by selecting McCormack's *I hear you calling me* as his first musical choice during his 2009 interview on the RTÉ programme *Miriam Meets.*

An annual cultural highlight of the time, and ever since, was the finals of the All-Ireland Amateur Drama Festival, run by a committee chaired for many years by P.J. Lenihan. P.J., who played a leadership role in so many activities, was also one of those involved in the revival of the Gaelic League in Athlone, although he soon dropped into the background. Its activities culminated in the winning of the Glór na nGael trophy in 1964 for Athlone, as the town that had made the most progress in promoting Irish. President de Valera visited Athlone for the presentation of the award. But the Irish-revival movement failed to plant deep roots in what its local chairman rather pejoratively described as a *seonín* town and its influence soon waned. Brian Senior had little interest in Irish, perhaps in reaction to his father P.J.'s somewhat cynical view that it was necessary to know it 'in order to get on in Dev's Ireland.' However, Brian Junior had a lifelong interest in the language, perhaps as a result of Brother Seamus's influence and because of his mother, who could speak Irish, having spent a year in Ring as a child: certainly he said in later years that he preferred Munster Irish to other dialects. The Gaelic League encouraged school drama and Brian Junior played a leading role in school plays, with in one case a dialogue in English, Irish and – curiously – Catalan. Appropriately he took the part of the king in one production.

The alleged *seonín* character of Athlone was most manifest in the town's deep-seated commitment to soccer. Sport was (and remains) a major feature of local life, possibly more so than in other provincial towns, which may be due to the military character of Athlone. The 1960s saw improved sporting facilities, executed or planned, for rowing, Gaelic games, rugby and swimming. However, it was soccer that had the deepest roots. Gentex had its own soccer team, which played junior football in the Athletic Union League. Brian Senior was an accomplished soccer player, until injury ended his career. He played with Gentex as a youth, and later as centre forward for UCD,

Shelbourne and Bohemians. He was capped on the Irish amateur team. He retained his enthusiasm for the game and on Sundays was a regular attender at St Mel's Park, the ground of Athlone Town, the principal local team. Soon after the club regained full League of Ireland status in 1969, Brian Senior was elected club president. Brian Junior and his younger brother, Conor, accompanied their father to matches. Athlone Town had no more avid supporter than young Brian. By the age of ten, he was travelling on excursion trains to matches in Dublin. Soccer featured strongly in his table talk at home. In adult life, he retained his interest in Athlone soccer: this writer recalls meeting him at a law lecturers' conference in the 1980s, where the topic of conversation quickly turned from the conference deliberations to the current fortunes of Athlone Town FC, on which he proved well informed.

In the 1960s there was little adult organisation of schoolboy soccer in Athlone. An early manifestation of Brian Junior's administrative capability was his recruitment and management of a schoolboy team in the Retreat area. The team was based at Ardagh Lodge, the home of his grandfather, 'Pop' Devine. The residence had a large disused tennis court at the rear, which provided the home ground for East End United, as Brian named his team. The team headquarters was in a disused kitchen at the back of the house. Brian's coordination was poor, preventing him from emulating his father as a star player, but he certainly enjoyed the game. He particularly revelled in the role of manager, organising training sessions, keeping a roll of those who attended, arranging fixtures with teams from other parts of the town, such as Coosan and Tormey Villas, and supervising match preparations. All this was done with great intensity of purpose, attention to detail, drive and determination, an early manifestation of some of the characteristics that marked his later career.

Commuting to Dublin virtually daily and servicing the sprawling Roscommon-Leitrim constituency at weekends was physically exhausting, especially in the pre-motorway era. In 1971, after Brian Senior had suffered a health scare, the family decided to re-settle in Dublin. His mother, Ann, did not regret the change, preferring the anonymity of Castleknock to the small-town intimacy of Athlone, where, as the minister's wife, she was constantly on parade. But Brian

Junior hated leaving Athlone, vowing as he went that when he grew up he would 'run away' to Athlone. In fact, the time was probably right for him to make the change. He had just completed primary school and for a teenage boy of his promise the twin experiences of Dublin and Belvedere were probably a more appropriate challenge than the provincial environment of Athlone. He did, of course, return as an adult visitor and could point out without difficulty the many haunts of his youth. According to his mother, he considered Athlone to have been his true home and he cherished the memory of his childhood there throughout his life.[1]

14 A MONUMENT BROUGHT DOWN BY GARGOYLES

MARIE LOUISE O'DONNELL

HE WAS SITTING LOW in a black Mondeo. A lopsided, leaning boyish form looking keenly out the window, as the car swerved into the car park. It circled around, spotted me standing hoping to be noticed, parked awkwardly at the far corner, and waited for a moment. Then he got out of the car.

He walked in my direction with a kind of dishevelled order and a slight sideways limp. He was grand looking and handsome. Not an offensive or disgruntled grin in sight. Soft baby features, oil black hair and a wide evident smile. A centurion, in the making.

'Hello you must be Marie Louise,' he said.

'Yes Minister,' I replied.

'Ah stop all that,' he said, 'call me Brian. I hear you want to spend some time with me in the area.'

'Yes, and maybe we could talk.'

'Talk ! Not sure I'm good at that.' He laughed as he opened the pub / restaurant door. I found a table and ordered some tea.

'Excuse me,' said a middle aged man, as he sidled slyly in our direction,

'I want a word with Brian.'

'Hold on a minute Marie Louise, I have to talk to someone over there.' Brian said, and he was gone.

It gave me a chance to look around, and to watch him across the pub cuddled into a table, bending in evident pain, and whispering to the gathered conclave. A filmic moment, from the core and the heartbeat of all true Lenihan politics. The shape and sound of what he had learned at his father's knee.

He returned to the table, all business, anxious to tell me how things really were, how his analysis, and only his analysis of the national financial engulfing problem, was the route to the solution. I was all business too, so I asked him to explain his historic pen. The pen that protected banking incompetence, and financially finished off the ordinary citizen for the next few decades.

'Historic pen,' he exclaimed 'I thought you came here to learn something about Dublin West. Historic pen,' he repeated to himself, as he ushered me out of the door and towards the car.

'Get in and I'll show you around. Don't tell anybody I let you into the car. It would be all over the papers. Security, and all of that stuff.'

I sat in, and we began our journey around his political background. Brian in the front like a young boy on a new world holiday, marvelling and pointing at the shopping centres, and at the sprawling new, newer and newest flat treeless housing estates.

We drove on past Draiocht, Blanchardstown Library and Hospital, past rugby, soccer and GAA sports clubs, past the Institute of Technology, the Quinn Tower, the high-tech pharmaceutical factories, and the Crown Plaza Hotel. Past built and rebuilt primary and secondary schools, and around, across and through, a growing thriving, mini-city.

'I have lived here for 39 years,' he began. 'I came here when I was twelve. This is my home and my life. I love this part of the city. I was involved from the beginning, twenty-five years building a good Dublin 15 structure. This is an ethnically and socially diverse area, from the well-manicured lawns of Castleknock right across to Mulhuddart.' And he laughed as he used the word manicured.

'What's funny?' I ask.

'Ah! That word manicured. People love using it, especially when they are talking about Castleknock. It always makes me laugh. It's not true at all.'

He paused looking out the window, and breathing gently down through his own personal memory.

'My father was here in 1992. Now in 2011 there are only about 1,500 of his voters left. There are huge changes here.'

He remained silent, as the satellite painting of another and new Dublin went by. Sitting down low and awkwardly in the car, he absorbed the sight of every road, avenue, alleyway, roundabout, lane, gate and hedge with sheer delight and enthusiasm, speaking as the true architect and designer of the young city at the end of his national garden. A gap appeared in his Dublin West travel guide. I took my chance.

'How do you answer the public anger at Fianna Fáil? The public anger at you. What do you say to all of that?'

I ask as we twist around the abundant roundabouts, my voice pitching high and anxious, and in direct contrast to his throaty whisper. I want him to be more urgent, more revealing and more answerable. I do not want to go on a horsey horsey journey, with no direction.

'That won't get me anywhere,' he says. 'Somebody has to pick up the pieces. There must be a reduction in living standards if there is to be a future for children. Our problem is that we do not have average living standards when compared with Europe. Ours are so high. Fianna Fáil will be punished, that's for sure, but I have very little faith in opportunist politics. I have even less faith in opportunist promises. I feel I personally worked very hard for the country and for my constituency. The people are capable of dividing personnel allegiance. The decline did not begin with me, far from it. The party actually began to decline during the Haughey era, then through Albert, and finally with Bertie, who tried very hard to mask it.

It is very hard for me to comment on those who ran away from their desks. I will not comment on it. I have a grudging respect for those who are giving up their pensions, and staying here.

Politics is not easy. I see it as a vocation. It is a calling, not a career. I have much more than just a generic passion and interest in Ireland. I read avidly about Ireland. As a lawyer, I feel that I was and I am, in a strong position to settle cases. I feel that I have a balanced view and

I am very capable of giving advice.'

'But are you capable of taking it?' I ask. He ignores the question for a minute.

'In this state,' he continues, 'there are 1.5 million people working. That's good advice. We do not know about the economic challenges of the thirties.'

'But your narrative is that we all partied.' I say 'and it isn't true. I was not at any party.' (Not admitting to my house extension, which was priced like a Trump Tower apartment and the builder is bankrupt and in Brazil.)

'We did party,' he insists 'there were children in helicopters making their communion. I feel that people during the Celtic Tiger retreated into a private space and lost an interest in public space and civic spirit. We cannot continue an incantation of the past. A new Ireland must ask the question as to how we can rebuild civic personal pride.'

'When will we get out of this?' I ask.

'We will get out of it when we adjust,' he answers 'When we come to terms with the mismanagement and squander. But nobody wants to talk about adjustment. In Ireland there is a kind of controlled lawlessness. Politics has to change. There is great reform on the way. There is a changed character going into politics. Politics needs to adapt to the people out there. Politics is really about the long distance runner. Micheál Martin came into politics 1985, Enda Kenny in 1975, Mary Hanafin in 1985, John Bruton in 1969. I came in 1974 and I only got a cabinet position in 2007, thirty-three years later. It is about long distance runners. That is what we all are, long distance runners.'

I am losing him in the poetic description and knowledge of political history. He will not open up on the now and the why of now.

'I loved working in Justice,' he continues. 'I was asked to take on Finance in 2008. I learned quickly. I never felt that I had been given or had taken up a poisoned chalice. I felt it was a challenge. There is good politics in good times and hard times.'

'But from Justice to Finance?' I question. 'It had to have been the greatest disaster considering what you faced, what you signed, and what you found out.'

'Listen,' he says undaunted, 'they think I know nothing about figures and that the portfolio is above me. They forget that I had lectured in law and more importantly in commercial law generally, so I did know about figures.'

We continue to drive fast and furiously across the plains of Dublin West. General Election posters appear everywhere, like ignorant leaves on steel trees. Faces, staring out in fright, fear and fakery. On some lamp posts Brian's head has been cut out, with circular spherical precision, leaving a perfect hole for us to see through.

'Ah ha!' he laughs undaunted, 'my face is whipped out on many of the posters. Modern Art eh! It will probably end up at some parties in the area after the election.'

We stop at Archbishop Troy Bridge in Carpenterstown. 'Come on,' he says, 'let me show you something.'

He gets out of the car with difficulty and limps slowly towards the railings to steady himself. I pretend not to notice. We stand and look down past the double track train line.

'You can see Farmleigh from here. I am steeped in this area from the Phoenix Park to the Meath border, bred to it. A new city in fifty years. Imagine that. My father worked here. He had a slogan. "*The team that's best for Dublin West.*" I liked that slogan and I particularly like the slogan that says "*Ignore all the promises – examine the facts!*" That's what we all should do, examine the facts. We have a very informed electorate. I can rely on the facts.'

And he stares into the distance.

It was a breezy day and we watched the trees in the distance waving at us and the dotted straight lined and cul-de-sac estates, peeping out in-between the greenery. We looked over the bridge like children searching for something. I far more lost than him, although he did not know it and with much more futility. He stared in a kind of wonder and perceptive silence and I knew he was miles away from the grey suits of Finance and the untruths that the banking ink pots had revealed. Then on an unprompted breeze, he said,

'I know I am unwell. I have a serious cancer. Sometimes when I go into the Mater Hospital for my treatment and there are other patients waiting, I can see the pain and the worry on their faces. I feel very sorry for them. I want to be able to help them, to give them some comfort, to share the reserves that I have, to get them through their suffering and fear.'

'What do you mean by reserves ?' I ask quietly.

'Reserves, I have spiritual reserves. Plenty of them. They are part of me. Don't write that down, they'll say I'm overly religious.'

'Are you afraid?' I ask only because I am afraid myself.

'No, I am not afraid. I have learned not to be afraid. There is nothing to be afraid of. That is what spiritual reserve has taught me. Politics has taught me this also. In politics, I have learned that you can never be fixed or disconnected. You have to renew yourself. There are politicians that are obsessed with consistency. They cannot live with a change of mind or situation, or loss of face. This is ridiculous. We must keep responding to the crisis like we do to the weather. Spiritual reserves are about renewal.'

I do not know what to say or ask. I continue to look at the distance, a much weaker and more fragile person than the one who is slowly losing his life's breath to the wind.

We return to the pub, where we began our journey.

'Fair dues to your balls Brian that you cut the dole,' says a hardshaw coming out of the pub, nicely plastered in the late sun afternoon.

Brian laughs 'I love the Dubliners, they will always tell you the truth, I have enjoyed myself greatly,' he says.

'I feel I know you,' I say sounding a bit familiar.

'You do, do you?' He laughs, sounding surprised, 'I'm not too sure about that!'

And he was right.

I did not know him at all. What I knew or thought I knew was the Lenihan legacy and the televised minister. What I met was a unique intelligence. An intelligence uninterrupted by the trappings and carpets of office. A man with a different approach to the persuade of power with the capacity for duty unparalleled and with an unyielding courage to stand on any bridge, face his own mortality and fading heartbeat, and not run away.

15 A CALL TO PATRIOTIC ACTION

FEARGAL O'ROURKE

WHILE REVIEWING IRISH TAXATION policy is something which I publicly do on an annual basis during the budgetary and Finance Act cycle in my role as head of tax in PwC, this piece is different. Firstly, it is a retrospective look at some of the most dramatic budgetary events in my professional lifetime through the prism of hindsight. Usually such reviews are contemporaneous with the budget cycle. Secondly the man and the minister who was at the helm in the Department during the most tumultuous financial times since the foundation of the State was my cousin. This does not make me blinkered – there were times when we disagreed on taxation matters. However, my admiration for him as a person of integrity, of intellect and of selflessness remains undiminished today.

Growing up, it was clear to me, and to all of the 'Lenihan' cousins, that Brian was going to be the one who would be a torch bearer for our generation. As I grew interested in reading about American politics in my teens, it struck me that we all viewed Brian in probably the same way that the Kennedys viewed Joe Kennedy Junior – the leader of the next generation who appeared to us to have the skills and the commitment to public service that would see him make a mark on society.

My mum was the youngest of four Lenihans and their children, my cousins, broadly speaking arrived in three 'waves.' Brian was part of the first wave, the cousins who were four or five years older and always seemed to be doing something exciting. Brian was five years older than me and I was part of the second wave along with Brian's brother Conor who was a little over a year older than me.

It's fair to say that Brian and Conor were different characters in their outlook and approach. Even physically, Brian was a Lenihan and Conor was a Devine. When I was in my early teens, one of the highlights for me was going up to Castleknock for a week to stay with the Lenihans. While Castleknock then was a little bit on the outskirts of Dublin, it was still a world removed from the Athlone of the mid-to-late 70s with multi-channel television, pirate radio stations and trips into the city on the 39A bus.

Even then I can recall Brian as a serious teenager, dressed way too sensibly, discussing wide ranging historical topics with Brian Senior ranging from the Anglo-Irish negotiations of 1921, the Franco-Prussian war of the nineteenth century and Garibaldi's role in the foundation of Italy. I must confess that while part of me wanted to listen in on these discussions, I did find myself more drawn to Conor's rebellious streak, including his frequent and loud playing of the Stranglers 'No More Heroes' album with its (even now) 'out there' lyrics.

Brian's progression through Trinity, Cambridge and the Bar with flying colours was no surprise to any of us. When the by-election arose in 1996 on the death of his father, it was obvious to all of us that if a family member were to run, it would be Brian. (Conor was to get elected the following year in the neighbouring Dublin South West). While he was not the favourite to win the seat – Fianna Fáil did not have a great record in by-elections in this period – his ability to win transfers from a wide range of candidates saw him elected.

Again, the career progression that followed surprised none of the cousins. Chairman of the All Party Oireachtas Committee on the Constitution, followed by Minister of State for Children in 2002 and then his appointment as Minister for Justice in 2007, a position also held by his father. This is where Brian was destined to be and during that period his passion for the post was clearly evident.

However, his tenure there lasted less than a year when newly-elected Taoiseach Brian Cowen appointed him to the post of Finance

Minister. I have to confess my initial thought on hearing the news was one of surprise. I had always felt he was 'made' for Justice and despite my background in the financial world, any discussions we had on taxation or budgetary policy were at a very broad high level. I recall meeting him very early on and telling him laughingly that I had been in the taxation world long before he arrived in Finance and expected to be there long after he left, so he was not to muck it up!

But he was never going to do that. The pros and cons of the bank guarantee will be examined and argued over for years to come and I do not propose to go into that here. But on general fiscal and taxation matters, I believe history will treat his tenure well.

Meeting Brian in those early months, I never ceased to be amazed by how quickly he was getting to grips with his brief in true barrister fashion. Over a short few months, his observations became more focussed and detailed. He devoured the briefings and papers given to him and outside the Department had a small number of friends and acquaintances in the financial and business world that he used as sounding boards. As they will testify, it was quite common to get a call at any point up to midnight when he was heading home after another day of crisis and he wanted to talk. In fact I'd say most of our interactions came outside normal working hours! Sometimes he had questions. Sometimes he just wanted to talk about an issue out loud and explain where he was coming from and just have you listen. Sometimes he was arguing a position where you knew he believed the opposite, but he wanted you to try and deconstruct it. He loved to intellectually engage.

His questions were not only about the theory of tax, but how things were likely to play out in the real world. On taxation matters he was fortunate to have the benefit of a very small group of excellent civil servants, including one in particular who gave him good practical advice but also interlaced this advice with the political (with a small 'p') implications of some of the things he was considering.

Very quickly on taking office, Brian recognised the gravity of the situation which Ireland was facing and announced he was advancing the date of the annual budget from its traditional December to mid-October. The crisis seemed to sharpen his focus even more. On 14 October 2008, he delivered the first austerity budget, reversing a trend of almost two decades. Economic activity had declined in the first two quarters of the year and the Department forecasted that GNP would decline by over 1.5 per cent in 2008, the first decline since the early 1980s. (Subsequent data would show it declined by nearly 3 per cent).

One of the major issues which he was facing on the taxation side was a structural one. By 2008, two of every five income earners were not within the income tax net. For example, a minimum wage worker was comfortably outside the tax net. Taking these into account, four of every five income earners were paying tax at no more than the standard rate of tax (20 per cent). A person earning the average industrial wage (approximately €34,000 in 2008) was comfortably below the top rate threshold. However, this 'hollowing out' of the income tax base which had taken place in the good times meant that the Exchequer was relying on an ever reducing number of taxpayers to fund income tax, which was not sustainable when the economic tide turned.

Brian's philosophical view was that that any tax changes needed to be progressive and that the better off should shoulder more of the burden. He indicated that close to €2 billion in tax revenues would have to be raised to keep within fiscal targets. This budget's big change saw the introduction of a crude but effective – in terms of revenue raising and ease of collection – income levy of 1 per cent on gross income from January 2009 rising to 2 per cent on income of over €100,100 and 3 per cent on incomes over €250,120. Income of less than €18,304 was exempt from this levy. It met his desire to have something which was equitable in that it was at a higher rate for those on higher income while, at the same time, was straightforward and easy to collect.

At the time, he felt that the levy would need to stay in place for at least five years, but given the simple but effective nature of the measure, I believe we will see many more finance ministers before it is phased out.

He concluded his maiden budget speech with the phrase 'It is.... no less than a call to patriotic action,' which was met with a degree of cynicism in some quarters. But to watch him deliver these words and to speak to him about it was to see for one's own eyes that he truly believed this and was prepared to lead by example.

His second budget was delivered less than six months later on 7 April 2009 and was against the backdrop of an expected 8 per cent contraction in GNP (following on a decline of 3 per cent the previous year). He identified his first priority as stabilising the public finances. In terms of raising additional taxation, the newly-implemented income levy was doubled to 2 per cent, 4 per cent and 6 per cent and the thresholds at which it was charged were reduced. He also doubled the Health Levy rates to 4 per cent and 5 per cent and reduced the entry point for these rates.

Philosophically, Brian had grasped another structural concept that the tax code had been biased in favour of property for many years and he introduced measures which sought to reduce the tax expenditures in these areas. Specifically, he reduced the level of interest relief which a residential property landlord could use against rental income from 100 per cent of the income to 75 per cent with immediate effect. In private, he recognised that if times had been better it could have been phased in for existing second property owners such that the change would have been a tapered and gradual one, but the change was introduced with immediate effect. He now understood that had such a change been introduced in the 'good times' of the previous decade – as one of his predecessors Charlie McCreevy had tried to do with the Bacon Report – the property market could have been a lot less frothy than it was in the years leading up to the crash. So a coincidence of necessity and philosophy saw him make fundamental changes to the tax code and it will take a brave Minister for Finance who might reverse this in future years.

In a similar vein, he restricted mortgage interest relief for a principal private residence to the first seven years of a mortgage, although the impact of this was relatively limited given it had effectively been frozen in value over many years. He also abolished the low 20 per cent rate of tax from profits from dealing in residential land and terminated a number of property based tax reliefs in the health sector.

Where was he to get inspiration and support for further structural tax changes? One of the commitments of the Programme for Fianna Fáil–Green–Progressive Democrats Government in 2007 was the establishment of a new Commission on Taxation to review the efficiency and appropriateness of the Irish taxation system. This read:

> While the Commission will have a wide remit to consider the structure of the taxation system, it will be specifically charged with considering and making recommendations on the following:
>
> • Examine the balance achieved between taxes collected on income, capital and spending and report on it.
>
> • Review all tax expenditures with a view to recommending the discontinuation of those that are unjustifiable on cost/benefit grounds;
>
> • Consider options for the future financing of local government;
>
> • In the context of maintaining a strong economy, investigate fiscal measures to protect and enhance the environment, including the introduction of a carbon tax.

In late 2007 the then Finance Minister Brian Cowan asked me would I be interested in being a member of the Commission and it was formally constituted in early February 2008. However, the eighteen months between the formation of the Commission and the delivery of our report saw a dramatic change in the financial position of the country. What was meant to be a report for the Government to consider how the system could be improved became one which was cherry picked to help raise incremental tax revenues. As Brian pithily put it one evening: 'A report conceived in peacetime but delivered in war-time.'

Being a member of the Commission was one of the most interesting experiences of my professional career. Eighteen people from varied walks of life, with only a few of us having any detailed knowledge of the tax system – but everyone having strong views! Huge credit must go to the chairman, Frank Daly, who stood down as Chairman of the Revenue Commissioners to chair this commission, and his secretariat, for keeping everyone on (broadly) the one track. Brian was keenly interested in the progress of the Commission and regularly quizzed me as to how the 'big picture' things were going, although he was also interested in the personal group dynamic.

The Commission report was delivered in time for his third budget on 9 December 2009 and many of the structural changes around Carbon Tax, a Property Tax (coupled with a significant reduction in Stamp Duty) and water charges appeared in this and subsequent budgets or are earmarked for the near future.

His speech was marked by his phrase 'we have turned the corner,' which even at the time and certainly with hindsight, notwithstanding the green shoots, was premature. Progress had been made – a budgetary adjustment of more than €8 billion over the preceding eighteen months was a staggering achievement – and a further €4 billion adjustment was planned for 2010 and Brian wanted to give hope and some sense that a lot of the 'heavy lifting' had been done. There was a broad pause on the raising of personal taxes with the main change being the amalgamation of the income levy, the health levy and employee PRSI into the Universal Social Charge. It would be paid by everyone at a low rate on a wide base as a 'collective contribution to public services.'

One of the issues that he grappled with was the whole area of 'tax exiles.' These are essentially wealthy individuals who are Irish by birth and one might say inclination, but, who, while spending significant time here in any year, are able to arrange their affairs such that they do not spend sufficient time here to be resident for tax purposes. The Irish test for tax residency is an objective one which is determined by reference to the number of days which an individual spends in the State. In summary, an individual will not be tax resident in Ireland if they are here

- for fewer than 183 days in a year and

- for fewer than 280 days, in aggregate, in a tax year and the preceding tax year

This test has the benefit of clarity, but other countries apply additional qualitative criteria which broaden the scope of residency. The Commission Report concluded that the existing regime should be supplemented by additional criteria to tighten the existing arrangements for determining residence for Irish citizens. Having regard to the position in other countries, the report suggested a permanent home test coupled with a test based on an individual's centre of vital interests should be added to the tax code.

However, a directly contrary proposal was being promoted at the time which would allow such individuals to spend extra time in Ireland in a year by effectively 'buying' days. (This proposal again came to light in 2013 when the Government-backed Forum on Philanthropy put forward a similar proposal, which would see such individuals get an extra 62 days per annum in Ireland in return for investment in charities and other worthy projects).There was significant lobbying of Brian for this proposal, including politicians past and present and he told me amusing tales of being buttonholed by one or two of these individuals at various events.

Brian was genuinely torn by the contrasting recommendations. On the one hand, there was the prospect of getting additional investment into the county at a time when it was most needed. However, at a time when every taxpayer in the country was having to tighten their belts and suffer increased taxes, he recognised that the tax system not only needed to be as equitable as possible, but to be seen as equitable.

Ultimately, when faced with these divergent conflicts, he maintained the status quo by leaving things as they stood, but, at the same time, he introduced an Irish Domicile Levy, which provided that Irish nationals and domiciled individuals who had Irish assets of greater than €5 million and income of more than €1 million to pay a levy of €200,000 per annum. While the move would have helped with the optical equity of the tax system, it has not been a money spinner to date and the debate on the taxation of non-resident Irish nationals is still not a settled issue.

For high earners in Ireland he increased restrictions to ensure a higher effective rate of tax was being paid by those on very high incomes by restricting their ability to utilise tax expenditures and reliefs.

The final chapter of his budgetary times occurred in a two-week period in November-December 2010. The publication of the Four Year Plan on 24 November against the backdrop of the Troika negotiations; the finalisation of a deal on Sunday 28 November and his final budget on 7 December.

The National Recovery Plan set out what it saw as the steps necessary to overcome the economic difficulties the country was facing at the time. To put this in context, the Plan noted that the 2010 GDP and GNP levels would be some 11 per cent and 15 per cent respectively below their corresponding levels in 2007 in real terms.

Indeed, as the then Taoiseach said in the Dáil, announcing this Plan in 2010, people

> understand that the idea behind this plan is that our taxation system needs reform and we need to see increased levels of taxation coming into the national Exchequer to bring income for national purposes up to levels of the order of what we had in 2006. We also know that the level of spend in our economy has to reduce to levels people saw around 2007.

The urgency and emergency was clear.

The Plan was a substantial document and the point was made in its chapter on taxation that it placed two-thirds of the required fiscal adjustment on expenditure (€10 billion) and one third of the adjustment on taxation (€5 billion). Referring to 'Macroeconomic Effects of Fiscal Consolidation' by Daniel Leigh, IMF, the Plan noted the broad acceptance that 'that this distribution of the burden of adjustments is less damaging to our future economic prospects than if it were more heavily placed on taxation.' Therefore, the key focus was on recovery with the least amount of damage inflicted.

According to the Recovery Plan, the list of tax measures to be adopted by the Government was substantial. The summary plan noted that the Government would:

Maintain the 12.5 per cent corporation tax rate;

Raise additional revenue through income tax changes and implement pension-related tax changes;

Abolish/curtail a range of tax expenditures;

Increase the standard rate of VAT from 21 per cent to 22 per cent in 2013 with a further increase to 23 per cent in 2014;

Introduce a local services contribution to fund essential locally-delivered services;

Increase the price of carbon gradually from €15 to €30;

Reform capital acquisitions and capital gains tax;

Transform the Business Expansion Scheme (BES) into a new Business Investment Targeting Employment Scheme.

The Recovery Plan noted that over the 2010-14 period of the Plan, the top marginal rates would remain the same at 52 per cent for PAYE workers and 55 per cent for self-employed. The current Programme for Government promised to 'maintain the current rates of income tax together with bands and credits' so one could see the theme emanating from the Plan in that regard.

Prior to the Plan and the economic downturn in 2008, Irish tax receipts had been focused on property transactions so the overall intent of the Recovery Plan was to widen the tax base. As part of that process, the Plan suggested that legacy costs associated with property incentives would be phased out over the period of the Plan. Significant restrictions on the use of property based capital allowances and Section 23 type relief against rental income were included in Finance Act 2011, but these measures were deferred pending the completion of an economic impact assessment. The related assessment was published, which considered the impact of any tax changes on investors, the banks and the State and the specific sectors which benefited from the tax reliefs. Its conclusions were incorporated into the next Government's Finance Act 2012, which brought about a 5 per cent surcharge applied to certain investors who availed of property reliefs with income of at least €100,000. Investors in certain capital allowances arrangements would not be able to use the capital allowances beyond 2014 in certain circumstances, but this was determinant on the building's tax life. As noted earlier, the blueprint for all of this was written in 2010!

Financing local services was an issue highlighted by the Recovery Plan and it intended to introduce a site value tax in 2012. It also suggested an 'interim fixed "household charge" of €100 per annum in 2012.' The interim measures happened, but the site charge was not to be. That said, a Local Property Tax came about in 2012 and is still being paid by householders at the time of writing. It, like a site tax, is a tax on property, so though it has a different name, it has the same effect. However, the substantial changes to carbon tax suggested in the Plan have not yet materialised.

One of the great successes in the Troika negotiations and the aftermath was the retention of the 12.5 per cent corporation tax rate. There was significant political pressure from the Germans and the French to concede on this issue which would have been a disaster for Ireland's 'brand' in the Foreign Direct investment sector. Brian understood the importance of this issue and was helped by the unanimity of the body politic on the 12.5 per cent rate. The IMF also turned out to be helpful allies in this exercise and eventually the pressure receded.

The rate preservation statement made in the Recovery Plan is still (rightly) recognised today when the current Taoiseach recently noted that 'our 12.5 per cent corporation tax remains a cornerstone of Irish industry policy.' This is the mantra which has been adopted since the 12.5 per cent rate came about in 2003 and, ten years on, it is not for turning. The maintaining of the rate was, is and will continue to be a red line issue for Ireland and when it was tested in the fire in 2010, Brian was equal to the task.

They say hindsight is 20/20, but one could make the same comment for foresight by the architects of the Recovery Plan given the changes brought about since the Plan was published. While some changes made were not a part of the Plan the inspiration behind some of those changes could be traced back to the pages of the 2010 document. The clue was in the title National Recovery Plan and three years on Ireland is now exiting the bailout programme.

In effect, the tax aspects of the plan were implemented by Brian in his last budget and by his successor Minister Michael Noonan over the subsequent three budgets.

Would Ireland have been in a position to exit the Bailout in December 2013 without the Lenihan budgets from October 2008 to December 2010? I believe the budgetary adjustments of that period were critical to Ireland's fiscal survival. Between the October 2008 budget and the December 2010 budget, the Exchequer savings between expenditure and revenues were in the region of €20 billion or over 12 per cent of GDP. But the tax raising was done by imposing the biggest burden on the more well off and the OECD reported that Ireland's tax system was the most progressive in the EU which reflected Brian's philosophy.

Minister Michael Noonan deserves much credit for piloting Ireland out of the bailout programme, but it was good to see at the time of the exit that some commentators recalled who had done the early 'heavy lifting.' Indeed, I have heard Minister Noonan say publicly on more than one occasion that while he disagreed with Brian on banking issues, he believed that his approach to fiscal consolidation was critically important in stabilising the national finances.

Perhaps I can finish with my fondest personal memory of that period. On a bright August Sunday in 2010 my wife Maeve and my two young children Jennifer and Sam got into our car to drive from Dublin down to Béal na Bláth. Brian was to be the first Fianna Fáil politician to address the Michael Collins commemoration. It was a glorious day and as we drove down the narrow roads to the memorial, the sense of occasion was palpable. Here were well over 2,000 people, not from his political tradition, but who were happy to welcome him to one of the most iconic sites of Irish history.

On that glorious day, the economic woes and Brian's health were put to one side and for a few hours all things seemed possible. The genuine affection in which Brian was held by the almost exclusively Fine Gael audience was testament to his standing right across the political spectrum. Brian was swamped by people at the end of his speech and I caught his eye and waved to him.

On the way home, we stopped at Bullys in Douglas, a good family restaurant, where for a treat the kids tucked into pizza and burgers and chips with some gusto. The mobile phone rang and it was Brian, clearly on a high after the occasion.

Fifteen minutes later he ambled into the restaurant and in true Cork fashion, no one blinked an eye. He sat down but announced he was not hungry and would not order anything. Then, in a manner recognisable by many of his friends, he proceeded to graze off all our plates as a wide ranging conversation ensued.

The kids had seen Brian on the television many times and had met him a few times, but they seemed fascinated by this man so clearly full of life but also a little miffed that he was tucking into their treat! While he was under pressure to head back up towards Dublin for a function, he was clearly at ease and stayed for about an hour until we all finished. We chatted a while more on the street and off he went into the evening.

We hoped we would have many such more evenings in the future, but it was not to be. Less than a year later as we walked behind his coffin, I recalled that day and the oft quoted Shakespeare lines from Romeo and Juliet:

> When he shall die,
> Take him and cut him out in little stars,
> And he will make the face of heaven so fine
> That all the world will be in love with night
> And pay no worship to the garish sun.

Why did the public hold one of the most severe Ministers for Finance in such high regard, as evidenced in part by the fact that he was the only Fianna Fáil TD elected in the capital in the 2011 election? The Brian I knew wanted to do what was right for the country, was warm, gregarious, intelligent and obviously passionate about his county and conveyed that passion when he spoke. He was clearly selfless and put the country first. That is the Brian I believe the public also saw. His family and the country are the poorer for his passing.

16 THE BREEN I KNEW – AB INITIO

MARY O'ROURKE

LET ME BEGIN AT the beginning. Breen Lenihan was the first born child of Brian Lenihan and Ann Devine. Brian Lenihan (Senior) was the first of four children of father and mother, Patrick Lenihan and Annie Scanlan. He was working in the Revenue Department and she had trained as a teacher, but at that time when you married you left teaching.

Patrick Lenihan's first posting was to Dundalk where in jig time my mother had her first child, who was Brian Lenihan, followed closely by a second son, Patrick Lenihan. Their journey then took them to Tralee, Dublin and Athlone in that order. In my father's job he got transferred to Tralee, where my sister, Anne, was born and then on to Dublin Castle and their life in Sutton, in County Dublin, where it appears I was conceived.

But, then on to Athlone where I was born and that completed the family – Brian, Paddy, Anne and myself.

Brian (Senior) went to the Marist Brother's College in Athlone, primary and post primary, and early on was marked out as gold medal material, winning prizes both in the study halls and on the fields of play. He was an all-rounder – a golden boy.

Later on, he went to UCD where he studied Law and in time began to practice as a Barrister on the Midland Circuit.

He started to date a young girl called Ann Devine, who was a student in UCG studying medicine. Ann was regarded as the Belle of Athlone and the most desirable and sought after young girl for all of the young swains to follow. He quickly established he was serious about her and in time they got engaged and then got married on 12 August 1958.

There was a great future mapped out for him. By now, beyond the budding stage barrister, he was well recognised and busy. He had also run as a very young man as a sweeper candidate for Fianna Fáil in Longford-Westmeath with Joe Kennedy and Frank Carter, so he was legally busy, politically busy and now a young married man living in Athlone in St. Mary's Place.

Nine months later, on 21 May 1959, young Breen arrived. Their gorgeous first-born and for all of us a child to wonder at and to love.

They were a lively young couple and he was a lovely baby for them both, following a very difficult pregnancy for Ann.

Breen in turn went to the Marist Boy's Primary School in Athlone. But prior to that, he attended the Fair Green Infant's School which was under the tutelage of the nuns from the Bower Convent – the order of La Sainte Union.

Again, Breen was the golden boy as a lovely nun in the Bower Convent liked to recite, Sister Thecla, and again in the Marist Boy's National School.

So life went on, we all got married and had children and Brian Senior's political life went on through several ministries and still the family continued to live in Athlone. Then came 1971, when Brian Senior and his family decided to move to Dublin. Brian was finding it increasingly tiring juggling the demands of running a government department in Dublin and commuting back and forth to the family home in Athlone. After some soul-searching, it was decided that it would be easier to move the family to Dublin and that Brian would try to spend as much time as possible at weekends in his Roscommon constituency. At this stage, they had Breen, Conor and Niall (in the interim period there had been the very sad death of five-year-old little Mark Lenihan).

Breen had just finished primary school and was twelve years of age when the family took the difficult decision to move to Dublin so there was all the fuss of buying a house and moving and all of that. Of course, we were sorry to see them leave Athlone, but the rest of us had families and children and were so occupied.

From early on, Brian's wife, Ann, became one of my dearest women friends. We soldiered together through many events in their life and in my life and I always found her a true, true person.

In anticipation of the trip to Dublin, Ann and Brian decided that Breen would attend the Jesuit College, Belvedere in Dublin and that Conor would attend the Prep School for Belvedere, the Belvedere Primary School. When both parents went to speak to the school head, he explained that most of the boys who would be coming into Belvedere for first year Secondary would have studied Latin and French in the last class in Belvedere Primary.

Ann worried about this and not to be outdone, came to see me and asked me if I would take Breen for Latin lessons that summer when he was twelve years of age and had finished in the Primary Marist Boys. She also asked Brian's mother, who lived in Athlone, if she would teach young Breen French.

So began that odyssey of exploration for young Breen and of a deepening in love of me for him.

He would come down on his bicycle to me say for 3 o'clock in the afternoon. At this time I had two boys – Feargal and Aengus, much younger than him, but able to be playing about on their own and they knew enough that it was my tutoring time. Breen would come on the bicycle and sit opposite the table from me and I can see yet his round earnest face and his eagerness to learn. Like any teacher (and I was at this time a teacher in a girls secondary school in Athlone), I always prepared my lessons overnight. I had started my teaching career by teaching Latin, but by this time it was long gone out of most of the second-level schools in Ireland, but obviously in some schools like the Jesuit and other boys colleges, it was still relevant.

I had kept my Longman's Latin Grammar which was the Bible for teachers of Latin. I would prepare a chapter each day that Breen was coming to his lesson and I would go over it very well and then we would have our lesson and oh, he was a joy to teach. He would, in turn, have studied beforehand what we had done but I invariably found that we would finish the lesson much quicker than I would have thought and he would say: 'Let's go to the next chapter Aunt Mary, Let's go to the next chapter,' but like any teacher I had only prepared for one lesson so I would say: 'No, we'll go over it again, we'll go over it again' and so we did. He would leave me and cycle up to his Grandma's and she would do her French with him. (Incidentally, on a note, my mother at her Matric had got first place in Ireland in French before she went into UCG). Breen always maintained that she was a far easier teacher because after about half an hour she would say: 'Oh it's a lovely day, we will go out and sit in the sun' and they would have glasses of lemonade, but they would do their oral French so maybe she had a method in that also.

So the Lenihan family packed their bags and went to Dublin. Of course I continued my friendship with them. As a minor point of interest, Ann always told me then and always repeats it that when young Breen went into Belvedere, he was better than most of the others at Latin and French and we always took a little secret bow of pride about all that.

Time went on and the two families remained very close, particularly through their children. My eldest son, Feargal, was a year and a half younger than Conor and my second son, Aengus, would have been friendly with another one of the Lenihan siblings so in that way the two families remained close with frequent trips to Dublin and frequent trips by the Lenihan children down to stay with Aunt Mary in Athlone and so it went through the childhood years.

I kept a keen eye on Breen, part aunt and part teacher and we delighted in his scholastic plaudits at both Belvedere and later on in Trinity College.

He was the golden boy all over again – Brian's eldest son.

In due time he became a scholar of Trinity following his law studies and then got a scholarship to Cambridge. From there, he went on to study for the Bar and again it was roses all the way.

He appeared to have a great facility for studying without being overwhelmed by it and without being too bookish.

Along the way, he always took an interest in Dublin West in his father's constituency and when Brian Senior's health deteriorated and he went to the Mayo Clinic for a liver transplant, young Breen took over the marshalling and organising of the General Election of 1989. Brian Senior won his seat while he was still in the Mayo Clinic and returned to Dáil Éireann to huge acclamation.

He lived six good years after the transplant and during this time young Breen more and more took the reins of attending to the constituency and to local political matters from his father's shoulders.

So much intervened with the Presidential Election, the replacement of Charlie Haughey by Albert Reynolds, the deposing of Albert Reynolds – all of the other extraneous political matters, but my topic for this essay is the times and themes of Breen Lenihan so I intend to concentrate on that.

Brian Senior sadly died in November 1995. In 1986 Breen Junior had married Patricia Ryan, a legal graduate like himself.

Breen was nominated by the Dublin West Constituency to run to fill his father's seat, which he did in the early spring of 1996. It was round about this time also that people began to call him 'Brian' Lenihan so from now in this narrative, I will call him Brian as well or Brian Junior. We were very content at this outcome. I was in charge of Laurel Lodge in Dublin West as a Dáil deputy in Bertie Ahern's opposition at that time. I was also Deputy Leader of Fianna Fáil. I was very active for the by-election and Laurel Lodge was a big urban district and we worked very hard in that by-election on Brian Junior's behalf. He worked very hard himself in an old-fashioned political sense – going to the churches, meeting the people, canvassing door to door, all of the detail of a by-election passed along very swiftly.

I discovered that Brian was very good under pressure. There were many large public meetings about a particular issue in the constituency when all of the TDs and would-be TDs were lined up and the people there would naturally be very anxious and, in some instances, overwrought and disturbed about something that was going on. Brian, because of his legal training, which gave him a clear brain, was able to always sum up the protests, put them in a coherent fashion, lay out what could be done and what could not be done and generally people coming out of meetings like that seemed satisfied that they had got their worth out of Brian Lenihan. That seems crude, just put plainly down like that, but that is exactly what happened on at least two or three occasions during that by-election.

He settled in very well to be a loyal backbench TD under Bertie Ahern as Taoiseach in waiting. John Bruton, Dick Spring and Proinsias De Rossa were the Coalition Government of the day – the Rainbow Coalition.

It was at this time that the bond between Brian Junior and myself grew much stronger. We were work colleagues under the one roof at Leinster House and while I was immensely senior to him in years and, I suppose, in experience, somehow he always seemed to me to have wisdom and knowledge in abundance. We had many conversations and cups of coffee along the way leading up to the General Election of 1997. That glorious June, Fianna Fáil returned to government and in the newspapers there was much talk that Brian Lenihan would get a Ministry or a Junior Ministry, but it was not to be. He fully understood, as did I, that at that time he was just a year in office and Bertie Ahern had the cautious approach that in general he would promote people who had served at least one term, but he did give Brian a very good committee appointment which truly mirrored his legal experience and gave him full rein to exercise his knowledge. He appointed him Chairman of the Constitutional Committee and in this role Brian excelled.

From 1997 to 2002 Brian happily undertook the Chairman's duties of the Constitutional Committee and they issued many reports. It was an all-party committee and it was run very much on all-party lines. Brian was fortunate in that Jim O'Keeffe, who had previously been the chairman, remained a member of the committee and he and Brian struck up a great friendship. (Just to digress, in fact, it was Jim O'Keeffe who later, when Brian was Minister for Finance, brought the invitation to Brian from west Cork from the Collins family to invite him to come to Béal na Bláth and speak on the anniversary of Michael Collins's assassination).

In January 2001, my dear darling Enda passed away. I have written extensively about this matter in my own book, *Just Mary*. But all my friends and family rallied to me. I missed Enda hugely and found life hard coming into the empty house on my own with not having my best friend, my husband, my lover to be with me. I found it a huge deprivation. So much so that my heart was not in the 2002 General Election campaign. The result was that I lost my seat and went into the Seanad as Leader of Seanad Éireann. After the 2002 General Election, Brian was appointed Minister for Children by the then Taoiseach, Bertie Ahern. He moved into an office in Leinster House which was next door to my office. During this period, we developed a very close, personal friendship. He would come into my office in the morning where Eamon McCormack and Lisa would be in the outside office and he would say: 'Is the Senator here?' in a semi-joking tone and they would say 'yes' and he would knock on my door and in he would come and we would sit down and we would talk and talk. Yes, the gossip of the Dáil, yes the gossip of the party, but our talk often strayed into family matters, into serious matters of history and literature. I so relished the physical closeness of our two offices together and the way our friendship blossomed during that period.

I am aware that Senator Jillian van Turnhout has written extensively on Brian's period as Minister for Children so I will not go into it. This was also the time of the breaking of the Church / child sex scandals and I would observe the various deputations which would troop into his office in Dáil Éireann. I know he took immense care and expressed great concern during that period.

In 2005, Bertie Ahern elevated Brian's role as Minster for Children to the cabinet table. Although Brian was not a full cabinet member and could not vote at cabinet, he attended all cabinet meetings. He took to government like a duck to water and continued on his path of reform in that section of the Department of Health, which encompassed the office of Children.

Then we had the 2007 General Election which Bertie Ahern, against all the odds, won again – his third win in a row. This was against the backdrop of great unease throughout the country and within the party about the various financial shenanigans in which Bertie was involved, the speeches and whip-rounds and a tearful interview with Bryan Dobson. Despite all of that, Bertie triumphed and he appointed Brian to be Minister for Justice – his first big, major portfolio. I know he was very moved about this because he spoke to me about his own father, Brian Senior, who had been the Minister for Justice and for whom Brian had a huge regard and affection. He was happy to get justice and he worked well in it with the civil service and with the party.

Of course, we know now the financial storm clouds were gathering in the US particularly and throughout the world. There is so much more I could write about this, but I do not want to take up my space.

Then came the resignation of our Taoiseach and the unanimous declaration of Brian Cowen as our new leader of Fianna Fáil and, therefore, Taoiseach. I maintained in my book, *Just Mary*, that Brian Cowen's elevation was that of a reluctant Taoiseach.

Anyway, in May 2008, over that weekend, prior to the announcement of the new cabinet, there was huge speculation that Brian would be the Tánaiste and various other guesses. However, I was sitting in my backbench seat, delighted to be back in Dáil Éireann after 2007, when Brian Cowen led his team down the steps and we saw Brian Cowen, Mary Coughlan, whom we knew immediately was Tánaiste, followed by Brian Lenihan as Finance and so on.

Brian took over the reins of Finance when, as he put it himself, the building boom and the revenues had come to 'a shuddering halt.' Very quickly Brian discovered that the clouds which seemed so far away in the UK and the US were now gathering for us in Ireland and he moved swiftly forward with his budgets. He delivered the first 'Emergency Budget', as it was called on 14 October 2008.

Before that, of course, came the drama of the night of 29 September 2008 and of the bank bailout. Brian, as Minister for Finance, learned quickly, moved quickly and acted calmly. He was a great believer in explaining what he was doing as he went along. The bank guarantee passed the Dáil and we know the various books and articles which have been written about it.

In December 2009, Brian began to feel bad and attended the Mater. The budget in early December, again, was carried in the Dáil and received a mixed but favourable reception in the press and with the public.

The news that Brian was suffering from pancreatic disease was very distressing. To me, Brian had become much more than a nephew or a work colleague; he had become a dear, dear friend.

Around this time, he had slipped into the habit of calling me on the telephone most weekends, maybe on a Saturday, maybe on a Sunday. In the midst of the financial turmoil he would talk to me, not about what he was going to do, because he was always very punctilious in that regard, but used me as a sort of a sounding board I think. I was an older person who had been through quite a lot in life and he was glad to have someone to sound off with.

As New Year 2010 dawned, Brian went on to the RTÉ *News at One* show with Sean O'Rourke and gave a lengthy interview in which, I do not use the words lightly, the sheer nobility and the hugely open and generous nature of the man was laid bare.

Can you imagine how difficult that must have been for him? Yet he spoke with such grace and elegance that it appeared effortless, but, of course, effortless it was not.

He spoke with courage and composure about where the tumour lay – at the neck of the pancreas and on a major blood vessel.

Of course, hope springs eternal in the human heart and through that spring of 2010 we began to hope, as Brian looked good and went about his daily work, and seemed to do so much that, perhaps, he was such a strong spirit and that perhaps he would surmount the cancer.

Brian continued on with his work. I continued my role as a very active backbencher.

At the August weekend of 2010, we had a very happy interlude for the family in Athlone. The local Lough Ree Yacht Club, of which my father had been a strong member, invited Brian down to re-launch my father's sailing boat called *The 67*. Brian came down with his wife, Patricia and with Tom and Clare and stayed in The Hodson Bay Hotel for two days. It was a very happy time and Brian walked from the Hodson Bay down to see his uncle, Paddy, with whom he had a great rapport. They sat and talked and talked. Looking back on that happy August weekend, it seemed a fairy tale time. The sun shone, everyone had a good time and definitely hope sprung in all of us that now, perhaps, Brian had seen off his deadly cancer.

That weekend in August had a dream-like quality for all of us and particularly, I imagine for Brian – the lovely trip on the lake; the launch of *The 67*; the coming together of old friends; the rare let-up in public pressure; the delicious meal in relaxed company in the Wineport Lodge and so on for the rest of us. It was easy to forget that weekend that Brian was as ill as he was.

He had a lovely visit with my brother, Paddy, who was to die some few months later. They talked and they talked of history, of politics, of the world, of family and I felt that whole weekend must have marked a time in Brian's memory of all that was good in his life. They visited Aengus, Lisa and their young family in their home. For us, we were content that he was content.

Paddy passed away in October 2010 and Brian came down to honour his family commitments, to pay the fullest of tributes to his uncle. He came to Flynn's Funeral Home in Athlone, came to the mass the next morning, he went to the graveyard and to lunch afterwards. He paid his uncle, Paddy, and his family all the honour he could at that very sad time for them.

In August, Brian had received the invitation from Dermot Collins, the Chair of the Organising Committee for the Béal na Bláth Commemoration. As I said earlier, in this essay, Jim O'Keeffe had initially conveyed the invitation to Brian from the Béal na Bláth Committee. Brian was immensely honoured to be so invited and he accepted. I will always be glad I went to Béal na Bláth. Micheál O'Faolain, Seamus Browne and myself travelled that lovely, sunny August day to hear Brian deliver his speech.

Do I remember what Brian said on that day? No, I cannot remember the exact words but I have so many perfect pictures in my mind – of the shining Cork sun, of the strong stirring words Brian spoke and of the tumultuous surging crowds. But most of all I remember coming back to Athlone with hope in my heart.

Of course, it was not to be. We have forever those memories of that Sunday Cork visit and the generosity and love of the Cork people of that region, who came out to meet him with full hearts and hopes, to give Brian an honour which he never forgot for the rest of his very short life.

By late autumn of 2010, despite the imposition of budget after brutal budget and the enactment of a series of aggressive cuts in government spending, it became clear that a new crisis point had been reached for Ireland.

By the beginning of November, it seemed that no one in the international financial markets was prepared to loan money to Ireland. Other European Ministers were putting Brian Lenihan under increasing pressure to accept a Bailout from the IMF/ECB/EU Troika, fearful that panic in Ireland might spread to other countries such as Spain and Portugal and indeed throughout Europe.

As Finance Minister, Brian Lenihan was determined to hold out for as long as he could against the pressure of seeking a bailout in order that Ireland would get the best possible terms from the Troika for the Irish people. He knew that in some ways we were in a stronger negotiation position that might have first appeared and he was intent in exploiting this advantage, however small it might be. It was a very difficult position in which to be.

It will be for others in their essays to deal in detail with that very difficult political period. Brian was under huge pressure to challenge Brian Cowen, but long years of loyalty to a leader would not allow him to do it – even though there was pressure on him to do so.

In January 2011, Micheál Martin challenged Brian Cowen and though Brian Cowen saw off that challenge he ultimately resigned a few days later. We went into that General Election knowing that we were going to be wiped out and we went from a party in the 70s to a party returning 20 TDs.

Brian retained his seat and we all felt great gratitude for the voters of Dublin West, who, despite all the calamitous financial pressure which the citizens of Ireland were undergoing, felt that they had faith in Brian Lenihan to return him to the seat that he had held and that his father had held with such honour.

I was a casualty of that election myself, but, in truth, was not a bit put out. I had had a great run at national politics. I felt I had worked hard for my constituents, worked hard for Ireland and luckily for us, Longford-Westmeath was one of the few constituencies which returned a Fianna Fáil TD so all the hard work over the years was not wasted.

Enda Kenny became Taoiseach and Eamon Gilmore Tánaiste and they slipped into the Dáil benches and the government roles easily and swiftly.

It was at this time that I started to write my own book. I continued to hear from Brian and, in March, he came down to Athlone to see myself and Paddy Cooney receive honorary degrees from the Athlone IT – in reward, they said, for the work we had carried out for and on behalf of education and, in particular, on behalf of the Athlone IT.

As well as all my own family, I invited Brian Lenihan to be my special guest and he brought Brian Murphy with him. I was always glad he came and in my mind's eye, as I write these lines, I can see him where he sat in the auditorium of the Athlone IT and the surge of delight I got when I saw him there to honour my honour which I was receiving.

The Institute of Technology were delighted to see him. He and his companion and friend that day, Brian Murphy, when I had gone home, took a drive all around Athlone and Brian showed Brian all of the sights where he went to school, where his home used to be, where he played soccer – all of the familiar places he knew as a child. It was later on that Brian Murphy told me that tale and, of course, I knew instinctively in my heart that it was Brian making his farewell visit to the town of Athlone which he truly loved and regarded as his home town.

We continued to keep in touch, mostly on the telephone to one another. I always relished his calls and would often call him back to go over a point or two again. He continued to go in and out to Dáil Éireann even though it was plain to those who saw him during this period that his health was slipping.

He always bore his illness stoically, but now there was a dignified air about him as he slipped away from all who loved him. I have written extensively about this in my book but I think I will repeat this incident again. He telephoned me one morning coming very near the end of May (he died on 10 June). His voice had got fainter like the voice of a very older person and he said to me in a puzzled tone: 'Mary, I am just up from bed. I slept all night and I am so tired, I want to go back to bed again.' I said to him, trying to be cheerful: 'Well sleep is good for one' and then I quoted the line from *Macbeth*: 'Sleep that knits up the ravell'd sleeve of care.' Brian said to me: 'Say that line again, Mary' and I did and he said: 'You were always a good teacher.' Those were the last words I had with Brian Lenihan, but his life has marked what remains of my life in a deep and personal way.

I think a lot about him and on more than one occasion, I have distinctly felt his presence with me, almost in a physical sense that he was there to be a support, a love and a help to me. On the occasions when it happened to me, it has not been frightening; rather it has been of a vibrant consoling nature.

I have to end this essay on a political note as I am writing about Brian Lenihan who, above all, was a political person. It amazes me that in all of the turmoil since the present government took office that apart from one or two references to Brian, they have never seen fit to say to the Irish people 'we are following the four-year National Recovery Plan, as laid out by Brian Lenihan'. I hold and treasure that plan.

Rather the present government would wish to denigrate the previous government and in many instances they have grounds on which they can do so. However, I am always disturbed that Micheál Martin, as leader of the party, never stands up for Brian or defends his memory in Dáil Éireann.

But on the work of Brian Lenihan, the government has no grounds to fault him. He worked for Ireland, he gave his life for Ireland and I say that not in a maudlin sense but in the real meaning of patriotism.

In the spring/summer/autumn of 2013, I did a lot of travelling around Ireland. I was fortunate to be invited to many literary festivals and gatherings of different kinds. Everywhere I went, people asked about Brian Lenihan. So many said he would have been a great leader for this country – someone for whom we would have respect. Throughout Ireland there is a genuine respect for him and a genuine sorrow at how quickly he passed away. He was truly a special person – a Lost Leader.

Requiescat in pace.

17 UNPRECEDENTED CIRCUMSTANCES

EAMON RYAN

I FIRST GOT TO know Brian Lenihan during the five years between 2002 and 2007 when I was sitting on the Opposition benches. I would pass him as we walked through on different sides of a Dáil vote, always with the customary nod which is the tradition in Leinster House. From the brief chats we did have I was uncertain what to make of him. He had a slightly distracted listening style. His glasses would be taken on and off as his gaze darted in different directions. You would find out weeks later in some follow-on conversation that he had, in fact, taken in everything you had said with an uncanny total recall. Other than that, I only had the same pen picture the public would have had of him. The sense that he had inherited the intellectual capability of his father and that some long standing internal Fianna Fáil feud had held him back from the senior ministry he seemed to deserve.

I got to know him a bit better in our first year in government together, but he was sitting at the far end of the cabinet table and our paths did not necessarily cross that often. The one exception was around our negotiations on the new Civil Partnership Bill. I found Brian Lenihan had an open mind and was someone you could work with. He was willing to pick up an idea and run with it, without the insecurities that someone less gifted might harbour in taking up someone else's suggestion.

In the summer of 2008 he moved to the seat directly opposite me as he took charge of the Finance ministry. He landed there at the very moment the Irish and global financial systems started to fall apart. Some say he didn't have the relevant experience for the scale of the crisis, but he had lectured in banking law, he had even greater expertise in constitutional matters and he had a remarkable knowledge of history, which is what you would need to put a perspective on what was to come.

I do not recall any hesitation that July as the implosion of our property bubble started. I will never forget the passing words of a finance official coming out of a crisis meeting in Government Buildings, 'the country is going down the tubes.' The official could see that tax revenues were collapsing and that we were left stranded following ten years of high spending and low taxation politics. We went straight into an unprecedented series of sharply contracting budgets, done not from any ideological hankering for austerity, but from an acceptance that an inevitable restructuring had to take place.

It was decided that the main budget should be brought forward to early October and the whole system started to focus on that task. In the background, there was news of problems in American sub-prime lending and a sense that our own banking system was starting to creak. The Green Party had gone into the Irish Bankers Federation in 2006 to share our concerns that the banks were overexposed to property lending. By 2008, my colleague John Gormley was innately sceptical about our prospects, even before we knew the true scale of the hidden losses. Like Brian Lenihan he spent September taking soundings from various people as to what needed to be done. I do not have good notes from that time, but I do recall going into the weekend of the bank guarantee with an understanding that some such mechanism was going to be needed. I resented the fact that the decision was taken in the middle of the night and was only approved by the cabinet over the phone and at a meeting the next morning. Brian regretted that he had been pressurised at the last minute to include dated and unsecured junior bonds within the guarantee. It was only out of luck that there were hardly any such bonds falling due within the two-year guarantee period.

The Department of Finance have real questions to answer about why so little scenario planning was done in advance of the crisis. One of the reasons might have been the culture which had developed where they bring memos to cabinet at the last minute, without going through the same review process that other departments are expected to follow. Brian Lenihan came into cabinet many times over the next two years with freshly printed memos under his arms. Perhaps, it was inevitable given the range of budgetary and banking policy decisions that would have to be made. I had confidence in his judgement, but in the long run it is not good for Government or even Finance itself to bypass the process of prudential oversight that they expect everyone else to live by.

My family have been involved in banking for years, I had studied and worked in the UCD business school and I had a long held interest in economics and finance. As the enormity of the crisis became apparent, I decided that I needed to get as close as possible to what was going on and try as best I could to provide a Green Party analysis of what Government needed to do. I went back to those same bankers we had called into three years previously and was told that while there might be some five billion in losses to cover, the system was still fundamentally sound. I approached Brian Lenihan to report what I had heard and started to get from him his sense of what was happening. It was a strange relationship because being in a separate party your job is to be sceptical and questioning and to put forward contrary views.

In early November, Brian Lenihan came to me with the news that a major share buying scheme to buy shares held by Sean Quinn in Anglo had been revealed. A few weeks later, he came with news that a transaction had been uncovered involving a transfer of funds between Anglo Irish Bank and Irish Nationwide Building Society. Never in that time did I feel that any information was being withheld. In subsequent months when the full truth was uncovered, the initial information that Brian Lenihan had shared with us was always shown to be true.

By early 2009, we had access to the bank loan books, via a confidential Price Waterhouse report. The scale of the reckless lending to the property sector was incredible, but still the advice from the leading accountancy company in the world was that the losses could be managed. It was hard to believe their analysis when you looked at the books. Little known builders had borrowed hundreds of millions on developments that would never turn a profit. Lending in genuinely productive areas such as energy assets accounted for less than 2 per cent of their book.

In early February, I was asked to a lunch with Michael Somers and John Corrigan of the NTMA, where we were joined by the former European Commissioner David Byrne and the economist Peter Bacon. A truly frightening picture was presented. Our banks were clearly insolvent and were now threatening the solvency of the state. Bacon had been asked by Brian Lenihan to assess plans for the management of those bad property loans. The choice was between giving some insurance cover similar to what the UK Government had provided and let the banks work out their loan books themselves or else take the bad loans off the banks and manage them in some sort of asset management agency. An estimated €70 billion in emergency liquidity would be needed from the European Central Bank to plug the hole that had been created as Irish banks were shut out from the short-term interbank lending market. The money would have to come from the ECB in return for bonds that the Irish state would issue for the purchase of the bank loans.

I remember returning to my colleagues to relate the frightening situation and resolving to keep a note from then on of every conversation and every internal document that came my way. Brian Lenihan was already clear that we were likely to end up owning most, if not all, of the six banks under the guarantee. The only question was whether we might end up with a minority share in Bank of Ireland. There were all sorts of opinions as to what to do, but I listened in particular to what former Taoisigh Garret FitzGerald and John Bruton and former Finance Ministers Ray Mac Sharry and Alan Dukes had to say. All articulated the same opinion, that what Brian Lenihan was trying to do was the least costly solution open to us.

There was a lot of anger at the proposal for NAMA to purchase property loans at what was known as their 'long-term economic value' where we would be paying more than the market rate that applied at that time, in the expectation that market would recover when normal activity returned. The fear from Finance was that if you priced the assets too low then the banks would go even further under and the taxpayer would be caught having to cover the gap. In the end, the idea of buying assets above the market rate was shelved and by April the ECB had said yes to the NAMA proposal. Before going into the Dáil, the NAMA legislation was presented to the Governor of the Central Bank, the head of the NTMA, and the Secretary General of the Department of Finance. They were each asked in turn whether this was the right way to go, to which they each said yes.

Critics have said that the clean-up of the banks and the clear out of the existing management should have been done quicker. I know that Brian Lenihan was himself very frustrated at the time it took to put the necessary legislation in place. Most of the boards and management of the banks were changed, but, in hindsight, some people should have been removed immediately and stripped of their gold-plated pensions.

In the subsequent months, Brian Lenihan built up a whole new team of people to help manage the crisis. Patrick Honohan took over in the Central Bank. Kevin Cardiff succeeded David Doyle in Finance, Matthew Elderfield became the Financial Regulator, John Corrigan replaced Michael Somers in the NTMA, and Frank Daly and Brendan McDonagh were given responsibility for NAMA. His more immediate team included his economic adviser, Alan Ahearne; Cathy Herbert, his political adviser, and Eoin Dorgan, his press officer. In the subsequent two years, working closely with those people, I do not think I was ever given any misinformation.

The other person who played a central role was the Attorney General, Paul Gallagher. The offices of the AG and the Minister of Finance face each other, watching over the gates into Government Buildings. The nature of those two offices told a lot about their occupants. Lenihan's was always a bit dishevelled, with paintings waiting to be hung, papers in loose piles on the table, business being done on his couch rather than at the desk. The AG's office had perfectly hung modern art and the in-trays and out-trays were scrupulously managed. The two lawyers clashed regularly over legal principles, but they respected each other and worked well together.

By that summer, we decided we needed a new Programme for Government which we would bring to our own party for approval in our participative democratic tradition. It was an important check on what was about to be done, in recognition that we were in a completely different territory to the one in which the Government was formed. We came to the negotiations with a myriad of policy ideas, but Fianna Fáil were tired after twelve years in government and in a state of shock at the dramatic reversal in the country's fortunes. The budget arithmetic was impossible, but in a number of ways we found Brian Lenihan an ally in the fundamental reforms we wanted to introduce. As the ESRI has acknowledged, the budgets introduced throughout that period were progressive. The Department of Finance wanted to cut several strategic areas for investment, including education which we particularly wanted to protect. Lenihan held the line against his own department's more conservative thinking. He understood the logic of a carbon tax and he saw the sense in using a site valuation system rather than a conventional revenue raising property tax. He was open to restructuring the social welfare system towards a basic income model, even if in the end the divisions between Revenue and Social Welfare were impossible to heal in our time in office.

Given that public sector pay accounted for 40 per cent of total spending, the only way to get the budget back in line was to either reduce pay or cut the numbers employed. The Taoiseach's department had faith that productivity gains could be agreed through the partnership process, but Finance was deeply sceptical. Brian Cowen came to cabinet in advance of the budget with a proposal where the unions had agreed to a cut in pay in return for additional days off. There was an awkward silence around the table when the proposal was announced and a majority seemed to oppose the measure. No decision was made, but later that evening the Taoiseach went public floating the idea. Brian Lenihan was out of the country at the time and a night of frantic phone calls ensued before the proposal was withdrawn the next day. This proposed plan damaged Brian Cowen's authority, but he had at least the humility to retract it, recognising that it had done real damage to internal confidence within the Government, as well as being greeted with disbelief by the public.

The loss of face for the Taoiseach was all the greater because public confidence was increasing in a Finance Minister who seemed to have a plan that might work. The closing line in his budget speech in December 2009 that 'the worst was over' was over optimistic, but it was understandable in the circumstances. International confidence in our banking solutions was increasing and we had a Finance Minister who seemed to be enjoying his role.

Two weeks later, we got the shocking news that he was suffering from pancreatic cancer. I knew nothing about the illness or the horrible prognosis it so often presents. You could sense across the country a deep sympathy for him and his family and a collective curse that the man in charge of pulling us out of the mess might not be around to see it through. When we returned after the Christmas break nothing was hidden nor was there any great debate about the choices that would have to be made. The Taoiseach said simply that Brian wished to stay in office as long as he could and we should all facilitate that approach unless it became no longer possible.

We went back to work while keeping an eye out for the man. Friends in the medical profession have rightly asked whether the drugs that Brian was taking for his treatment would affect his judgement at that critical time. It is impossible to know the inside of someone else's mind, but nothing that I saw indicated that to be true. He was fortunate in that the chemotherapy did not seem to hit him too badly. The radiotherapy was a different case. He described it as a hammer blow to his core. It never stopped him working, except on one occasion he asked to leave a cabinet meeting for a moment to deal with the pain. As he walked ashen faced from the table, every other head was frozen in silence. Half an hour later, he came back and picked up his pen.

As well as sitting opposite him in Cabinet, our offices in Government Buildings also faced each other. Early on in his illness, a massive black reclining chair arrived in his office, which was to serve the purpose of letting him rest in between bouts of work. I do not recall him ever sleeping in it, but I do think he enjoyed sitting there surrounded by the caravan of attendant officials working on his papers and diary arrangements.

For the first quarter of 2010, there was a faint hope of some sort of financial recovery, but in May the loan losses in Anglo turned out to be far bigger than had been expected. What made it worse was that a number of the banks were not fully co-operating with the Department, which meant that the figures only came through at the last minute. It looked like the Government did not know what was happening and people increasingly questioned the massive cost to the public purse. A conventional wisdom developed that if only we had not guaranteed the banks we would not have any of these problems. The narrative suited the Labour Party, who had been the only party in the Dáil to vote against the bank guarantee. Brian Lenihan was privately scathing about the Labour analysis and we all knew that once in government they would face the same decisions and come to similar conclusions, as has subsequently proved the case. Even with the much larger losses in the banks, the alternative of letting them go would, I think, have cost us more. You had to count the money that the UK Government was pumping into the country to prop up Ulster Bank. You also had to count what it would take to replace the low interest rates that were being paid on the emergency lending from the ECB. Finance also estimated there would be an immediate 2 per cent increase in every mortgage in the country if we had taken a different direction.

That summer the economic problems that had been developing in Greece evolved into a full scale crisis. No one believed the figures that the Greek Government were presenting and their people were rioting in the streets. The Cabinet returned in September to face a further worsening in the losses in the Irish banks, increasing the State's liability to over €60 billion. Public confidence in the Government and the Minister for Finance was evaporating and that loss of confidence was picked up internationally and amplified.

The German Chancellor and the French President met on the fringes of a G20 meeting in Deauville and without consulting anyone made the announcement that from 2015 onwards sovereign debt in peripheral countries might not be fully secured. It was as if they wanted to punish countries that they believed had squandered the low interest environment that the euro had created. They wanted a two-tier euro where one interest rate would apply in one country and a different one in another. It was a reckless mistake that immediately undermined an already weak Irish position. At the same time, the European Central Bank was losing its nerve as our emergency lending had grown to €130 billion. Rather than doing what a central bank should do and acting as a lender of last resort, the bank panicked. While the Fed was buying $85 billion of new US bonds every month, our ECB decided instead to start contracting economies that were clearly going into recession. It would take the arrival of Mario Draghi a year later to reverse the mistake.

The comments from Merkel and Sarkozy brought on the fully fledged sovereign debt crisis we had been trying to avoid. The Green Party suggested the formation of a National Government to manage our way out of the crisis and invited Enda Kenny and Eamon Gilmore to talks to discuss the idea. They came in for a meeting to see what might be possible; the books were opened to them to show the scale of the banking and budgetary problems. It came to nothing because neither Kenny nor Gilmore had any interest.

At the same time, local and international confidence in the Government hit a new low following a live interview Brian Cowen gave to RTÉ on the morning after a Fianna Fáil Parliamentary Party meeting in Galway. It was no secret that Brian Lenihan was considering a challenge to the leadership at the time and you could tell that he was itching to have a go, but in the end he decided against it. For all the problems that beset that Government and for all the mistakes the Government did make, the critical decisions were taken by a cabinet where every single member had the right to object to any provision and where there was real collective decision-making. Brian Cowen deserves credit for that approach and Brian Lenihan deserves credit for realising it was not a time for personal goals or ambitions.

As the economic and political crisis worsened the Government came to an agreement on the 2011 budget and the four-year plan that would bring us back to a 3 per cent budget deficit by 2016. There was pressure from the ECB and the Commission to make an adjustment of €6 billion in the first year, but other than that the plan was prepared and agreed by the Cabinet prior to any intervention by any outside agency. Because of the uncertainty that Merkel and Sarkozy had created and because of increasingly negative sentiment about the real shape of the Irish banks, a run of money started once again, this time from the wholesale money markets, as large corporations and other banks withdrew short term deposits from Irish accounts. One of the daily routines came to be the question how much money had gone this morning, how much left this afternoon?

In the second week in November, the EU Economics Commissioner Olli Rehn came to Dublin and met with each of the parties in Government and Opposition to discuss the four-year plan. At the end of our own meeting, he said he was satisfied with what we had put in place and that he would be taking the plan to the meeting of the G20 where the topic of Ireland was on the agenda.

Five days later and two days after the G20 meeting, I got a phonecall from Bloomberg asking did I know we would be entering a programme with the Trokia. I asked the journalist why would we be doing that when we still had €20 billion in cash reserves? He said the message was coming from Seoul, it was coming from Brussels, it was coming from Berlin. I said I didn't know anything about it and I would call him back.

I rang Brian Lenihan, who said he had heard the rumours but downplayed the issue saying there were only exploratory discussions without real substance. The next day I found out from officials that there was, in fact, some real substance behind the talks, which had already started between the ECB and our own central bank. I called my colleagues telling them to stay quiet until we had learnt more. Noel Dempsey and Dermot Ahern were not so lucky, without being fully informed they went out on national television to swear that nothing was happening. The images looked awful and the blow to public confidence was all the greater when it became apparent later in the week that talks on a possible programme had already started. Brian Lenihan's strategy was to try and avoid Ireland having to do a deal and failing that to play hard-ball to get the best possible terms in any deal. Whatever about the merits of that strategy I can understand how let down his Fianna Fáil colleagues felt, as he could at least have given them the fully story before going out to bat in the media.

It did not help that Brussels and Frankfurt were spinning against one of their own sovereign Governments and that we had no direct voice in that G20 room. By Thursday, 18 November, the situation was becoming impossible. I was in the *Morning Ireland* studio, due to take the slot straight after the eight o'clock news when at the last minute RTÉ asked me to hold back as they wanted to interview Patrick Honohan, who was ringing in from the ECB meeting in Frankfurt first. In that interview he confirmed that in his view the country would have to go into a facility, it would be large in scale and it would last several years. After his interview, I was asked to comment and said I could not disagree with anything the Central Bank Governor had said. Coming out of the studio Brian Lenihan gave me a call and maintained the civility that he had held right through that time. He was not mad at Honohan, but simply said that he was under tremendous pressure from the ECB and from the run on the banks and could not hold the line. The die was cast, we would have to go into negotiations and the IMF arrived in town.

It was the most surreal, depressing and scary of times. The international media were encamped in white vans with satellite dishes all along Merrion Street. Government Buildings and the Dáil felt like they were under siege, people came and went via side and back doors, trudging through snow and ice as woefully cold weather matched the national mood. I remember flying back from Brussels with Brian on one of those snowy days and having a long sad conversation about how the recovery of the country was going to take some years. Gone was all the talk about getting on well with Madame Lagarde or Strauss-Kahn. Lenihan recognised that we had few friends in the Council of Ministers and that the European institutions were structurally unable to manage the crisis that we were in.

Our negotiating team with the Trokia was made up of Matthew

Elderfield, John Corrigan and Patrick Honohan with Kevin Cardiff playing a co-ordinating role. I was as close as anyone to what was happening and we had our own team of advisers keeping in contact with the negotiators, but in truth while I trusted each of our negotiators implicitly, I did not like the remove from the political system in which the negotiations took place. I knew Brian Lenihan was looking to get a cut in senior bondholders included in the package. I knew that both Trichet and Timothy Geithner had set their respective institutions against it, even though the IMF were in favour. But I think everyone involved, including our lead negotiators were annoyed that that information only became available just before the cabinet meeting where we had to consider whether or not we would accept a deal. Both Patrick Honohan and John Corrigan had to change their letters of recommendation to Government to adjust to that fact. In the meantime, the Government had little or no room for manoeuvre. We had a run on our banks and no prospect of support from the European Central Bank unless we accepted the deal. It was a deal based on misconceptions about the nature of the problem. It was a deal where other European countries would borrow on the international markets at 2.5 per cent and then lend to their European partner at 6 per cent. It was truly horrible, but we had to sign it as by that stage there were no other options available, even if the debt was already close to being unsustainable. The only comfort was that there was a timeline for negotiation on key aspects of the deal, which could give a new government the chance to bring the cost down in the following year.

The four-year plan that underpinned the programme was written by an Irish cabinet and not by the Troika. It had been worked on over the previous four months and was agreed at Cabinet before the G20 meeting. The only variation that the ECB and the IMF insisted on was a reduction in the minimum wage. I regret deeply that we ever ceded to that one provision.

After the Cabinet meeting, Brian Lenihan had to report the agreement to a special meeting of the European Council of Ministers and myself and John Gormley retired to a meeting of our own Parliamentary Party. Politicians know more than anyone else the mood of the nation. That week we had been spat at, told we should commit suicide and one member summed it up best when he said for the first time in his life he felt unable to walk the main street in his town.

The Government was no longer viable and we knew it, but at the same time we decided we could not make the crisis even worse by pulling out straight away. We would pass the budget for 2011 and then immediately have a general election which would give a new government room to negotiate the various terms of the deal. The next morning we arranged a press conference. John had trouble getting through to the Taoiseach and I only got to Brian Lenihan just in time. I told him about our strategy and once again he was remarkably understanding and calm. He had as sharp political antennae as anyone and could see how continuing as normal was untenable. Knowing that an election was coming would release the steam from the situation, even if it would happen a couple of months later after we had put through one of the hardest budgets in the history of the State. It would also allow Brian time to put through some critical banking legislation allowing significant savings on the payment of junior bondholders. It would allow a new government to be formed with a lot of the necessary budget adjustments already in place.

Others in Fianna Fáil were furious and could hardly look at us as we passed in the corridor. The real question was what would the Taoiseach do and, to my immense relief, he decided to go with the option of keeping the Government together to get the Finance Bill through before then going to the Park.

The ending of that Government involved a comedy of errors that does not bear repeating. It was the only time I saw Brian lose his cool. But out of the dying embers one last move was yet to be made. I called Fine Gael and asked them would they be willing to hold off on a motion of no-confidence in the Government if we signed off on the budget process within days and then called an immediate election. I called Brian Lenihan, who was unusually brusque on the phone, but he was willing to do it, as was Brian Cowen. All of the parties met in the Department of Finance and played out their various theatrical roles. It took Brian Lenihan half an hour to get agreement on the means by which the Finance Bill would be passed. Fine Gael and Labour dropped their 'no confidence' motions and an election day was set. It was clear then that Michael Noonan agreed with the general approach Brian Lenihan was following and intended implementing the four-year plan that the outgoing Government had written. Between the lines, you could also see that the Labour Party would do the same thing even though their election campaign would say the exact opposite. Sinn Féin had the easy option of walking out the door saying they opposed it all.

It was the last time I spoke to Brian. We met in the Dáil the next day, but everyone was already in election mode. I miss him and regret that I never had the chance to talk to him outside those unprecedented circumstances, when I got to know him quite well.

18 CREDIT WHERE CREDIT IS DUE

JOHN TRETHOWAN

I KNEW BRIAN FOR a relatively short period of time, but was immediately impressed by the integrity and intelligence which shone from the man. As Minister for Finance, Brian asked me to help implement some ideas he had on ensuring that SMEs and farms have access to credit in a climate where the banks themselves were struggling for survival. These initiatives continue today in the Credit Review Office and, to date, over 2,000 jobs have been protected as a result of Brian's foresight in this area.

Brian had taken on the job of Minister for Finance in the most challenging economic circumstances imaginable: a collapsing world and domestic economy and a bankrupt Irish banking system.

We have seen recently the disruption to customers and businesses caused when Ulster Bank had trouble with its payment systems. If our banks had not been saved in 2008, it could have led to an immediate domestic crisis with all banks unable to settle customers' electronic ATM and debit and credit card transactions between each other, as each bank did not know which bank could afford to pay up to settle customers' payments transacted through other banks. Simply put, overnight the country's payment systems could have been at best severely constrained or indeed switched off, and people would have had to largely rely on the cash in circulation on that day, which would cover only a small percentage of the nation's requirements.

We are today starting to see the challenges in having only three main banks left operating in Ireland. It would thus have been unimaginable in 2008 for the future recovery of the economy to have lost our two main banks.

It is easy for commentators to criticise in hindsight how the bailout of the banks was enacted and implemented. Brian and his officials had to face what is described as a heuristic situation – one where there is no precedent or game-plan to suggest what to do next. The actions taken by Brian can now be judged over the longer term – six years on the Troika have been and gone and the country is returning to growth, with the madness and the lessons of the tiger years well learned.

So it was around 6 p.m. on a December Friday evening in 2009, that I received a call from the Department of Finance. 'Would you consider doing a piece of work for us? Minister Lenihan would like to announce it in the budget on Wednesday?' Having rescued the banks from their difficulties in that famous evening in September 2008, there were increasing concerns on the supply of credit to SMEs and farms, and the Government was seeking to use its shareholding to ensure that the widely held criticism that the 'banks were not lending' was addressed.

I had retired from banking in 2007 after spending nine years addressing the difficulties in National Irish Bank, then helping to sell it to Danske, and leading the bank through the transitional year in which new investment in systems and processes were implemented. As a banker, I had retained some credibility after the crisis broke in having had a due diligence performed on the NIB lending book in the sale of the bank to Danske at the height of the boom.

After the initial shock of being asked to help, I enquired what was envisaged and was told that it was really a matter for a banker how it was to be done. I was aware that there was already a Financial Services Ombudsman service, but that this office dealt with contractual issues and did not address access to credit. It struck me that this model could work to help SMEs and farms which had been denied credit – the right of appeal to an independent arbiter. The Credit Review Office was born and the genesis was Minster Brian

Lenihan's brainchild. To date, the Credit Review Office has protected or created over 2,000 jobs in credit appeals for SMEs and farms, and direct interventions to assist larger businesses at Ministers' requests.

More than a bit terrified, I worked all weekend at an outline framework and what would be required to set up and run the Credit Review Office and Brian duly announced the initiative in the budget on the following Wednesday, 9 December.

We met quite a few times in the following months to discuss progress in setting the office up. The necessary legislation was duly passed on 31 March 2010, allowing the Credit Review Office to be established on 1 April 2010. From the outset, Brian had been very clear that the Credit Review Office was to address what was seen then as temporary shortcomings in the supply of credit and that the structure had to be easily dismantled when no longer required. To this day, the Credit Review Office comprises a small core staff of three – myself, my deputy and the helpline or office administrator with the Credit Reviewers on contracts, which pay per case so that they are paid as required by demand for appeals.

In March 2010, as he was preparing to bring the legislation to the Dáil, Brian called me in to advise that in addition to the appeals mechanism, he intended to set the two pillar banks lending targets. He asked me to monitor and collate figures to be reported to him each month. We discussed the basis for the targets and he wanted to see credit activity and to ensure that no region, nor trade sector, would be disadvantaged by bank lending policies. We discussed the validity of figures that would indicate the level of lending activity and agreed that loan sanctions would fairly reflect what banks were achieving, as opposed to loan drawdowns which were at the discretion of borrowers.

Brian settled on a limit of loan sanctions of €3 billion per annum for each bank. This was an aspirational target, in truth set by the Minister without knowing the capacity of the economy for SMEs and farms to absorb credit, as at any one time this is transitory to the state of the underlying economy; and in our case in Ireland how it applies to just two of the banks. It is thus difficult to put a logical figure on such a target. Both the Central Bank and Forfás have since advised that no regulator or economic advisory panel in the EU has been able to determine any country's credit system capacity.

A further challenge is that the two banks' management information systems are geared to retrospective quarterly Central Bank balance sheet reporting, rather than 'real time' sanctioning activity.

This arbitrary target setting should not, however, diminish another of Brian's ongoing legacies in that the ongoing monitoring of the two banks' monthly performance has provided a really valuable measure of lending conditions, including the identification of seasonal trends and performance, which are the basis for the continuing routine monitoring meeting, held each quarter with the two banks and the Department of Finance.

Finally, I was dispatched by Brian to the two banks in spring 2010 to review their lending policies and to ensure that these were not constricting or biased against any sector. I spent some time in each bank with one common finding that the policies in themselves were not constraining, but that the policies were now to be strictly followed – which was a key change in that the madness of the credit boom was characterised by the widespread breach of banks' credit policies.

Over the months of 2010, I knew that Brian was fighting his illness, whilst carrying the huge burden of a broken economy and banking system. He carried both these separate burdens with great dignity, and I came to know a man of undoubted intellect, impeccable manners and courage.

As the months went on in 2010, it became more and more apparent that the bond markets had lost faith in Ireland's ability to deal with its problems alone. This was evident when almost every taxi driver in Dublin could, for some months, tell you the current sovereign bond rate for that day for Irish ten-year bonds. When this percentage rate reached the mid-teens it was evident that external help was required and it was Brian who called in the Troika.

The Troika arrived in the Dublin on the week I was to launch my second quarterly report on progress in the Credit Review Office. The media are always invited to cover these reports and to interview me as required. When I arrived in Merrion Street that morning there were twenty or thirty photographers and journalists at the door of the Department awaiting first sight of Mr Chopra from the IMF. As

I approached all the cameras went up and then a voice came from inside the throng to say 'it's alright, I know him,' and all the cameras duly went down again – needless to say I had a very quiet press conference that day.

The experience and monitoring of pillar banks' lending performance have assisted the Department in the SME section of the quarterly Troika monitoring visits and, without Brian's initiatives in 2010, it is doubtful if such a direct picture of this part of the market could have been presented. The Troika has now left Ireland to manage its own affairs and I would doubt if many Dublin taxi drivers could tell you Ireland's ten-year sovereign bond rate today.

Probably my final encounter with Brian was at the now infamous Fianna Fáil Parliamentary Party get together at Ardilaun Hotel in Galway in September 2010. I do not have political affiliations at all, but was invited by Brian as part of a panel comprising Frank Daly, Chair of NAMA; Cliff Taylor, the then editor of the *Sunday Business Post*, and myself from the Credit Review Office. We were the guest panel for the morning of the conference, following the dinner on Monday evening.

The pre-dinner drinks in the bar were no different from any corporate team event I have attended, with people enjoying each other's company and in good spirits. We then went into dinner where the three guests were seated with our hosts at the top table and the conversation with Brian was very easy and covered wide topics, including his enjoyment of visits to the North and the great walking trips and sightseeing there.

One of the benefits of getting older is knowing when to call it a night and I duly retired to bed after an enjoyable dinner. The next morning at breakfast in the restaurant, I noticed that RTÉ's *Morning Ireland* had a small table in the corner and were broadcasting live from the hotel. I was sought out and asked to give an interview on progress in the Credit Review Office. As I left the seat, it was taken by the then Taoiseach, Brian Cowen, who gave his now infamous radio interview, followed by that subsequent tweet. As I left the chair, Brian Cowen wished me good morning and I must say that I saw nothing untoward with the man on that brief interchange – one for the memoirs!

The election followed in the next spring and Brian was re-elected, although many of his party colleagues lost their seats in a reaction to all that had happened to the country since 2008. Having been unburdened of the weight of ministerial office and the affairs of the economy and State, Brian's illness returned with a vengeance and Ireland was robbed of a gifted and true gentleman; one that I had the privilege to briefly know and work for.

19 CHILDREN'S CHAMPION

JILLIAN VAN TURNHOUT

THE LATE BRIAN LENIHAN was a true 'children's champion' and I do not use these words lightly. His achievements during his time as Minister of State for Children from 2002 to 2007 speak for themselves. However, it is *how* he achieved these successes, as much as *what* he achieved, which stays with me. In my role as the then Chief Executive of the Children's Rights Alliance, I had the pleasure to work with Brian Lenihan to promote and further children's rights in Ireland. I would like to share some of my insights into the person I found behind the public persona.

On 19 June 2002, Brian Lenihan was appointed Minister of State at the Department of Health and Children; at the Department of Justice, Equality and Law Reform; and at the Department of Education and Science; with special responsibility for children. Certainly one of the longest ministerial titles I have ever seen! Based in the National Children's Office, his role required him to carry out duties for three senior ministers – which is some juggling act for a junior minister.

During his five years in the post, Lenihan transformed the role of Minister for Children. The game-changer occurred in December 2005, when the then Taoiseach Bertie Ahern announced that Minister Lenihan was to spearhead all Government policies on children and would attend Cabinet meetings. This decision to allow the Children's Minister a seat at the Cabinet table was a milestone. A Cabinet seat – despite his not having a vote – meant Lenihan had influence and was entitled to receive all Cabinet papers. It also sent out a strong message that, politically, children matter.

Lenihan had something to get his teeth into with access to Cabinet and an empire to build. His empire came in the form of the Office of the Minister for Children. He moved quickly to appoint a dynamic and experienced civil servant, Sylda Langford, as Director General. The Office of the Minister for Children adopted a cross departmental approach – an innovative move within a siloed civil service. The existing staff team was connected through a system of co-location, with staff from Youth Justice under the aegis of the Department of Justice, Equality and Law Reform; and the staff from Education for Early Years under the aegis of the Department of Education and Science.

My first substantial meeting with Lenihan came shortly after my appointment as Chief Executive of the Children's Rights Alliance in 2005. I was joined at this meeting and the many subsequent ones by my deputy, the Alliance's Policy Director, Maria Corbett, an expert on children's policy and a conceptual power house. I always remember, as we walked into the meeting, being advised that it would be a twenty minute 'meet and greet' with the Minister and some key officials. In fact, this first encounter lasted several hours. In advance of the meeting, I had submitted the Alliance's 'wish list' for children's rights in Ireland to the Department. My plan was to bring this list to Lenihan's attention during the meeting and hopefully arrange a follow up with his adviser, Cathy Herbert, and relevant civil servants. Instead, the Minister took each point in turn and grilled myself and Maria on it. It was a dynamic exchange in which he pushed us on our thinking about how best to progress the issues and he shared with us his views and identified areas where he saw potential difficulties and pitfalls. On leaving the meeting, I was both exhilarated and exhausted. I had also learned a valuable lesson – never go into a meeting with Lenihan without being fully briefed and ready for anything.

From this and subsequent meetings, I quickly appreciated that Lenihan had a very different 'modus operandi' from what I have experienced with other ministers or office holders. A senior civil servant remarked to me about his ability to read into briefs so quickly. His intellectual ability to grasp the complexity of an issue was remarkable. He encouraged his civil servants to speak openly and, at times, would park a discussion whilst one party or other did more research or fact finding. He was not afraid of being challenged. Indeed, I think he revelled in it.

Before deciding on something, he would pitch his ideas informally to several people and canvas their views. He seemed to go out of his way to find challenging opinions to stretch his thinking. He listened to anyone who had thought out views and never seemed to be concerned by a person's seniority, title or party affiliation. He had the ability not to take disagreement personally, once you were not being negative for negative's sake.

If you could convince him that there was a better way, then he would change his mind. On more than one occasion, after debating an issue with Lenihan, I would end the conversation unsure if I had convinced him or not. Then several hours or days later he would phone to advise me that he was now convinced. Once he made a decision you knew he had the energy and drive to bring it to fruition.

All too often I think we have an unrealistic expectation that a minister must be all knowing and, therefore, all powerful. The true power of Lenihan was his openness to canvass, debate and learn from others.

Above all of his achievements, I will remember Lenihan most for his work to strengthen children's rights in the Constitution. For decades a series of expert reports and numerous children's advocates had called for constitutional change for children. However, upon his appointment as Children's Minister, I believe Lenihan opposed these calls based on his legal experience; his work on the All-Party Oireachtas Committee on the Constitution; and his appreciation of the challenge involved in winning a referendum. He favoured instead a legislative route for achieving reform.

I believe there were a number of key factors and moments which led to Lenihan's change of heart on the need for a constitutional reform for children. The seeds of support were certainly sown by the work of Dr Geoffrey Shannon, a leading independent child and family law expert, who was retained by the Department of Health and Children to advise on future developments in the area of adoption law. The full reform agenda identified by Shannon in 2003 was not deliverable due to constitutional blocks. For the first time, in his role as Children's Minister, Lenihan was confronted by the limitations of the current constitutional provisions.

Two judicial cases in 2006 further demonstrated the need for greater constitutional protection for children. The case of Baby Ann was making its way through the courts and he knew the judgment – regardless of which way it fell –would be controversial. And, in May 2006, public outrage followed the Supreme Court judgment in the CC case, which struck down Section 1(1) of the Criminal Law (Amendment) Act 1935 on statutory rape. The Government was left scrambling to find an appropriate response.

Lenihan recognised that the Government, and especially the Minister for Children, needed to know what was coming down the track from the courts in relation to children. A colleague recalls him saying that he wanted to ensure that he was aware of 'incoming tsunamis.' He examined several international models on how governments receive advice, other than in times of crisis. In June 2006, Lenihan appointed Dr Geoffrey Shannon as the Government's Special Rapporteur on Child Protection – to be an objective eye on legal developments and best practice internationally. Again this clearly demonstrated his willingness to appoint people of calibre and expertise who would challenge his thinking and Government policy. With a legacy of numerous annual Special Rapporteur reports to-date, Shannon has provided an invaluable and comprehensive analysis of how the State can enhance and develop its legal framework to best protect children. The breath and value of this work is unrivalled.

A key personal moment in my relationship with Lenihan and on the journey towards constitutional change for children took place not in Dublin, but in Geneva, Switzerland, on 20 September 2006, in advance of Ireland's appearance before the UN Committee on the Rights of the Child. The Alliance had secured an important win at the previous UN hearing in 1998, where Ireland announced significant state funding for an awareness-raising campaign on children's rights. Against this backdrop and a big build-up to the 2006 hearing, I was very conscious that the member organisations of the Children's Rights Alliance had considerable expectations about the UN process and that I needed to deliver. I requested a meeting with Lenihan and was invited to meet a senior civil servant late on the evening preceding the hearing. We met in the lobby of the hotel in Geneva where the Government delegation was staying and I outlined the Alliance's key concerns and recommendations, at the forefront of which was our call for constitutional change. We had a robust and constructive discussion, but any agreement would need the Minister's approval and it was suggested that we met personally.

At that moment, Lenihan came bounding through the front door of the hotel. He was coming from a TV studio where he had just done a live link to RTÉ's *Prime Time* programme. I had done a pre-record for the same programme prior to travelling to Geneva. Lenihan did a double take when he saw me in the foyer. He joked that he had just had to answer to me telling him what he needed to do on TV in Dublin and then arrives to the hotel to find me waiting for him in person! His official brought him up to speed on what we had been discussing and Lenihan turned to me and said: 'Come on, let's have a drink and discuss your issues.' Lenihan and I talked and chatted into the early hours about all that needed to be done. We both agreed that the ultimate goal was constitutional reform. It was the win I was looking for, but I agreed with him that a referendum to change the Irish Constitution should be announced at home in Ireland by the Taoiseach, not on foreign soil where Ireland was under scrutiny from the UN.

I remember on my way to the UN hearing the next morning doubts creeping in. Would a commitment made in such an informal setting really stand? Was I naïve in thinking the path forward had been agreed? As we entered the hearing, I bumped into the Minister and within thirty seconds I instinctively knew that his decision was made and he was a man of his word. I think we both took a leap of faith in one another, one which held true throughout our relationship in our respective roles.

At the hearing, Lenihan gave a robust defence of the

Government's record to the UN, although he admitted there were certain shortcomings. In her concluding comments, the UN Committee's special envoy to Ireland, Lucy Smith, commented that she had been warned that 'the Irish people are very charming and it is easy to be taken in by their charm and elegance, but when this [the Committee's report] is being written, the Irish charm will be back in Ireland and there are several issues we have to take up.' It was an accurate summary, Lenihan was charming and the atmosphere was positive but that did not take away from the fact that much work was needed to achieve the ultimate goal of making Ireland the best country in the world to be a child.

In keeping with our discussion, Lenihan pledged at the UN hearing to undertake an 'article by article' review of the Constitution in relation to children and just six weeks later, on 3 November 2006, at an eve of a Fianna Fáil Ard Fheis event in City West the then Taoiseach, Bertie Ahern, announced his intention to amend the Constitution to acknowledge the rights of children. The Children's Rights Alliance was the only non-governmental organisation invited to hear the Taoiseach's announcement – I have a fond memory of racing down the M50 to hear that historic statement. Lenihan had delivered on his promise. The Taoiseach's announcement was followed by an invitation to the Alliance to take up a coordinating role among the non-governmental sector in working towards a constitutional amendment.

Another memory from that auspicious UN hearing concerns the Unmarried and Separated Fathers of Ireland group who staged an awareness raising protest outside the Palais Wilson. On his way into the hearing that morning, Lenihan approached the protestors to greet them and hear their concerns. I felt this was a very respectful gesture. Somewhere in the midst of the chaos and pressure of that day, Lenihan gave further thought to the men with placards outside. There was a small reception planned for that night for those involved in the hearing and Lenihan and his officials approached me to see if I could 'sound out' the protestors. Would they be happy to accept an invitation to the reception and to attend without using the opportunity to lobby the Minister? I knew Ray Kelly and his colleagues through my work and I was happy to act as a go-between. The group were very appreciative of the invitation and joined us that evening. It was a simple gesture, but it sticks in my mind. This was the type of man Brian Lenihan was.

Given the combination of Lenihan's constitutional law expertise and the Government's resources and ability to invest in favoured projects, it appeared there was never a better moment as 2007 for a children's referendum. I was equally aware of the scope for potential backlash against the proposed amendment by a wide range of organisations and individuals, who felt an explicit recognition of children's rights might serve to erode the rights of parents, undermine the special place of the married family in Irish society, or could encourage overzealous State intervention.

My work during this period was not without its stresses and strains, including receiving anonymous and abusive calls and mail from those who you could broadly describe as believing that 'the family always knows best.' One day I took a call from a woman who claimed to represent a large organisation and was seeking information from me. I told her that I was more than happy to send her the details she wanted and asked for her name and address. She refused to provide either and proceeded to harass me about several issues that the Alliance was promoting. As she raged from issue to issue, I was thankful for the training I had received in my first job on a help desk dealing with frustrated and disgruntled customers. Grasping at a final straw she accused: 'Van Turnhout, where did you get that name?' I replied that my husband was Dutch and that I took his name when we got married. I naively thought that this was a safe answer. She then shouted at me that she now knew where I got my morals from since 'they all sleep with one another at twelve in that awful country.' She then slammed the phone down. I was gobsmacked and thankful that none of my staff had taken the call.

A few weeks later, it transpired that Lenihan had agreed to meet with the same woman regarding the proposed changes to the Constitution. During the meeting she repeated her insults about my morals. I heard both from Lenihan and his adviser that at this point in the meeting Lenihan stood up and advised her that he would be leaving the room and would return in fifteen minutes. If she was still there, he would continue on the basis that she had withdrawn her remarks. If she was not in the room, that was her choice. To this day I am impressed with his handling of this situation.

In the first few days of New Year 2007, I received a phone call from Lenihan. It was clear that over the Christmas period he had read every book, opinion and judgment that could inform him about how best to move forward on the wording of the amendment. Now, with ministerial engagement, our activity levels ratcheted up several gears with meetings, phone calls and broad consultations. From early morning to late evening, you could expect a call from Lenihan testing out a point in that comprehensive and holistic way of working that was quite unique to him in Government. It really kept me on my toes. We were also called into numerous meetings, either directly by Lenihan himself or by an official to discuss and debate possible formulations. There was considerable to-ing and fro-ing at this stage as we worked hard to build a case for strong wording.

I remember at one meeting, Lenihan advised us that we would have to pause and resume in a few hours. He said that, while he was minister for all children in Ireland, he was also a father and his son had an important rugby match, which he could not miss.

During that period, there was one issue that led us to have a formal meeting that could only be described as confrontational. I requested the meeting as an issue had emerged in the wording that I knew the Department of Justice were promoting in the background, but which represented an uncompromising 'red line' for the Alliance. It was a tough meeting where I was unequivocal in saying that the Alliance would not be able to support the wording if this issue remained. Had we reached an impasse? I left the meeting very disheartened.

Several days passed before Lenihan called me to say he realised that the wording was not everything that we were hoping for, but that he also had to be mindful of the need to persuade the electorate.

He had taken on board what we had said at our last meeting and brought it to the highest level. The Cabinet had agreed on a formulation of wording that did not cross the Alliance's 'red line.' We had won that battle. Over the next six years, through several iterations of amendment wording and the discussions leading to the final wording put to the people in 2012, that 'red line' issue never came back on the table.

On 19 February 2007, on behalf of the Government, Lenihan published the wording for a constitutional amendment on children. In his speech, he mentioned having had 'a series of consultations with political party representatives, the Ombudsman for Children, non-governmental organisations (represented by the Children's Rights Alliance) and faith-based groups.' The Chairperson of the Alliance, Dr Nóirín Hayes, and I issued a press release on behalf of the Alliance to warmly welcome the publication of the Twenty-eighth Amendment to the Constitution Bill as a significant step in the right direction. We announced that the Alliance would consult with its members to review the likely impact of the proposed wording and would then take a formal decision on whether to support the amendment.

It was clear that the Government would only proceed if there was all-party agreement and the Opposition was wary of rushing into constitutional change. Significantly, the Ombudsman for Children, Emily Logan, said more time was needed to debate the issues and that many parents were fearful of State intervention. This concern was soon followed by non-governmental representatives, politicians and legal professionals advocating differing positions on the wording. The momentum was ultimately lost. However, to this day, I stand by my decision to 'seize the moment' and push for an early referendum.

A few weeks after the wording was published, the Dáil was dissolved and a General Election called. This put the proposed referendum on hold until a new Government could be sworn in and agree its Programme for Government.

Over this period, the Alliance had meetings with members of the main political parties to encourage them to commit to a referendum on children's rights. Each of the 2007 General Election manifestos of the main parties contained a commitment to holding a referendum. This led the new Government to establishing the All Party Oireachtas Committee on the Constitutional Amendment on Children and, as Minister for Justice, Equality and Law Reform, Brian Lenihan was an ex-officio member of this committee.

In this way, Lenihan continued to play a role in shaping the wording for the children's referendum. I remember one occasion when he was present at the Committee, which was chaired by Mary O'Rourke TD. It was a particularly busy time in Government and, after the meeting, I remarked how good it was that he was able to attend. He quipped that if Aunt Mary tells you to be there, then you do not really have a choice!

He will probably be remembered by most people for his role as Minister for Finance. During this time, I only had a few exchanges with him through pre-budget meetings he held with the Community and Voluntary pillar. He had a voracious appetite for information and over the years I had noticed, at various conferences, that when his attention was not being held by a speaker he would delve into his jacket pocket for something to read. With this in mind, I would bring our points on one page and would find an opportunity to give them to him when he was walking out of the room. I knew that he would put the page into his jacket pocket, and that in all likelihood at some point during the day he would come across it. It was an unusual, but effective way of communicating our key asks.

As Minister for Finance, it was clear that his time as Minister of State for Children never left him and, in April 2009, he announced the introduction of the Free Pre-School Year stating: 'Pre-primary education significantly enhances the subsequent educational achievement of students and in turn increases the return for State investment in education generally.' He also continued to keep alive the momentum of constitutional change for children by ear-marking €3 million in the budget to hold the referendum in 2010.

In closing, it would be remiss of me not to mention some of the additional achievements made by Brian Lenihan during his tenure as Minister of State for Children. Recognising the contribution children and young people can make to policy development and the planning of services, Lenihan oversaw the publication of several reports and initiatives that provided guidance and a platform for children's voices. He oversaw the development and growth of Dáil na nÓg and Comhairle na nÓg, which gives children and young people a voice in matters which affect them. And, in March 2004, Ireland became one of the first countries in the world to produce a detailed National Play Policy which led to a significant increase in spaces for children to play and be children.

He oversaw the publication of the Ferns Inquiry Report in 2005, which identified more than 100 allegations of child sexual abuse against 21 priests, made between 1962 and 2002. Upon publication, and on behalf of the Government, he expressed dismay at the 'repeated failure and gross dereliction of duties' highlighted in the report. Following its publication, he initiated the first national review of compliance with the Children First Guidelines and launched an awareness campaign on child abuse.

Lenihan played a significant role in broadening the scope of the vetting of staff and volunteers working with children and vulnerable adults. In late 2004, he announced a major phased expansion of the Garda Síochána's vetting service to enable all organisations that recruit persons or volunteers to work with children and vulnerable adults to apply for vetting, and saw the establishment of the National Vetting Unit in Thurles, County Tipperary.

The first State of the Nation's Children report was published during Lenihan's tenure, fulfilling a commitment in the National Children's Strategy to publish a regularly updated statement of key indicators of children's well-being. In March 2006, he launched the National Childcare Investment Programme 2006–2010, which provided groundwork for an integrated national policy on childcare and early education and informed policies and regulations for early year's education and care sector. He also worked to increase investment in the area, including capital funding to deal with the lack of appropriate infrastructure. In April 2006, he announced a major investment into the first seven-year phase of the National Longitudinal Study on Children in Ireland, *Growing Up in Ireland*, one of the most exciting developments ever in children's research in Ireland.

In the area of Youth Justice, he oversaw significant developments, including the establishment of a new Youth Justice Service; new detention arrangements for all youth offenders under 18 years; changes to the age of criminal responsibility from 7 to 12 years; and the introduction of the concept of anti-social behaviour orders (ASBOs) for young persons between 12 to 18 years. I learned from officials that Lenihan went to battle on behalf of children to ensure that a similar system of ASBOs modelled in the UK, which many regarded as an over-zealous and regressive response to youth offending, was not replicated in Ireland.

Lenihan played an instrumental role in securing significant advances for children during his time as Minister of State for Children. It was clear that he had a personal and professional commitment to children's rights in Ireland. He sought the best advice and regularly stepped outside of his comfort zone. He very much worked on the basis of trust, knowledge, analysis and clear evidence-based solutions.

I, along with many others, will carry on the fight to strengthen children's rights in Ireland and will do so knowing that Brian Lenihan gave us a helping hand that was above and beyond the call of duty. Brian will always be remembered as a 'children's champion.'

APPENDIX ONE

DEATH OF MEMBER: EXPRESSIONS OF SYMPATHY DÁIL ÉIREANN, WEDNESDAY, 15 JUNE 2011

An Ceann Comhairle: We will take expressions of sympathy on the unfortunate and untimely death of our dear colleague, the late Deputy Brian Lenihan. I understand the Taoiseach proposes to give way to Deputy Martin in order that he might deliver the opening contribution.

Deputy Micheál Martin: Duine éirimiúil ab ea Brian Lenihan agus polaiteoir den chéad scoth. Duine lách, sibhialta, cúirtéiseach a bhí ann. Bhí gach éinne geanúil air agus bhí spéis aige i ngach éinne freisin. Bhí am aige do gach duine. I rith a shaoil ba léir gur thuig sé níos mó ná aon duine eile go bhfuil dualgais orainn uile don tír agus don Stát. D'oibrigh sé go dian dícheallach ar son mhuintir na hÉireann mar pholaiteoir, mar reachtóir agus mar Aire Rialtais.

It is fitting that we are remembering Brian Lenihan in this House which he graced for the past 15 years. Brian's passing is deeply felt on all sides of Dáil Éireann. Many of us have been numbed by the loss of a brilliant politician, a patriotic Irishman and, to so many of us here, a great friend.

Brian fought a brave and courageous battle with a serious illness during the past 18 months. In all of that time, he never once flinched from his public duties and he showed an unceasing and untiring commitment to tackling the economic crisis facing this country. Even when receiving debilitating treatment, Brian continued to work assiduously in the best interests of this country. For Brian Lenihan, that was always paramount. Brian's commitment in doing his utmost for the Irish people defines modern patriotism and all that is laudable in our politics. His loss to Irish public life is immense.

Brian Lenihan was a superb lawyer and academic, as well as a politician of rare ability and great talent. He had already accomplished much on Ireland's behalf and had the potential to achieve so much more. He was a politician with few peers and a man in his prime, which makes his passing all the more distressing. To quote William Butler Yeats:

> *Soldier, scholar, horseman, he,*
> *As 'twere all life's epitome.*
> *What made us dream that he could comb grey hair?*

Of course, we could never have been certain that what Brian once light-heartedly described, in an interview with Sean O'Rourke, as his 'famous dark indestructible hair' would ever have turned grey. However, we all would have liked to have seen Brian get the chance to age with dignity and to live a much longer life.

As a young man, Brian Lenihan studied law in Trinity College, Dublin, and Sidney Sussex College, Cambridge, graduating from both institutions with first class honours. He subsequently worked as a barrister and as a lecturer before devoting himself to politics. He was elected to Dáil Éireann in a by-election for the Dublin West constituency in April 1996, following the death of his father, Brian Lenihan Senior, who in his time had also been a much loved and respected political figure in Irish life. P.J. Lenihan, Brian's grandfather, also served in this House in the 1960s, having joined Fianna Fáil in the early 1930s. In his youth, P.J. Lenihan had been strongly associated with Michael Collins. In later life, however, he became a close confidant of Seán Lemass. Brian served in this House for many years in the company of his aunt and former Minister, Mary O'Rourke, and his brother, Conor.

Last summer, Brian was extremely honoured to have been asked to speak at the Michael Collins commemoration at Béal na Blath where he touched upon his grandfather's – and his own – admiration for Collins and Lemass as two of Ireland's greatest ever leaders. At Béal na Blath, Brian said:

> 'Years after the Civil War, after a decade as a civil servant, my grandfather joined Fianna Fáil, attracted in particular by Seán Lemass who shared many of the same qualities he had admired in Michael Collins: the talent for organisation, great energy and a modernising tendency.'

Brian Lenihan was rightly proud of his family's immense contribution to public service in this country. The highest compliment I can pay Brian is to say that by his own impeccable career he has added further lustre to the proud record of distinction of a truly great political family.

Brian Lenihan was undoubtedly an outstanding public representative of this generation. He had an unrivalled combination of skills and an unstinting work ethic, which he generously put at the full disposal of the Irish people. He had a formidable intellect and was a gifted communicator. He was full to the brim with ideas and had a great grasp of policy. He was an intellectual powerhouse, but he wore his learning lightly. He was witty, he was good humoured and he was full of fun. He was engaging, he had charisma and he loved meeting people. He was one of the best-read people I ever met and although he was a first-rate academic, he always retained the common touch.

Brian's academic prowess was not just confined to the law, brilliant though he was in that sphere. His knowledge of literature and history was also breath-taking. A former party official and friend of Brian's told me of a recent conversation he had with him on evolving political attitudes to the Presidency in twentieth-century Ireland. As part of their discussion, Brian referred in detail to a Dáil debate that had taken place in 1947. When Brian was asked how he had come across this interesting but slightly obscure information, he matter of factly informed his stunned friend that he had read every single Dáil debate from the 1940s.

Brian, of course, read those Dáil debates in hard copy. When future scholars come to study the Dáil debates of our time, they will have the benefit of online technologies and search engines. They will need to do no more than insert the words 'Brian Lenihan' to find some of the most outstanding Dáil speeches of the second half of the 1990s and the first decade of this century. His contributions to this House were consistently erudite and always impressive. Just as Brian was a voracious reader of history, especially Irish history, he also had an immense passion for languages. He was a Francophile and had a great command of French, so much so that in his contacts with the French Finance Minister, Ms Christine Lagarde, Brian would regularly discuss technical and complex fiscal matters with her in that language. Many people will have heard Ms Lagarde's interview at the weekend in which she described Brian as 'heroic' and as a politician who was 'calm, solid and very analytical when we had major issues.' This weekend, *The New York Times* praised Brian for his 'tenacity,' while Commissioner Ollie Rehn observed: 'this is a loss which will be shared by many people across the political spectrum in Europe, who have had the honour to know Brian Lenihan as a politician and as a person.'In life and in death, Brian Lenihan is respected at home and abroad as a great statesman. He brought credit and distinction to our country and represented Ireland with superb diplomatic skills in a challenging international environment.

Bhí grá daingean ag Brian don Ghaeilge chomh maith. Mar chúlbhinseoir d'oibrigh sé go crua chun a chuid Gaeilge a fheabhsú. Tá scéal ag chara Breen faoi chuairt a thug Brian ar shiopa leabhar anseo i mBaile Átha Cliath chun Bíobla Naofa, Sean-Tiomna, as Gaeilge a cheannach. Chaith Brian go leor ama ins na seachtainí ina dhiaidh sin ag léamh an Bhíobla agus ag déanamh aistriúcháin ar an téacs. Is féidir a rá go raibh a mhódhanna foghlama neamhghnách, ach bhí Brian cinnte de gur slí chliste í chun a chuid Gaeilge a fheabhsú agus, ag an am gcéanna, a chreideamh a neartú.

Ar bhás Bhrian, is féidir focail Thomás Uí Chriomhthain a thabhairt chun cuimhne, 'Ní bheidh ár leithéidí arís ann.' I gcás Bhrian is féidir a rá, le bród agus le huaigneas, nach mbeidh a leithéid arís ann.

As a ministerial colleague, I was privileged to observe Brian Lenihan at close quarters. He had my complete admiration. He was, quite simply, brilliant and often in a league of his own. He was a solutions based politician with a sharp and incisive mind and an uncanny ability to get things done. He served first as Minister of State with responsibility for children, where it was my pleasure to work closely with him as Minister for Health and Children. Brian was a conscientious and compassionate children's Minister of State and he brought forward a number of fresh and valuable policies relating to child protection, child care and youth justice. In June 2007, Brian Lenihan was appointed Minister for Justice, Equality and Law Reform. In this Department, he was a reforming and innovative Minister with political and legal mastery of his portfolio. He was particularly focused on putting the rights of victims of crime centre stage.

Brian Lenihan's time in the Department of Justice, Equality and Law Reform was relatively short and, in May 2008, he was appointed Minister for Finance. He was in this key economic portfolio when the worst financial crisis ever to hit independent Ireland emerged. Brian Lenihan faced events at a scale and a pace of magnitude that no other Irish minister has ever previously had to contend with. He rose to this unprecedented challenge and he never complained. His performance characterised grace under pressure. He was tested, and tested hard, but he played a stellar role in meeting the fiscal crisis head-on. When Ireland was in the eye of the storm, Brian Lenihan never faltered. Day in and day out he continued to step up to the plate and he did not shirk his responsibilities. He was tenacious and he never gave up. He did his utmost to communicate with clarity the hugely difficult predicament the country found itself in. In a hugely volatile and rapidly evolving political and economic climate, Brian Lenihan was always cool and clear-headed in his decision-making. He was willing to take unpopular choices if he believed these were necessary and in the country's best long-term interests. His unyielding determination to do his duty, in spite of a serious illness, was remarkable and inspirational. It was truly a profile in courage.

History will record that Brian Lenihan did an outstanding job in extraordinarily difficult circumstances. I believe Brian Lenihan will be remembered with affection, gratitude and enduring respect by the Irish people. The poet Stephen Spender wrote:

I think continually of those who were truly great.
Who, from the womb, remembered the soul's history
Through corridors of light where the hours are suns
Endless and singing. ....
The names of those who in their lives fought for life
Who wore at their hearts the fire's centre.
Born of the sun they travelled a short while towards the sun,
And left the vivid air signed with their honour.

The Truly Great captures the essence of Brian Lenihan's contribution. Brian's untimely death robs this country of a hugely talented politician and someone who had so much more to give.

The greatest loss belongs to Brian's family, the people who knew him best and loved him most. I wish to extend my deepest sympathies to Brian's wife, Patricia, his son, Tom, his daughter, Clare, his mum, Mrs. Ann Lenihan, his brothers, Conor, Niall and Paul, his sister, Anita, his aunt, Mary O'Rourke, his extended family and many, many friends.

My own abiding memory of Brian Lenihan is of a politician who was never deflated, who was always optimistic and restless to achieve more. He spent all of his time in politics in vigorous pursuit of the public interest. He packed so much into too short a life, and he did it all with great humanity and wisdom and always with a smile upon his face.

Well done Brian, you have done us all proud. Now rest in peace, my friend. Ar dheis Dé go raibh d'anam dílis.

The Taoiseach: Chuir sé isteach go mór orm nuair a chuala mé faoi bhás Bhrian Uí Luineacháin. Ar son mo pháirtí-se agus ar son an Rialtais ba mhaith liom mo chómhbhrón a ghabháil lena pháirtí, Fianna Fáil, agus le ceannaire Fhianna Fáil, Mícheál Ó Máirtín. Déanaim rún comhbhróin dhílis dá mháthair, Áine, dá bhean chéile Pádraigín, dá chlann, Tomás agus Clár, dá dheartháireacha, Pól, Niall agus Conchúr agus dá dheirfiúr, Anita, as ucht bhás Bhrian.

No words of mine can adequately deal with the sense of loss felt by Brian Lenihan's family. I recall the eloquence of the silence, and indeed the applause, in Porterstown church yesterday, where I attended his funeral. I spoke to Brian Lenihan on a number of occasions in the House, particularly on the last occasion I met him before his last attendance here. He said, 'I really shouldn't be here'. The job he held in the Department of Finance gave him that extra challenge to cope with his debilitating illness and the job of getting on with life. I listened to his open and candid interview when his problem was first diagnosed. The openness and courage with which he explained what his medical problem was and how he intended to cope with it was a revelation.

Brian Lenihan exhibited a great sense of humanity, particularly when he chaired the All-Party Oireachtas Committee on the Constitution and during the five years when he was Minister of State with responsibility for children. When he was appointed Minister for Justice, Equality and Law Reform, he had a real attraction to the work and showed a real inclination to make serious changes in the way our judicial and legal system operates. Events moved on and he was appointed Minister for Finance. The scale of the chasm in front of him became apparent to him very quickly.

He exemplified a love of politics and an association with people. Far from being locked into an individual or political rut, Brian Lenihan would always break off to talk to people from other parties, of other persuasions or with other interests. He demonstrated that ability on a regular basis.

His facing up to a terminal illness as he did and the openness with which he spoke about it to everybody is a lesson for every person. His funeral brought home to everyone elected to this House, and those who might think they are above their station, that at the end of the line the tricolour will fly at half mast for everyone who is in this Chamber.

I like to think Brian Lenihan will be remembered as a politician who made a contribution and constantly strove to bring out the best in politics. We argued and had many reasons to argue differences of political opinion but as a person, as a representative of politics and of the country and in the constitutional Ministries he held, I always regarded Brian as a friend.

The words of Louis MacNeice come to mind: 'By a high star our course is set.' Brian Lenihan's course was set by a high star. Fate and time intervened to prevent him from, possibly, achieving higher office in which I know he had an interest.

I offer with Deputy Martin and the Fianna Fáil Party my condolences to Brian Lenihan's mother, Ann, his wife, Patricia, his children, Tom and Clare, and the broader Lenihan family. I commend them on their contribution to public life and sympathise with them on the loss of a husband, father, political representative and politician. That was epitomised by the numbers who turned up to pay their last respects to somebody for whom they had an affinity, regardless of whether they agreed with his politics. Ar dheis Dé go raibh a anam dílis.

Minister for Social Protection (Deputy Joan Burton): Ba mhaith liom mo chomhbhrón a dhéanamh ar son Pháirtí an Lucht Oibre mhuintir agus le clann Brian Lenihan. On behalf of the Labour Party, I offer my sincere condolences to Brian's family: his wife, Patricia; his children, Tom and Clare; his mother, Mrs. Ann Lenihan; his brothers, Conor, Niall and Paul; his sister, Anita; and his indefatigable aunt, Mary O'Rourke, a former colleague of ours and a very good friend to every woman who has had the honour of being a Member of this House.

I first met Brian during the presidential election campaign of 1990, when he was one of the principal campaigners and strategists for his late father, Brian. That was a hard campaign for the Lenihans. Many different things happened as they do in different campaigns. Politics is not all about the glory days; there are many hard and difficult times in politics for most people. Although in many ways Brian Lenihan, coming as he did from such a distinguished lineage in politics, was, if one likes, a political aristocrat, political battles had to be hard fought and hard won by the Lenihans as they are by everybody in this House.

Yesterday, I was as happy as one could be in such a sad situation that the sun was shining on St. Mochta's church in Porterstown. When I first represented Dublin West, that constituency was represented not just by the Lenihans, but also by the Lawlors. That particular road and lane and the fields leading down to the Liffey were the subject of many pitched political battles on rezoning and development. For those who had fought to keep some green fields in Dublin West in the context of a population of 92,000, nature collaborated in a way that on the evening of the removal a swallow was high up in the roof of the church. I know there are some myths that sometimes when a person's soul is passing, one sees something like a bird and it expresses the soul of the person going away to another space and into another realm. It was nice that the service, which was so intimate and personal to Brian, the Lenihan family and to all that he loved and cherished, was attended by so many people not just from the community of Dublin West and his own family and friends, but also by people from throughout Ireland.

The Dublin West issues are in many ways the issues of the development of modern Ireland in the past two or three decades – schools, the hospital, public transport, community development and infrastructure. I am happy to say that although Brian was very competitive in politics – I am certainly a competitive person – we were happy to co-operate as do most Members of this House at a local level on behalf of the interests of their constituents, of the families and the children who make a home and a community in an area such as Dublin West, which grew over 30 years from approximately five small villages into a population of 92,000, which makes it bigger than the cities of Limerick, Waterford or Galway.

Brian was a consummate lawyer and had the lawyer's great ability to read and master a brief. He was enormously wrapped up in the law, and he loved the law. Many lawyers were present yesterday and the very fine words of Paul Gallagher summed up the respect his fellow lawyers had for him.

He was happiest in ministerial service in the period after he became Minister for Justice, Equality and Law Reform. It was a personal joy for him to achieve that, particularly as his late father had been Minister for Justice. He was always tremendously conscious of his responsibilities in terms of the Lenihan dynasty and of achieving things that would have made his father proud.

To be made Minister for Finance was a great honour but also brought great responsibility. I differed with him and his predecessor on their approach to the famous tax breaks that fuelled the property bubble, the bank guarantee and NAMA. However, these were political and ideological differences and arguments about matters that were fundamental to the well being of the people. I am happy that despite these clashes, it never ran to personal rancour or bitterness, which was one of the things that made Brian so respected across the political spectrum. There were long nights in this House when Brian was sitting where the Taoiseach is, the Minister, Deputy Richard Bruton, was sitting where Deputy Micheál Martin is now and I was somewhere hereabouts. We three carried the debates on our own with four or five people from the different parties coming in and out at different times. We often took time to talk privately in a quiet corner about the best way forward for the country. In the early months after the introduction of the bank guarantee, I gave him a short paper I had written about approaches to bank failures, bank resolution and so on. For months and even years afterwards when I met him, he still had the details of the eight or nine points on the paper, which he had taken in and analysed. He came back and discussed them with me as the situation evolved.

Above all Brian was a Fianna Fáil man born and bred. He loved Fianna Fáil with all his being as his father had done before. He, like Brian Senior, loved the fun and mischievousness that people could get up to at election time and the little tricks that rivals in constituencies often played on one another, including why someone managed to appear at an event and someone else managed not to appear, the little things that make up the bread and butter of political experience. He also loved Ireland and its people – most people in politics, regardless of party, love their country and try to do their best.

He was immensely brave about his illness, and by doing so gave so much hope to other people afflicted by serious illness. He had that great ability of courage and grace under fire, and great fortitude.

Many people who have been ill themselves have told me that they found the way he approached and coped with his illness deeply inspiring and comforting. His passing reminds us that there is more to life than just politics. Ultimately it is his family – his children, wife, mother, brothers, sisters, aunts and uncles – who will really miss him and grieve very sorely for him. Politics is a bit like diplomacy – one has interests rather than friends. When times are tough, we go back to our families and core communities, the people with whom we are most at ease. All the people who gave care and attention to Brian during his final illness and the months when his strength began to wane – he acknowledged that privately to many people here in this House – really did him a great service. In many ways it was being a politician and being a Minister which I often felt kept his adrenalin going in the face of the great challenges he faced at a personal level.

We mourn his passing. I hope he goes gently into that good night and I know that he did. Ar dheis Dé go raibh a anam dílis.

Deputy Gerry Adams: Ba mhaith liom mo chomhbhrón a dhéanamh fosta le clann Lenihan. Bhí an-bhrón orm nuair a chuala mé go bhfuair Brian bás agus tá brón orm fós. I express my deepest condolences to Brian Lenihan's family, his wife Patricia, son Tom, daughter Clare, mother Ann, sister Anita and brothers Conor, Niall and Paul, and his aunt Mary O'Rourke. I extend my sympathy to the Fianna Fáil Party, which was so much a part of Brian's life and which was enriched by the contribution he and his family made over many years.

Mar a dúirt na cainteoirí eile, bhí Brian Lenihan an-láidir agus an-mhisniúil leis an tinneas a bhí air. Bhí meas agam ar an tslí a rinne sé déileáil leis an chruachás a bhí air le déanaí. Ag an am seo, aithníonn cairde theaghlaigh Lenihan go bhfuil siad ag iarraidh ama dóibh féin. Brian's courage and fortitude in the face of his illness were an inspiration. We all knew he was seriously ill but he never seemed to let it get him down. He set an example for all of us. In many ways, he was a role model for other citizens suffering from debilitating illness. In his work in this Chamber and public interviews and engagements, there was no sign of the obvious emotional impact his illness must have been having on him and his family. Bhí sé go han-chróga.

Throughout his ordeal, Brian was an articulate and able advocate for the Fianna Fáil Government and its policies. Brian was a talented and gifted politician who worked diligently on behalf of his constituents and party. At the funeral yesterday, four or five people approached me to pay testimony to him and the work he had done in this regard.

Brian was also a considerate person. On the first day of the new Dáil, he was very open. He stayed behind after business and sat here when most other Deputies had left to engage with some of the first-timers, and he did so in a very cordial and welcoming way. I remember meeting him during the recent election campaign. I was chiding him gently – we were talking one-to-one about what was going on – and he said with a smile, 'You'll just have to do what you have to do, and good luck with that.'

Above all, Brian Lenihan was a husband, father, brother and son. To Patricia, Tom and Clare in particular, I extend again, on behalf of Sinn Féin, my sympathy and solidarity. Brian's death will leave a huge gap in their lives. All his family, particularly Patricia and his children, can take comfort from knowing that, in his relatively short life, he helped many people and was genuinely liked. Sometimes people use a lot of plámás when speaking of others. Irrespective of political differences, Brian was genuinely liked by all sides, by friends and political opponents alike. Perhaps there is no greater legacy than that. Go ndéanfaidh Dia trócaire ar a anam dílis.

Deputy Mattie McGrath: I am speaking on behalf of the Technical Group and the Independents. Ba mhaith liom mo chomhbhrón a dhéanamh le muintir Lenihan, a bhean chéile Patricia, a pháistí Tom agus Clare, agus an Lenihan family go léir. The huge turnout of Brian Lenihan's constituents since last Friday was a true testament to the man who served them for so long. Brian was a man of immense talent and had a magnificent ability to deal with any situation, no matter what presented itself at any given hour. He was a man of enormous intellect. Brian had an innate sense of decency and was totally committed to public service, which he always saw as his first duty. He was a true patriot. With his love of country and family and his commitment to his party, he was able to transcend all political views and ideologies. Service to his constituents was his first dedication. He, as a member of the Fianna Fáil Party, was truly honoured to be the first person independent of Fine Gael to be asked to speak at Béal na Bláth. What a job he did on that occasion.

He excelled as a Deputy, Minister of State with responsibility for children, Minister for Justice, Equality and Law Reform and, latterly, Minister for Finance. During the last Dáil, he was available at all times to meet colleagues, of any party or group, at any time of the day or night.

The tributes paid to Mr. Lenihan, including those by Commissioner Olli Rehn, Christine Lagarde and many other foreign politicians and dignitaries, demonstrate clearly that Brian was an astute politician who understood totally the gravity of the circumstances in which Ireland had found itself, and who wanted at all costs to deal tenaciously and honestly with the financial crisis for the sake of the people of all of Europe, but primarily the people of Éire.

Unyielding determination to continue in the Ministry for Finance during a debilitating illness displayed the true Brian Lenihan, a man of courage and bravery with an interest in his country. Brian was a shining beacon that illuminated the sky and gave inspiration and hope to all of us in this House and to his family, party and community. During many an animated debate that backbenchers and I had with him during the tough 18 months of his illness, Brian never showed any bitterness. On the morning on which he was leaving Baldonnel to go to serious discussions with the IMF and the European Union, which discussions history will judge, he telephoned me because my mother was being laid to rest. He found the time in his schedule, as he did for everyone, to telephone me to apologise for his absence at her burial. This meant an awful lot to me. That was the true style of Brian and that is why he meant so much to so many.

The biggest loss will be to Brian's family. I thank the parish priest for his lovely ceremony yesterday and all the people who attended. A wonderful eulogy was delivered by Brian's colleague, the former Attorney General. We can reflect on that and on thoughts of Brian. We will have many a happy discussion about him in the future. Again, I extend my sympathy to his family. Ar dheis Dé go raibh anam dílis Brian Ó Luineacháin.

Minister for Transport (Deputy Leo Varadkar): I join the Taoiseach, party leaders and other Members in extending my condolences to Patricia, Tom, Clare and the rest of the Lenihan family on their sad loss. I extend my condolences to the Fianna Fáil Party, for which a bright light has gone out.

I first got to know Brian when I was a young councillor in about 2003, at which time he was Minister of State responsible for children. He was already the senior politician in the constituency. As an ambitious young councillor looking to make a name for myself, I always made a point of taking Brian on and holding him to account for pretty much everything that went wrong in the constituency in the hope that criticism would give rise to provocation and, perhaps, publicity for myself. More often than not, Brian's good humour and unflappable nature thwarted my objectives. He always seemed to be able to rise above the cut and thrust of normal politics. When Brian was speaking at constituency functions as a Minister of State, as he always did at that time, he always began by acknowledging the presence of politicians from other political parties, who potentially would have gone unnoticed had he not done so. I promised myself at the time that if I ever had the opportunity to be a Minister, I would make sure to do the exact same. I do so. He was a very good constituency colleague. He was always willing to share information and listen to suggestions, and his first instinct when a problem was presented was to try to solve it rather than rush to the media or the barricades.

Brian Lenihan was the only Fianna Fáil Deputy to hold a seat in the Dublin area in the recent general election. Most politicians believe they have a personal vote but it is only when the tide goes out for one's party or one decides to go it alone that one finds out who does and does not have a personal vote. In the most recent general election the tide went out for Fianna Fáil as it had never gone out previously but Brian held on, and the genuine personal vote he had stuck with him.

His legacy and achievements are etched into the fabric of the Dublin West constituency, for example, St. Francis Hospice in Blanchardstown for which he secured the land and funding –

in a bitter irony Brian became one of its first home care patients; playgrounds across west Dublin and Ireland were built on foot of the national play policy, which was developed while he was Minister; and also school buildings.

When Dublin West faced a very serious school places crisis in 2006 Brian took it upon himself to try to solve that problem. He went into the Department and worked with it to establish a new model of national school, the community national school, of which we now have two in Dublin West, Scoil Choilm and Scoil Grainne. Neither of those schools are called after saints because they are run by the State and are non-denominational. They were given a random Irish language name to give them some identity but the next time we build a community national school in Dublin 15 we might call it Scoil Brían after Brian Lenihan and to remember him in that way.

Brian was extremely intelligent but always grounded. He was patrician but never superior. Sometimes he was wrong but he always tried to do what was right. When others were weak he was strong. When others gave up, he fought on. When others complained that they could give no more, Brian gave everything.

Members will be aware that he was a very learned man and from time to time liked to quote the great Greek philosophers. I will end with a quote from Aristotle: 'The beauty of the soul shines out when a man bears with composure one heavy mischance after another, not because he does not feel them, but because he is a man of high and heroic temper'. May he rest in peace.

Deputy Joe Higgins: In the Dublin West by-election of April 1996 the late Brian Lenihan, on the final count, secured 11,754 votes. I happened to be the nearest rival candidate, just 370 votes behind. In the context of that by-election and since we clashed sharply on political issues, and it has to be said that our differences would have grown wide as a chasm, especially on issues relating to the EU-IMF-ECB agreement. This is not the time to rehearse all that.

Cancer is an awful disease. Those of us, and we are very many throughout this country, who have had friends and family claimed by it at untimely ages of their lives know the anguish of Brian Lenihan's loved ones. To them and to his extended family I wish to extend our condolences and sympathy.

An Ceann Comhairle: I call on Deputy Healy-Rae to speak on behalf of the Independents.

Deputy Michael Healy-Rae: The former Deputy, Jackie Healy-Rae, was most anxious to ensure that we expressed our sympathies on Brian Lenihan's sad passing. When I first came into this House a few months ago he was extremely kind, warm and welcoming to me and I appreciated that very much. His constituency and Ireland have lost a brilliant, hard-working and dedicated politician. His family have lost a caring and loving son, husband, father and brother.

The Lenihan family are highly thought of the length and breadth of this country. In County Kerry in particular they are highly regarded as his aunt, the former Deputy Mary O'Rourke, spent a great deal of time holidaying in the county. They were very well respected.

I sympathise with Deputy Micheál Martin, the leader of the Fianna Fáil Party, as Brian was an extremely committed party man. I also sympathise with all of his colleagues who worked with him during the different Administrations.

Jackie Healy-Rae asked me to record Brian Lenihan's kindness, ability to do his job and helpfulness to everybody in this Chamber. When he was riding high in the Government he was also very kind to everyone in all quarters of the House.

Life is very short for all of us but we must try to pack whatever living we can into each day, and Brian Lenihan did that. He did not waste time. He used every minute to the betterment of his constituency, his country and everybody he encountered. May he rest in peace.

Members rose.

An Ceann Comhairle: May he rest in peace.

APPENDIX TWO

MICHAEL COLLINS COMMEMORATION – BÉAL NA BLÁTH
ADDRESS BY MINISTER FOR FINANCE,
BRIAN LENIHAN T.D. 22 AUGUST 2010

FIRST, MAY I SAY how great an honour it is to be invited to speak at this annual commemoration of the life and legacy of Michael Collins. When the generous and quite unexpected offer of the Collins family and the Commemoration Committee was conveyed to me I was delighted to accept.

I am acutely conscious that while in recent years there has been a range of speakers at this event, this is the first time someone from the Fianna Fáil party, has been given this privilege. It is true that over time the painful divisions from which emerged the two largest political parties in the State have more or less entirely healed. The differences between Fianna Fáil and Fine Gael today are no longer defined by the Civil War, nor have they been for many years. It would be absurd if they were. This period of our history is gradually moving out of living memory. We ask and expect those in Northern Ireland to live and work together despite the carnage and grief of a much more recent, and much more protracted, conflict.

Nonetheless, keen competition between Fianna Fail and Fine Gael remains – as I am very aware every time I stand up in the Dáil. But the power of symbolism cannot be denied, all the more so as we move towards the centenaries of the Easter Rising and all that followed. If today's commemoration can be seen as a further public act of historical reconciliation, at one of Irish history's sacred places, then I will be proud to have played my part.

Today is a day to recall the remarkable qualities of a man who, along with O'Connell, Parnell and De Valera, is part of our national Pantheon. As Dr Garret FitzGerald has written, these other three political leaders 'had not only the capacity and ability to play a major political role over an extended period of time, but also the opportunity to do so.' Dr FitzGerald adds: 'There are others who if they had lived…might have rivalled or even outshone some or all of these three – most notably Michael Collins in this century.'

Fine Gael has of course been the political custodian of the memory of Michael Collins, including at a time when some in Fianna Fáil were unwilling to recognise his importance and to salute his greatness. It may be that De Valera himself felt a sense of challenge from the ghost of Collins. Political partisanship led to their followers championing one or the other.

But, notwithstanding the very real polarisation in the post-Civil War period, there was more fluidity in the early decades of our politics than is often recalled. My own paternal grandfather, Paddy Lenihan, greatly admired Michael Collins and took the pro-treaty side in 1922. Indeed, he referred to this fact when he was a Fianna Fáil backbencher in the Dáil in 1969. Speaking during a debate on the eruption of the Troubles in the North he recalled that when he was a young university student in Galway during the Truce, Collins called for Volunteers to invade the North. 'I remember putting my name to it,' he told the House. 'It was rather stupid when one thinks of it. These were the things done in those days but 1969 is a different day… I appeal to younger men to keep sane about these things, to catch themselves on'.

Years after the Civil War, after a decade as a civil servant, my grandfather joined Fianna Fáil, attracted in particular by Seán Lemass who shared many of the same qualities he had admired in Michael Collins: the talent for organisation, great energy and a modernising tendency.

I should add that my maternal grandfather, Joe Devine, having been in the IRA during the War of Independence, immediately joined An Garda Siochana on its formation in 1922 and loyally served the State, under governments of several different complexions, for many decades.

De Valera's reputation may have suffered from the fact that he stayed on too long as Taoiseach and leader of his party. But so much of our thinking about Collins is dominated by questions whose answers we will never know. One of the many imponderables that arise from his untimely death is the impact he would have had on the politics of the new State of which he had been a key architect. No man is fully formed at the age of 31. Had Collins lived, would the Civil War have ended sooner and would its legacy have been less bitter? What kind of leader would he have become and what would have been the shape of the political party he would have fashioned? Would the party to which I belong have been pre-empted by the party he would have created? How would he have approached Northern Ireland and relations with Britain?

There are tantalising questions. As Professor Joe Lee has written: 'Almost any answer is plausible, depending on one's assumptions'. Indeed Professor Lee rightly urges students of Collins to spell out explicitly those assumptions so that debate can take place on a proper historical plane and can be rescued from the purposes of propagandists.

In recent decades, however, the full magnitude of Collins's achievements has, I believe, come to be appreciated and valued by Irishmen and women right across the political spectrum. But at times this has, regrettably and unnecessarily, been accompanied by a denigration of Eamon de Valera, as if only one of the two could win the approbation of history.

But even if we can never know how the relationship between Collins and de Valera might have evolved, surely now we have the maturity to see that, in their very different styles, both made huge contributions to the creation and development of our State. They shared much, in terms of their devotion to Ireland, their interest in its language and culture, their piety, their social conservatism. While in some ways they were temperamental opposites, nonetheless each was quickly identified by his peers as a natural leader. Neither was without flaws, but each had great strengths. Each was, at different periods, prepared to operate within the constraints of the realities facing him, without losing sight of his greater vision of a free, prosperous, distinctive and united Ireland.

It is also true that part of the healing process on our island must be an acknowledgement, aided by the work of modern historians like T. Ryle Dwyer and the late Peter Hart, that, alongside great patriotism and self-sacrifice, terrible deeds were done on all sides during the War of Independence and the Civil War. We cannot know today how we as individuals might have thought or acted in those convulsive years. Nor must we forget that many people with little or no connection to the struggle died or suffered by accident, or because of where they worked or where they worshipped.

In the round, however, the generation which laid and built on the foundations of our modern state achieved remarkable things. Collins stood at the very forefront of that generation, and his qualities were remarkable.

Collins was a man of energy and action;

An astute politician;

A man of extraordinary organisational and administrative ability;

A pragmatist who believed he could over time bring Ireland total independence;

A driven, ambitious man who was born to be a leader.

I have been re-reading some of the Collins biographies and historical analyses of his career. You will forgive me if I have taken a particular interest in his work as Minister for Finance between 1919 and 1922. In a meeting room in the Department of Finance where I have spent many hours over the last two years, hang pictures of all previous Ministers. They are in sequence. Eoin McNeill's portrait is the first because he was actually the first to hold that office in the First Dáil, though he served for less than ten weeks. The picture of Collins is placed second and regularly catches my eye: he is the youngest and, I daresay, the best-looking of us all.

It was Michael Collins who set up in its basic form a system of financial administration, important elements of which persist to this day. Of course, it was the task of raising the loan to finance the work of the revolutionary government that preoccupied him most as Minister for Finance. History has recorded the extraordinary success of that venture in the most adverse circumstances of suppression and constant hindrance by the British authorities. It was a truly remarkable feat and it added greatly to the authority and capacity of the first Dáil at home and abroad.

What is less often recognised is Collins's work in putting in place an accounting system that required government departments to give full reports of expenditure to the Dáil, and also required that any financial proposal brought to Cabinet should be first submitted to the Minister for Finance. Here was a man at constant risk of arrest and death, running a ruthless guerrilla war and masterminding the highly efficient intelligence system which secured its success. Yet he still had the time and the ability to build the foundations of a system of financial control. He recognised that such a system was essential to the running of a State. His talent for state-craft was also evident when in the period between the signing of the Treaty and the outbreak of the Civil War he continued to build the administrative apparatus which still serves the modern Irish State.

There is no substantive connection between the economic and financial position we confront today and the totally different challenge faced by Collins and his contemporaries. But as I look at those pictures of my predecessors on the wall in my meeting room I recognise that many of them, from Collins through to Ray Mac Sharry, had in their time to deal with immense, if different, difficulties. I am comforted by what their stories tell me about the essential resilience of our country, of our political and administrative system, and above all of the Irish people. That is why I am convinced that we have the ability to work through and to overcome our present difficulties, great though the scale of the challenges may be and devastating though the effects of the crisis have been on the lives of so many of our citizens.

The resolution of the current economic and financial crisis is the key challenge for this generation. The depth of the crisis, and the scale of its human cost has inevitably given rise to sharp and, of course, entirely legitimate disagreement between political parties and between individual commentators about how it can be resolved. Very few even of the most eminent economic experts, domestically, within the European Union, or internationally, foresaw the speed and extent of the crisis, either here in Ireland or worldwide. By the same token, none of us should be dogmatic in our certainties. Moreover, I hope that we can all accept that our differing approaches and viewpoints do not call into question our sincerity and good faith.

But we must be resolute in our determination to do what is right. Those of us in government have to make decisions in real time based on the best information and advice available to us.

We know we must address the severe difficulties we face with a sense of realism and an awareness of the international environment in which we work.

Whatever our disagreements, I believe we can and must all work together to build a viable economy which can sustain jobs for all our people.

We need a national understanding and acceptance that three elements are essential to the recovery and maintenance of future employment:

1. We must improve our competitiveness
2. We must restore sustainable public finances
3. We must ensure that credit is available for businesses and households

In a small open economy like ours, competitiveness is essential to creating sustainable jobs. We know from our own and from international experience that only the private sector can create enough good jobs to meet the demands of our highly-trained young people and to solve the unemployment problem. We need businesses to compete successfully in the global marketplace so that they will expand employment to meet increased demand for their goods and services. Last year, we recorded a significant improvement in competitiveness relative to the rest of the eurozone. This helped to keep our exports constant while those of many other countries slumped. We must build on this improvement in competitiveness in the coming years, throughout all sectors of the economy. That means that costs must be kept under control and reduced wherever possible, especially relative to our European partners. But we must also continue to invest in infrastructure, in research and in education, as the Government is committed to do.

Job creation requires that the public finances be put back on a sustainable path. We know from the 1980s that unless businesses are confident about the Exchequer's long-term position, they will not create new jobs. What we spend on our public services must be funded by an efficient tax system. In the medium term we cannot borrow to fund day-to-day services. As I made clear last December, I am committed to delivering budgets for 2011 and 2012 which continue to bring expenditure and revenues towards a sustainable balance. It is also now abundantly clear – as the pressures on the eurozone this year have made manifest – that neither the bond markets, nor our major EU partners, would tolerate any slippage on our part. So far, they are confident that we will keep to the path we have mapped out.

This inevitably means that future budgets will continue to require strict control of expenditure. What I can promise is that as Minister I will try to ensure that the burden is borne by those who can best afford it. Recent budgets have, according to the ESRI, made a positive contribution towards a fairer tax system. The budgetary measures have been progressive: those who can afford to pay the most, are paying the most.

Credit must be available to businesses that want to invest and create jobs. To provide such credit banks must attract funding which they can then lend on to these sustainable businesses. The measures adopted to resolve the banking crisis, including the creation of NAMA and support for individual financial institutions, are grounded in realism. Some elements of these measures have received the support of other political parties. Some have not. I have welcomed the approval of all parties for the appointments of Professor Patrick Honohan as Governor of the Central Bank and Matthew Elderfield as Financial Regulator. In advancing solutions to our economic crisis we must listen to these acknowledged experts and other experts to ensure our solutions are realistic. Their expertise cannot be dismissed just because it points the way to rigorous and difficult solutions.

I appreciate and understand continuing public incomprehension and anger at the scale of the funding necessary to rescue the banking sector – above all the vast sums being channelled into Anglo Irish Bank. Fury is a quite reasonable response to the incredible recklessness and incompetence which fuelled the banking mania of the last 'Celtic Tiger' years. Like others I hope that anyone who broke the law will face its full rigours. But anger is not a policy on its own. The Government has made the difficult decision to support the banks based on the expert advice available to us here at home and also from the EU and IMF. That advice has strongly been that we must stand behind our banks in order to ensure that a sustainable financial system is established and, in the case of Anglo, to ensure that the resolution of its debts does not damage Ireland's international credit-worthiness and end up costing us even more than we must now pay.

The successful resolution of the three key challenges – competitiveness, the public finances, and the supply of credit – requires that all those in positions of leadership be straight with the people. Solutions that would make Ireland an international pariah, walking away from our financial commitments or from our EU obligations, are just not credible. We must be realistic in our approach to this crisis.

Collins and the founders of this State were determined that all citizens should have equal rights and equal opportunities. The job of government is to strike a balance between the legitimate interests of individual groups and the greater good. Sometimes, and quite frequently in times of economic difficulty, achieving this balance requires governments to take unpopular decisions. But that is what leadership in a democracy is about: the exercise of power in the interests of the common good. Governments must face up to realities and act; to procrastinate and hope that problems solve themselves is not an option.

Over the last two years our country has been severely shaken. But our economy is beginning to heal. Exports are growing and consumer spending has moved off its lows of late last year. New order books are expanding and business confidence has improved markedly. Most forecasters now expect Ireland to register the strongest pace of economic growth in the eurozone next year. Tax revenues are stabilising and our underlying budget deficit will shrink next year.

As in other countries, our recovery is likely to be somewhat uneven. And it is a very unfortunate reality that a reduction in unemployment will, as is usually the case internationally, lag behind other indicators. But let there be no doubt that if we continue to make progress in the three key areas – improved competitiveness, sustainable public finances, and the proper availability of credit – we will return to high employment levels and maintain an average standard of living that is still among the highest in the world.

The challenges we face today are different from those that confronted previous generations since the foundation of this State. But we need to remind ourselves that many of those challenges were as daunting as our own.

In the 1920s, the apparatus of the State was created in the face of conflict and political division. In the 1930s, the first economic enterprises of the State were established in the face of the most severe global economic downturn ever. In the 1940s, the State survived and protected its citizens throughout the greatest conflict in history. In the 1960s, the State began the transformation from an agrarian economy and society to a more balanced modern economy and society. The 1970s saw an opening up of Ireland to the world and the extensive further modernising which that required. The 1980s saw a more severe unemployment crisis than the one we face today, and we overcame that through the resilience of our people and our investment in education. The benefit of this transformation was seen through the 1990s and the start of this decade with Ireland experiencing one of the most sustained and remarkable expansions in recent history.

Yes, the current crisis is deep and severe. But we have surmounted similar difficulties in the past.

In meeting challenges and seizing opportunities, the Irish people have shown their courage, determination and creativity – just as Michael Collins and his comrades and colleagues did in the campaign for independence and in the establishment of our State.

The spirit of Collins is the spirit of our nation, and it must continue to inspire all of us in public life, irrespective of party or tradition.

NOTES

3 A Personal Reflection, *Paul Gallagher*

1   For reasons of confidentiality, it would be inappropriate to comment on the important role played by so many others in events and decisions referred to in this reflection.

2   This was work that had been commenced by Michael McDowell, his predecessor.

3   and under the present Treaties.

4   Article 125 TFEU.

5   See, for example, Alan S. Blinder, *After the Music Stopped* (Penguin, 2014), p. 91.

6   Speech of Jean-Claude Trichet, Frankfurt, 3 June 2008.

7   It ultimately passed into law on 3 October 2008.

8   Donal Donovan and Antoin E. Murphy, *The Fall of the Celtic Tiger: Ireland and the Euro Debt Crisis* (Oxford University Press, 2013), p. 103.

9   The Financial Emergency Measures in the Public Interest Act, 2009.

10 Donovan and Murphy, *The Fall of the Celtic Tiger: Ireland and the Euro Debt Crisis*, p. 229.

11 On 9 May 2010, an extraordinary meeting of the ECOFIN Council and the European Council decided to create the European Financial Stabilisation Mechanism (EFSM) based on TFEU Article 122(2) and an intergovernmental agreement of Eurozone State Members. Also, on 9 May 2010, representatives of the Governments of the Eurozone committed to stand ready to provide temporary financial assistance to each other through the European Financial Stability Facility (EFSF).

12 *Lycidas* by John Milton.

5 Brian Lenihan and the Nation's Finances, *Patrick Honohan*

1   A direct external pressure came in the form of the near-collapse of a big German bank with an important Irish subsidiary. The weekend before the Irish guarantee Hypo RE bank's Dublin subsidiary DePfa was running out of cash. Here the Irish authorities stood firm, resisting foreign pressures to provide government or central bank support.

2   The two big banks clearly had an interest not only in securing as wide and categorical a guarantee as possible, but also would have been happy to see their troublesome competitor Anglo taken off the pitch. They did not shrink from presenting their point of view.

3   With hindsight of the scale of the hidden losses in Anglo's books, it may seem obvious now that to have pushed Anglo into bankruptcy at that time, leaving depositors and bondholders, domestic and foreign alike, to take their losses would have provided a better allocation of those losses. But it is worth bearing in mind the spill-over effects, i.e. even ignoring the likely market consequences, such action would likely have given Brian

and his Government pariah status, given the general perception at the time that the US Government's decision to let Lehman's fall into bankruptcy had triggered the global crisis just a couple of weeks before. A bankrupt Anglo could have been seen as the European Lehman's.

4   €7 billion had flowed out in the previous five days; almost a billion in retail deposits that day alone.

13 Athlone Background, *Harman Murtagh*

1   I wish to acknowledge the assistance I received in the compilation of this article from Mrs Ann Lenihan, Ms Anita Lenihan, Mrs Mary O'Rourke, Mr Martin Hanevy, Dr Henry Walker and Ms Miriam O'Callaghan. I am especially grateful to Mr Gearoid O'Brien and the staff of the Aiden Heavey Library Athlone.

INDEX